THE FUTURE OF RESEARCH

THE FUTURE OF RESEARCH

Geoffrey Oldham
(Editor)

Stuart S. Blume   Michael Gibbons
R. J. H. Beverton   and   G. W. D. Findlay
Cyril S. Smith   David Daiches   Wendy Hirsh
Kenneth Durham

SOCIETY FOR RESEARCH INTO HIGHER EDUCATION

378
.0072
F996

The Future of research

Research into Higher Education Monographs

The Society for Research into Higher Education, At the University, Guildford, Surrey GU2 5XH

First published 1982

© 1982 Society for Research into Higher Education

ISBN 0 900868 86 4

Printed in England by Direct Design (Bournemouth) Ltd. Printers
Butts Pond Industrial Estate, Sturminster Newton,
Dorset DT10 1AZ

THE LEVERHULME PROGRAMME
OF
STUDY INTO THE FUTURE OF HIGHER EDUCATION

This is the fourth report of a programme of study focusing informed opinion and recent research findings on the major strategic options likely to be available to higher education institutions and policy-making bodies in the 1980s and 1990s. The programme has been made possible by a generous grant from the Leverhulme Trust to the Society for Research into Higher Education and is entirely independent of governmental or other organizational pressure. The present volume arises out of a specialist seminar on the research function of higher education. We are extremely grateful to Kenneth Durham for his chairmanship as well as for his important contributions to the present volume and his considerable interest in the whole programme. We are also grateful to Unilever for inviting the seminar to be guests of the company at its International Management Training Centre.

A fundamental question facing higher education is the extent to which consensual arrangements and assumptions that generally worked well during the long postwar period of its expansion can cope with the much more stringent conditions likely to prevail in the 1980s and 1990s. Is there sufficient common purpose amongst the various institutions and interest groups that constitute 'the higher education system' to permit the development of viable long-run policy objectives or must higher education policy increasingly become merely the outcome of a struggle for survival and dominance among conflicting interests and ideas?

This is both a substantive and a methodological question. Substantively it will be faced squarely in the final report of the programme of study. Methodologically it will be tackled in the way the conclusions of that final report are reached.

In brief, the programme of study is an experiment in formulating long-term strategies openly, taking into account the best available specialist knowledge about a complex system, the legitimate interests of a wide range of conflicting pressure groups, and wider public interests as perceived by disinterested individuals with no direct day-to-day involvement in higher education. The final recommendations will be the result of an iterative process in which proposals are made, then discussed, then revised, then reconsidered. Stage one is to commission research reviews by acknowledged experts in various specialist areas. Stage two is a seminar at which others with detailed knowledge and experience of the area discuss these reviews. Stage three is publication of the reviews together with a report of the discussion and of the policy implications highlighted by it. Stage four is wider debate in the press and in specially convened conferences. Stage five is reconsideration of the policy issues in the light of the wider reaction. Stage six is the preparation of a final report. A seventh stage is of course intended, in which public authorities and institutions of higher education will take up the report's recommendations.

Publication of this volume represents the conclusion of the first three stages in the part of the programme concerned with research in higher education institutions. To consider the research function in long-term perspective is particularly timely in view of the many changes that are currently being forced on higher education institutions.

The first three volumes published by the programme of study have been *Higher Education and the Labour Market*, *Access to Higher Education* and *Agenda for Institutional Change in Higher Education*. In the first a careful review of the evidence suggested that there is little scope for any simple manpower needs principle replacing the Robbins principle of student demand as a basic criterion that ought to determine the allocation of resources in higher education. However, there appears to be a good case for allowing subsequent employment opportunities to have a more explicit influence on the pattern and content of courses. There is convincing evidence that most students do expect their higher education to bring improved job prospects and disappointment on this score was almost certainly largely responsible for the stagnating demand for higher education during the 1970s.

The Access volume starts from the view that current indicators give little hope of any significant increase in demand for the existing pattern of courses for many years. However, there is interesting evidence of considerable regional variation in participation rates and also evidence that the wastage of talent at sixteen through differential social class participation in post-compulsory education is no less than it was at the time of Robbins. The volume suggests various policies which might encourage significant increases in participation to the advantage of the higher education system and the community at large.

The Institutional Change volume proposes a variety of ways in which higher education institutions can become more responsive to the social, economic and cultural needs of a wider society without infringing essential academic freedoms. While many obstacles to a responsive higher education system are identified the volume concludes on the optimistic note that already, in the face of the problems of the past two years, 'considerable learning and adaptation has taken place in a relatively short period'.

Four other main themes remain to be treated: some of the issues are outlined below.

THE ARTS IN HIGHER EDUCATION
The role of the arts in education has for some time been a special concern of the Gulbenkian Foundation, which has made a special grant to enable the

topic to be included in this programme. A consideration of courses in the arts (music, painting, theatre) raises a number of issues relevant to the future development of higher education as a whole. The nature of academic knowledge, the problem of assessment in activities that are at least partly expressive, the relationship between course provision and labour market opportunities are three of the generalizable issues that will be treated.

THE TEACHING FUNCTION

The largest task of higher education institutions is the teaching of students. In scope it ranges from training in specific vocational skills to the provision of opportunities for self-development in a wide range of general analytical and creative activities. Since 1960 there has been a huge increase in the curricular content of higher education; at the same time considerable attention has been devoted to the improvement of teaching, particularly through the use of new educational technologies. However, with rather few exceptions, of which the Open University is the most outstanding example, there has been little change in the ways in which the teaching function has been carried out. During the 1980s new problems are likely to emerge, particularly as the result of the aging of the stock of teachers and the lack of opportunities for mobility within higher education and out of it. The existence of a healthy higher education system in the 1990s is likely to depend at least as much on the attention that is paid to the content and methods of teaching as on external circumstances. This seminar will therefore give consideration to what is taught and how it is taught.

RESOURCES AND THEIR ALLOCATION

There are two levels of discussion about financial policy for higher education which ought to be brought together. The first is consideration of radical changes in present financial arrangements, such as greater dependence on private finance of various kinds and the replacement of student grants by loans. The second is whether the existing financial mechanisms for disbursing public funds do in fact ensure an allocation of resources which is consistent with public policy objectives. The tension between academic freedom and public accountability is one which needs to be kept constantly under review.

STRUCTURE AND GOVERNANCE

The Robbins Report recommended the establishment of what was in effect a unitary system of higher education dominated by the universities and regulated largely through the University Grants Committee. In fact a binary policy was established which aimed to give the public sector parity of esteem with the universities, largely through the concentration of advanced level courses in thirty polytechnics in England and fourteen central institutions in Scotland. This policy has never been entirely satisfactory and there have been numerous attempts at improving the ability of the public sector to respond to changing social needs. The most recent development was the establishment in 1981 of the National Advisory Body of public sector higher education. At the same time growing financial stringency has raised questions about whether the machinery of the UGC is appropriate for the likely conditions of the 1980s. The problem of co-ordination of resource and course provision between the university and public sectors is increased by resource stringency.

All the seminar reports, together with comments on them from interested organizations and individuals will form the basis for a final report setting out the conclusions and policy recommendations of the programme as a whole. This will be drawn up by the chairmen of the seminars and the editors of the accompanying monographs under the chairmanship of Lord Scarman, and will be published in May 1983.

The scope of the SRHE Leverhulme programme of study is very wide. The need for a major review of higher education has been recognized by informed commentators for some time and the financial stringency of 1981 has made it even more apparent. In its report *The Funding and Organisation of Courses in Higher Education* the Education, Science and Arts Committee of the House of Commons commended the programme and·concluded: 'We believe that higher education is at a watershed in its development and that the time is ripe for a great national debate. . . .' The SRHE Leverhulme programme offers that debate both a structure within which the main issues can be considered and an assessment of the evidence on which future policy should be based.

Professor Gareth Williams
Programme Director

FOREWORD

by Kenneth Durham

I felt privileged to chair and take part in the discussions of the SRHE/Leverhulme seminar on the research function in higher education. Our discussions were lively and interesting and a task which I felt would be onerous was, in the event, very enjoyable. Aside from our recommendations I took away three personal impressions from the seminar which were unexpected and somewhat disturbing.

My first impression was that it is virtually impossible to consider research in the natural sciences and the humanities within one framework of higher education. Nor had I realized so clearly before how easy it is to overlook the importance of scholarship in the humanities when faced with the task of trying to assess priorities for the heavy funding requirements of scientific research. We must be vigilant.

Secondly, I had not fully appreciated the disarray into which our academic institutions had been thrown by the cuts in funding for both teaching and research. These are clearly having a divisive effect which could be harmful if allowed to continued for long.

Thirdly, I gained the impression that our higher educational institutions have neither the organizational structures nor as yet the management skills to deal with what will be a difficult situation over the next few years. Industrialists have had to learn how to manage change in difficult times and I hope the need for academics to do the same will be an important lesson from our seminar.

Kenneth Durham
Chairman

CONTENTS

INTRODUCTION AND ACKNOWLEDGEMENTS   1

SEMINAR PARTICIPANTS   3

1   A FRAMEWORK FOR ANALYSIS   5
By Stuart S. Blume

Changing conceptions of research — The legacy of the Golden Age — The new context of research — The crisis of research — A strategy for the future — Notes — References — Seminar discussion

2   THE FUNCTIONS OF RESEARCH   48
by Michael Gibbons

Introduction — Context —
The higher education sector in the UK —
The organization of the scientific community —
Policy alternatives — Conclusion —
Seminar discussion

3   FUNDING AND POLICY FOR RESEARCH IN THE NATURAL SCIENCES   83
by R.J.H. Beverton and G.W.D. Findlay

Introduction — Constitutional background —
Sources and treatment of data —
Expenditure and manpower for university scientific research 1965-1980 — Support for university scientific research 1965-1980 —
Expenditure on research at the polytechnics —
The immediate future — Emergence of a policy for the longer term — Appendix: information requirements — Acknowledgements —
Seminar discussion

4   THE RESEARCH FUNCTION IN THE SOCIAL SCIENCES   150
    by Cyril S. Smith

    The University Grants Committee —
    The polytechnics and the local authorities —
    The research councils — Direct department
    funding — The response of the scientific
    community to funding opportunities —
    Could we do better next time? — Notes —
    Seminar discussion

5   THE FUNCTIONS OF RESEARCH IN THE HUMANITIES   171
    by David Daiches

    Notes — Seminar discussion

6   POSTGRADUATE TRAINING OF RESEARCHERS   190
    by Wendy Hirsh

    The development of postgraduate training
    in Britain — The employment of higher
    degree graduates — Student demand —
    The contribution of research students
    to research — Practical problems with PhD
    training — Current policy trends —
    Unresolved policy issues — References —
    Seminar discussion

7   CONCLUSION AND RECOMMENDATIONS   210
    by Kenneth Durham and Geoffrey Oldham

    Our recommendations — Statistics —
    University research policy —
    National research priorities —Funding
    research — University/industry relations —
    The social sciences — The humanities —
    Postgraduate training — The polytechnics —
    In conclusion

INTRODUCTION AND ACKNOWLEDGEMENTS

This book on the research function of higher education in Britain is one of a series on the future of higher education, and its preparation has followed the pattern of the others. The centrepiece in the process was a seminar which took place in March 1982 at the Unilever International Training Centre in Kingston-upon-Thames. Some forty-five people from a wide range of institutions concerned with university and polytechnic research met for three days to discuss the issues. The list of participants is shown on page 3.

Starting point for the seminar discussions were background papers which had been specially commissioned. The content and coverage of the background papers had itself involved a considerable process of consultation and discussion. Research in universities and polytechnics is a subject on which many people have an opinion. There are relatively few, however, who have themselves thoroughly investigated the topic.

The process of selecting authors took place in two stages. First, Raymond Beverton, Stuart Blume, Geoffrey Findlay, Michael Gibbons and myself met to allocate the topics to be covered by each of the papers. Several months later it became apparent that gaps remained in the overall coverage. It was then that David Daiches, Wendy Hirsh and Cyril Smith were also asked to contribute.

The six final papers suggest that the health of the university and polytechnic research system today is not good. Without a healthy system the ability to respond to the different demands imposed on the system is impaired. Deterioration began in the mid-1970s, and the current crisis in higher education has served only to hasten the decline. Several of the papers examine the historical evolution of the system in order to diagnose the nature of the ills and to explain how they have arisen. They then go on to suggest how these ills might be cured and how a revitalized higher education research system could play an important part in Britain's economic recovery.

The seminar discussions were lively, and there was broad agreement on the diagnosis of the problems. There was far less agreement about what should be done to overcome them. There was also surprisingly little discussion about the demands likely to be made of the higher education research system over the next twenty years. Most people seemed to be preoccupied with coping with the immediate problems.

After the seminar the chairman, Ken Durham, and I drew up our conclusions and recommendations. While it is imperative, given the differences of opinion which existed at the seminar, to emphasize that these are our own not those of the group as a whole, both Mr Durham and myself wish to acknowledge the extent to which we have drawn on the papers and the seminar discussion as a whole and hope that those who disagree with our recommendations will join in the public debate which this series of books is intended to stimulate.

ACKNOWLEDGEMENTS

As convenor of the Research Function seminar I have been greatly assisted in what has been a most enjoyable task by a large number of people. First I would like to thank Gareth Williams, director of the programme, and Kenneth Durham, chairman of the seminar. Ken Durham has played a particularly active role in planning the seminar, selecting participants, chairing the meeting, and joining with myself in preparing the conclusions and recommendations.

The authors of the papers formed an informal steering group and met several times to help provide the shape of the seminar programme as well as to discuss the content of their own papers. They were a good team to work with.

I would like to thank Unilever Limited for their hospitality in providing the facilities for the seminar, and especially Dr Don Markwell, director of the International Management Training Centre, and all of the staff. Finally I owe a special vote of thanks for their patience and support to Betsy Breuer, the programme administrator and Anne Tyrrell of the Science Policy Research Unit.

Geoffrey Oldham
Editor

SEMINAR PARTICIPANTS

   Mr Kenneth Durham (Chairman)
   Prof. Geoffrey Oldham, University of Sussex (Convenor)
   Sir Geoffrey Allen, Unilever
   Prof. John Ashworth, University of Salford
   Mr Jack Barnes, Department of Health and Social Security
   Prof. Ian Beattie, University of Southampton
+ Dr Ray Beverton, formerly Natural Environment Research Council
   Prof. Tessa Blackstone, University of London Institute of Education
   Dr Donald Bligh, University of Exeter
+ Dr Stuart Blume, London School of Economics
   Sir Hermann Bondi, Natural Environment Research Council
   Dr John Collingwood, formerly Unilever
   Dr Peter Collins, The Royal Society
+ Prof. David Daiches, University of Edinburgh
   Dr Jack Edelman, Rank Hovis McDougall Research Ltd
   Dr J. Fendley, Science and Engineering Research Council
+ Dr Geoffrey Findlay, Science and Engineering Research Council
   Mr Paul Flather, *The Times Higher Education Supplement*
+ Prof. Michael Gibbons, University of Manchester
   Prof. Michael Hart, King's College London
   Miss Ros Herman, *New Scientist*
+ Dr Wendy Hirsh, Institute of Manpower Studies, University of Sussex
   Prof. Alan Johnson, University of Sussex
   Prof. Maurice Kogan, Brunel University
   Dr Bernard Langley, ICI
   Dr John Langrish, Manchester Polytechnic
   Dr Robert Lindley, University of Warwick
   Sir Norman Lindop, Hatfield Polytechnic
   Mr Brian Oakley, Science and Engineering Research Council
   Dr Jennifer Platt, University of Sussex
   Dr Kenneth Robinson, Calouste Gulbenkian Foundation
   Prof. Stephen Rose, The Open University
   Dr Ernest Rudd, University of Essex
   Mr Clive Saville, Department of Education and Science
   Mr Peter Scott, *The Times Higher Education Supplement*
   Prof. John Sizer, Loughborough University
+ Dr Cyril S. Smith, Social Science Research Council

Mr David Tanner, Department of Education and Science
Dr Ronald Tress, The Leverhulme Trust
Mr Phillip Whitehead, MP
Dr Noelle Whiteside, University of Bristol
Sir Bruce Williams, Technical Change Centre
Prof. Gareth Williams, University of Lancaster

1

A FRAMEWORK FOR ANALYSIS

by Stuart S. Blume

CHANGING CONCEPTIONS OF RESEARCH

'In the early part of 1940, two professors, A and B, were talking about the havoc which the War had wrought upon the staff of the Arts Faculty of their University. "You know," said A, "poor old C has lost so many of his lecturers that he's had to give up his research altogether." "I should think better of him," replied B, "if he had given up his teaching altogether." '

(Truscot 1951, p.143)

The discussion of the situation of the British universities written during World War II under the pseudonym Bruce Truscot provides a useful starting point for this chapter. Truscot argued passionately that research is the principal duty of the university teacher.

'To reveal hidden knowledge, to present fresh modes of thought and to train one's successors to do both these things are amongst the noblest activities in which anyone can hope to engage. And, of all people on earth, members of universities — and, most of all, university teachers — have the greatest opportunities, and obligations, to engage in them.'

(Ibid p.149)

Truscot's plea for research evokes the traditional culture of British universities, in which the essential harmony of research and teaching was widely proclaimed, as, for example, by the UGC in its 1936 report, cited by Truscot, and quoting the inaugural lecture of the first principal of Owen's College, Manchester:

'He who learns from one occupied in learning, drinks of a running stream. He who learns from one who has learned all he is to teach, drinks "the green mantle of the stagnant pool".'

It was a culture which, paradoxically, sustained but a minimal research activity. Truscot refers scornfully to the publications emanating from the arts faculty of one university in the 1930s:

'Twenty professors who in their twenty-two weeks of vacation produce a single article each and three books between them! Eighty lecturers, each the proud author of an eighth part of a book and less than half an article!'

(Ibid p.158)

The significance of this book, which appeared precisely thirty years ago, is that whilst pointing the way forwards (these thirty years having seen a veritable explosion in research activity) it does so from within traditional academic culture. The conception of research which Truscot (in reality a professor of Spanish) puts forward is essentially traditional scholarly activity. He is scornful of the expansion of doctoral research in American graduate schools because, for him, the very notion of research is debased and trivialized.

'Research is undertaken, from no spirit of adventure or inquiry, but as a piece of drab routine of which the only cheerful aspect is that one day it will all be over. (So thesis topics are chosen which make) the least demands on qualities which he either does not possess or has no desire to use — such as imagination, critical insight, judgement, and calls into play chiefly . . . industry and perseverance. . . . Hence the prostitution of research by the choice of unworthy subjects — the theses on dishwashing, cheer-leading, and the buying of women's garments by mail. . . .'

(Ibid pp.145-5)

To most of those who at present concern themselves with research policy the idea that there should be 'worthy' and 'unworthy' subjects for research seems anachronistic. The idea of research which largely underpins policy today is a different, but also more complex one. For Truscot university research was important because on the one hand it was in itself a cultural good, and on the other it prevented the stagnation of teaching. But it was not such a view which brought about the tremendous post-World War II expansion in research. The literature of the history of science policy shows that this was due above all to the lesson of war itself: the demonstration that research could be useful.

Through the 1950s and 1960s scientists had little difficulty in convincing society and its political leaders that there should be a substantial national commitment to research, including fundamental research. Technological (and thence economic) development was coming to be seen as dependent upon a stock of basic discoveries which was in need of continuous replenishment. The university system had to train in research the large number of scientists who would be needed by what was to be an increasingly research-based industrial system. 1963 was the year of (Sir) Harold Wilson's famous speech 'Labour and the Scientific Revolution', heralding the beginning of a 'white-hot technological revolution' in British industry. Research was seen as essential in itself to national prosperity as well as (now echoing Truscot) an indispensable adjunct of university teaching. The Council for Scientific Policy (which was an advisory body to the Secretary of State for Education and Science), in its first (1966) report, expressed this view.

'We are entirely at one with the (Robbins) Committee's insistence that "It is of the utmost importance that the ablest (undergraduates), who are capable of going forwards to original work, should be infected at their first entry to higher education with a sense of the potentialities of their studies. . . . There is no border-line between teaching and research; they are complementary and overlapping activities. . . ." We consider that the volume of research conducted in universities should keep pace with the growth of teaching functions.'

(CSP 1966)

Though it was a belief in the utility of scientific research which fuelled expansion, it was a belief consonant with traditional notions of free inquiry. For example, it was the growing complexities of policy making, and the design of social policies in particular, which led to recognition of the potential importance of social science, and establishment of the Heyworth Committee on social studies. The report of this Committee (Heyworth 1965), which led to establishment of the SSRC, though much concerned with utility, showed a remarkable sensitivity to the particular nature of the social sciences, and the ways in which they could be useful. I shall not explore the process here by which this sensitivity has been lost from official doctrine, and through which a natural science model has come to be imposed (and gradually accepted) in all fields of inquiry. The point I want to make here is that this model, to which all fields have been assimilated, is itself now based upon a notion of the utility of science quite different from that of the 1960s. In other words, I shall suggest that as considerations of utility have come to dominate discussion of the support for university research, the idea of *how* science is to be useful has changed. It would be wrong to say that the term has been 'redefined' for this would be to ignore the debate which the term itself now occasions (especially in the social sciences).

The variety of notions which I have sketched of what research, and preeminently university research, is and does have become piled upon one another. Old notions of scholarship have not been wholly abandoned, for example, though they are rarely paraded in public these days. The result is that university research is now called upon to *be* many things: to perform a complex variety of functions: for the educational process itself, for industry, for government, and so on. From this follow a number of central questions. How compatible are these functions? Can the university system accommodate what may be entirely different, even conflicting, notions of research? Are there research tasks which the universities cannot and should not be required to perform? Why are such demands made of the universities, which account for only 10% of our research system? But in order to understand these problems of the 1980s it is necessary to go back and trace developments of the last twenty years in somewhat more detail. These two decades both contain the roots of present difficulties and throw light upon what might be achieved in the future.

THE LEGACY OF THE GOLDEN AGE

What is today often described (internationally) as a crisis of academic research, only exacerbated by the cuts of 1981, can only be understood by reference to the 1960s, a period often described as a 'golden age' for science. Developments of that time are important in two distinct ways. First, there are the concrete manifestations of the expansion of higher education and research: the structures set into place and the resources of money and talent provided to maintain them. Second, there are the attitudes, beliefs, and aspirations which developed, and which came to be seen as in some ways expressing the inherent nature of science and of the scientific career.

Expansion — Structures and Resources
Although I have already referred to the expansion of the 1960s in available research resources, this was in fact a less significant determinant of the expansion of academic research than was post-Robbins expansion in the higher education system itself.

As is well known, acceptance of the Robbins doctrine that higher education should be made available to all those wanting it and possessing appropriate qualifications was accompanied by considerable expansion. The overall size of the system was thus to be determined by numbers qualifying at 'A' level, whereas it was intended that the existing rough balance in provision, between the universities on the one hand and the colleges of further education on the other, was to be maintained. In order to provide for the universities' share of the expansion, a number of new universities were created and the ex-colleges of advanced technology upgraded to university status. In terms of student numbers, the university sector grew by over 50 per cent over the five years 1962/3-1967/8. Academic staff were recruited, rapidly, to cope with the expansion. As Table 1.1 shows, the number of full-time academic staff grew at a similar rate to student numbers, doubling over the decade of the 1960s. These figures probably underestimate the growth in staff. There were in addition large — and undoubtedly growing — numbers of staff paid from other funds, for example from research funds. There is no statistical series for this group: in 1966/7 they numbered 3,862 (including 121 professors) (UGC 1968 p.128).

Some idea of the place of research in the view which this expanding number of academics had of their role may be gained from the survey carried out by Halsey and Trow in the early 1960s. There, some two-thirds of respondents described themselves as 'leaning towards research' (rather than teaching), a figure which varied between faculties. The research orientation was strongest in medicine, followed by natural sciences, arts, and technology, with social sciences coming last. There was also a strong age bias, with the younger academic staff being most particularly committed to research (Halsey and Trow 1973 Chapter 12). And of course expansion meant that it was the younger group that was growing most rapidly. Halsey and Trow account for their findings not in terms of a generational effect, but rather 'that for many older men, the motivation to do a good deal of research grows weaker, and the competitive demands of teaching and administration are greater than they are for younger men.'

Accompanying the expansion of the universities was the expansion of the 'public' or non-university sector. The reasons for this expansion, and its

TABLE 1.1
Full-time teaching and research staff[1] 1955-56 to 1977-78: universities (excluding the Open University)

Academic years	Professors	Readers and senior lecturers	Lecturers and assistant lecturers	Others	Total	Percentage annual change
1955/56	1,467	1,806	7,182	1,070	11,525	3.8
1956/57	1,505	1,925	7,336	1,061	11,827	2.6
1957/58	1,522	2,048	7,579	1,067	12,216	3.3
1958/59	1,555	2,111	7,781	1,050	12,497	2.3
1959/60	1,606	2,265	8,262	1,108	13,241	5.9
1960/61	1,677	2,426	8,621	1,185	13,909	5.0
1961/62	1,761	2,629	8,990	1,264	14,644	5.3
1962/63	1,853	2,868	9,206	1,755	15,682	7.1
1963/64	1,970	3,089	9,870	1,952	16,881	7.6
1964/65	2,230	3,578	11,478	1,526	18,812	11.4
1965/66	2,448	4,228	14,728	815	22,219	18.1
1966/67	2,686	4,531	15,846	962	24,025	8.1
1967/68	2,924	4,830	17,054	1,031	25,839	7.5
1968/69	3,051	5,170	17,485	948	26,654	3.2
1969/70	3,200	5,368	17,989	983	27,540	3.3
1970/71	3,432	5,646	18,606	983	28,667	4.1
1971/72	3,492	6,034	19,215	914	29,655	3.4
1972/73	3,649	6,475	19,651	969	30,744	3.7
1973/74	3,753	6,972	19,698	1,031	31,454	2.3
1974/75	3,906	7,398	19,883	914	32,101	2.1
1975/76	3,989	7,617	19,722	880	32,208	0.3
1976/77[2]	4,124	7,877	20,025	712	32,738	1.6
1977/78	4,164	8,163	19,982	677	32,986	0.8

1 Full-time teaching and research staff in post wholly financed from general university funds.
2 Revised figures; the entries therefore differ from those shown in Table 33 of *Education Statistics for the United Kingdom 1976 and 1977*.

enshrinement in the 'binary' principle, are one manifestation of an issue crucial to the theme of this paper. This is the continuing attempt, through the 1950s and 1960s, to create a system of higher education which adequately met the needs (not the demand) of industry for highly qualified scientific and technological manpower (Burgess and Pratt 1971). In 1956 the colleges of advanced technology (CATs) were designated from within the public sector, the intention being that they should rapidly increase their advanced work in technology. As Burgess and Pratt point out, government was here not so much responding to existing shortages: 'a powerful spur to policy in 1956 was the thought that there "ought" to be a greater demand for technologists from industry.' In 1962 the ten CATs were placed under the direct (and then benevolent!) aegis of the DES; in 1963 Robbins recommended their upgrading to university status, and in 1965 the transition process was complete. In 1966 government once more spelled out its intention to expand non-university higher education preferentially: this time by creating thirty polytechnics. These were to combine full-time and part-time study, advanced and non-advanced work, and to cover not just technology but a wide range of fields. Research was not mentioned in the 1966 White Paper, but in 1967 the then Secretary of State pointed out that, although the polytechnics were to be essentially teaching institutions,

'It will be necessary to make the provision for research which is essential to the proper fulfilment of their teaching function and the maintenance and development of close links with industry, particularly local industry, so as to promote the rapid application of results to its problems.'

These various initiatives may be understood as expressing a single continuing concern: with the inability or unwillingness of the universities to meet the needs of the community (and particularly industry) for manpower and research. There has been a continuing attempt to create a sector of higher education committed to these needs and not sharing what has been believed to be the anti-industrial values of the universities. I cannot deal with the truth of this belief here,[1] although there is much to be said for it. Halsey and Trow noted the particular status of Oxford and Cambridge, which '. . . serve as status and intellectual models and thereby both reflect and reinforce a traditional view of academic life.' It need hardly be pointed out that for 100 years the ancient universities stood aloof from the process of industrialization, obliging the rising industrial and professional middle classes to create new academic institutions better suited to their needs. Precisely this reaction is of course behind the creation of the great nineteenth-century civic universities.

We have witnessed a variety of attempts to create something equal but different: a model of higher education seemingly more suited to the industrial age. Yet it appears difficult to establish a distinctive, alternative, model of university-level education in this country. An alternative philosophy for the polytechnics *was* expressed in those early days, including by some of those involved in their creation. Eric Robinson, for example, made a passionate case, including a distinctive role in research.

'A major part of the work of the polytechnics must be to act as research, development and retraining centres for engineers, executives, and teachers working in the vicinity. . . .

'To fulfil its educational function in improving teaching and its function as a service to the community research is generally most effective as a group activity and every encouragement should be given to this type of research. . . . (In) the allocation of resources priority should be given to the creating of strong group interests.'

In addition there would be research

'related to the function of the polytechnics as a servant of industry, business and the public services. This would have an important emphasis on development and design work and on the propagation of modern techniques in industry. In general this work should be financed by the outside bodies which benefit from these services. . . .'

(Robinson 1968 pp.168-172)

But, as we shall see, no really distinctive role in research has in fact emerged: indeed it is doubtful if many staff would have shared the view that one was desirable.

To summarize, the 1960s saw a rapid expansion in students and in staff within the universities, and this at a time when basic, mind- (and career-) enhancing research seemed to be legitimated by all possible arguments, including the national interest. The decade also saw a still more rapid expansion of the non-university sector of higher education, with the polytechnics conceived as having a limited but different research role. There was, then, a vast expansion in the numbers of academic staff wanting to do research.

The resources for them to realize this aspiration were, by and large, made available. We have seen that, taking account of the incorporation of the CATs into the university sector, university staff numbers doubled over the decade. Through the same period, research funds available through the research councils (reorganized, and confirmed in their independence of government following the Trend Report of 1963) also grew at an average of 10 per cent per annum in real terms over this period (1965/6-1966/7 13.3 per cent, 1969/70-1970/71 7.1 per cent; see Table 1.5, p.22).

A third manifestation of the growth of academic research in the 1960s was the expansion of postgraduate education. Taking both research training and advanced courses together (but excluding teacher training), Robbins had argued that the 20 per cent going on to postgraduate work in 1961 should rise to 30 per cent by 1980. In fact, expansion of postgraduate studies was more rapid than this. On a somewhat different basis from Robbins, Layard King and Moser estimated that new home full-time postgraduates as a proportion of those who had graduated the previous summer rose from 44.7 per cent in 1961/2 to 59.5 per cent in 1966/7, again excluding teacher trainees (Layard King and Moser 1969). What these postgraduates were doing actually varied from one faculty to another. In the social sciences about half were doing advanced courses. But in the pure sciences almost all were doing research: about one-third of all graduates in the natural sciences (in 1965 72.5 per cent of those with firsts, 43 per cent of those with seconds) remained in the university on graduating, almost all to do research.

There were many factors beind this expansion of postgraduate work: the status of science, university expansion, economic climate, and good prospects of a scientific career. There were large numbers of new faculty anxious to build up research programmes, and funds were available. In science and technology the Science Research Council (now the Science and Engineering Research Council) played a major role, financing about 40 per cent of postgraduate work in these fields. However, it seemed that even the majority of these turned down for an SRC studentship nevertheless obtained the means to remain in the university doing research! Through the 1960s the SRC determined to maintain the number of studentships awarded as a constant proportion of the (rapidly rising) number of new graduates. The Swann Committee, set up in 1965, rapidly came to the conclusion that the extent of retention of (the best) science and technology graduates within the academic system actually posed a major threat to industrial development (Swann Committee 1968).

Expansion — Attitudes and Beliefs
The significance of the decade 1960-1970 for the problems of academic research today is not fully captured in statistics of growth. Material conditions both sprang from and influenced ways of thinking about science and higher education. Beliefs and attitudes then engendered continue partly to condition perceptions of, and reactions to, the situation of the 1980s.

I have already suggested that the rapid expansion in scientific and technological research was based upon a view, widely shared in the community, that science is *useful*. To compete successfully in the world, it was felt, required a substantial national commitment to research. Such arguments could thus be deployed effectively by scientific spokesmen. The Council for Scientific Policy (CSP), for example, in its *Second Report*, wrote

'We believe that with (proper encouragement) science is a prime mover: supplying the vital new knowledge, both immediately useful and otherwise, and the individual leaders, without which progress and indeed industrial survival are hardly possible. If we could summarise the purpose for our existence in a single sentence, it would be to understand the scientific environment, to advise on its preservation in current difficult conditions, and to convince both scientific and lay opinion that the nation wills its proper support.'

(CSP 1967 p.1)

In other words, though the innate value of science was not questioned, it was its perceived utility (supported by economic analyses suggesting an astonishingly high contribution to American economic growth) which was the persuasive argument for resources. Scientists and technologists came to believe implicitly in the value for the nation of what they were doing: whether it was basic science or applied.

But the conception of utility which lay behind this support for science could not easily be extended to all subjects. Research in the humanities, for example, was not seen as useful or necessary. It was seen as desirable, an essential accoutrement of civilization, and so had to be supported to an extent. But on the whole the humanities were on the defensive, neither criticizing the extent to which notions of utility were coming to dominate the university (with great compensatory rewards) nor seeking redefinition of these notions. One exception, of course, was the critic F.R. Leavis, who argued passionately against Snow, Robbins, and the 'technologico-Benthamite civilization' which for him they represented. These it was, he argued, who had diverted the universities from their proper critical function (Leavis 1972). But Leavis was fighting a lost battle. In contrast to the majority of European countries the idea that there are useful (or potentially useful) disciplines, and useless (though desirable) ones has come to dominate research and higher education policy in Britain. For the social sciences there was in a sense a choice, for it was clear that stress could be laid on either the critical or the instrumental function. Acceptance of the utility criterion, liaison with the natural sciences, was the route chosen (eg the fledgling SSRC within a few years joined the other councils under the aegis of the CSP). This led, in Britain as in the USA, to acceptance of natural science models of the organization, finance, and nature of the social sciences, which some eminent practitioners thought misconceived (eg Nisbet 1971).

But if science and technology were useful, this did not mean that they should be pressed too firmly into service. The Trend Report of 1963, which gave us our present research council structure, reaffirmed the importance of preserving the councils, and research, from considerations of immediate usefulness or government control (Trend 1963). Though it was not always acted upon, a similar view gained wide international currency at the time. It was expressed authoritatively by the sociologist of science Joseph Ben-David, in an influential report:

'investigations of the relationship between scientific research and technological growth are consistent with the view that there is no direct relationship between specific kinds of fundamental research and the eventual application of the findings in practice, and that success in exploiting science for practical purposes does not, therefore, result from the guidance of fundamental research by practical considerations but from constant entrepreneurial activity aimed at bringing to the attention of potential users whatever may be relevant for them in science, and vice versa.'

(Ben-David 1968 p.56)

In other words it was believed to be in the best interests both of science and of its application that the research enterprise should not be put under too much pressure.

Scientific research came to seem to have other kinds of needs. The most important one, widely believed and convincingly articulated, was for continuing growth. The term 'sophistication' came to express the *necessary* growth in real expenditure on new instruments, if research was to remain at the forefront of knowledge. Estimates of this essential growth rate, based on past trends, were worked out to be of the order of 10 per cent annually (Cohen and Ivins 1967). Of these estimates, the CSP wrote:

> 'we believe that (unless there is redeployment of the interests of a laboratory) the sophistication factor, when established on sufficiently broad data, represents a characteristic growth rate for short term projections. To go below this would represent an actual reduction of effort, at a time when very much more sophisticated techniques . . . are now becoming much more widely appreciated'
> (CSP 1967 p.26)

Thus what were taken to be the inherent needs of science were seen as a proper basis for policy, and generally accepted as such for much of the 1960s.

Finally, it is perhaps necessary to refer once more to the research aspirations of the polytechnics, and their staffs. Despite the limited and particular role in research envisaged initially, the polytechnics gradually came to wish to engage in research little different from that of the universities. Though this will be an issue more particularly for the 1970s, in which their development largely took place, its roots lie here. This identity of interest is hardly surprising, since their staff gradually came to be little different from those of universities, with similar professional socialization and research training, and similar interests and aspirations. Much the same happened in comparable non-university institutions of higher education elsewhere in Europe (Blume 1974). Thus it was that the polytechnics pressed for adequate representation on research council committees, and for a 'fair share' (if not for positive discrimination) in the allocation of grants.

By and large, the expansion of the 1960s documented here — in students, postgraduate training, university research activity and funds for research — was an international phenomenon. Demographic factors, prosperity, beliefs about science and technology, produced comparable patterns throughout most of the OECD area (OECD 1981a Chapter 1). There are similarities too in the very different decade which followed: it is only now, in the 1980s, that the British situation begins sharply to diverge.

THE NEW CONTEXT OF RESEARCH

As I have tried to indicate, the research expansion within the higher education sector which took place in the 1960s was fuelled from within both higher education policy and science policy. The fact that these two sets of policies were not always adequately co-ordinated with each other was of no great moment, since the general tendency of each was the same. Amongst the effects of expansion had been a gradual acceptance in the academic world that more didn't necessarily mean worse; the creation of a permanent, distinctive, non-university higher education sector which nevertheless came to share many of the traditional values of the universities (though in some cases inhibited in the realization of their aspirations by local control); the development (or reinforcement) of a set of beliefs about the needs of science and the nature of its usefulness. Values such as these were necessarily carried over into the 1970s, where they soon came to be confronted (or affronted) by very different conditions gradually emerging.

Once more these conditions were a consequence of developments both in higher education policy and in science policy. But whereas previously the lack of articulation between these two sets of policies had not in itself been a source of difficulty, this was slowly ceasing to be the case. Growing uncertainty was partly responsible, as financial planning began to break down. The effects of inflation, from the mid-1970s, upon mechanisms of public expenditure planning is of course an issue which extends far beyond my present theme, and cannot be treated here. But it is important to note that the 1970s saw the end of the quinquennial system of university grants: from the mid-70s the universities had to live in an almost constant state of financial uncertainty. The effects of this uncertainty were compounded, so far as research is concerned, by the fact that the research councils were similarly having to adapt to uncertainties. The Advisory Board for the Research Councils (ABRC), which in 1972 had taken over the responsibilities of the CSP, still engaged in its 'Forward look', but there can have been little confidence in the meaningfulness of this exercise other than as a way of ascertaining research council priorities. In December 1973 the funds available to the Research Council were cut at short notice, with specific categories of expenditure singled out. The ABRC had to contend with a science budget for 1974/5 4 per cent less in real terms than had been envisaged. Those research councils with significant permanent commitments to tenured staffs of their own (ARC, MRC, NERC) could cope only by reducing funds available for project support of academic scientists. Uncertainties were compounded. We had travelled far, and quickly, since the CSP had in 1966 written:

> 'We accept the necessity for forward planning. Indeed the chief danger for science . . . arises from a failure to plan: the sudden imposition of a financial ceiling without full consideration of the long-term effects would strike most at new men and new projects simply because there are already heavy commitments for the old. . . . Good morale among scientists is vital to the evolution of science, and the consequences of even temporary loss of confidence severe. . . . If we are to avoid these problems we must lean how to maintain scientific vitality and excellence on relatively stable economic resources.'
>
> (CSP 1966 p.3)

Tied in with the breakdown of financial planning was the loss of the intellectual coherence which, in that part of science policy impacting upon academic institutions, had derived from the attempt to give expression to the supposed 'needs of science'. In place of this basis for the work of the CSP there developed an increasingly desperate emphasis upon utility. But for whom? For what? For a range of 'customers' with requirements not always properly specified, nor necessarily compatible. British science and technology policy fell apart, demolished by the axe which Lord Rothschild put into the hands of government.

Finally, the division of responsibilities for the support of academic research between the UGC and the research councils — the so-called dual support system — became increasingly unclear. The councils were being called upon more and more frequently to provide for the purchase of basic equipment which had previously been available from UGC funds.

In considering the developments of the 1970s it is necessary more clearly to distinguish between the effects of higher education policies on the one hand and of science policies on the other.

Higher Education Policies
In a White Paper of 1972 the general outline of higher education expansion envisaged was set out. Broadly speaking, the government anticipated a continuing, but slow expansion, of which the bulk was to be accommodated in the polytechnics. The White Paper suggested that planning (the word still had some currency in 1972!) should proceed on the basis of a slight shift from the sciences to the arts (to 'reduce the present disparities between the opportunities for arts candidates and science candidates to obtain admission'). Attempts would be made to reduce unit costs. The share of postgraduates within total student numbers would be reduced somewhat. This statement of intent more or less reflects what happened through most of the 1970s.

Table 1.2 shows that the universities found themselves with student numbers still growing, though rather more slowly than before. But in contrast to the 1960s resources provided did not quite match up to this slow growth. From Table 1.1 we see, for example, that growth in the number of university staff did not quite match that in student numbers: indeed from the mid-70s there has been virtually no growth at all. Although the number of postgraduate students did rise through the 1970s, their share in the total body of full-time students did fall. These trends are summarized in Table 1.3. Moreover, we see from Table 1.2 that postgraduate study has been slowly becoming a part-time activity, and from Table 1.3 that there has been (at least until recently) a slow movement from postgraduate *research* to other forms of advanced training.

The availability of financial resources, combined with changing costs (eg wage/grade drift as the new faculty recruited in the 1960s collectively aged) produced one other important effect. This is demonstrated by looking at the share of total expenditure accounted for by academic salaries, administrative costs, and the costs of maintaining premises (wages, rates, repairs, light/

heat, etc.). Table 1.4 shows that whereas these costs, as a percentage of total current expenditure by the universities, fell through the 1960s, over the 70s they rose from just over half to over two-thirds. I have usurped the term 'fixed costs' to reflect the fact that this growing share of total resources was *not* available for redeployment in line with changing needs of research (and of course teaching).

Developments in higher education policy over the 1970s were thus characterized by a number of factors relevant for research performance. The very slight growth in teaching faculty resulted in a slight deterioration in staff/student ratio and in the ageing of the faculty (a matter to which I shall return); there was a reduction in the share of postgraduates in the student body (with a movement away from research and from full-time study); and a growing share of university resources taken up by salaries and overheads.

But this was also a time at which the polytechnics were growing more rapidly than the universities and were at the same time seeking to realize their aspirations in research. Information on the scope of polytechnic research at that time is scarce. However, inquiries which I myself made in 1973, in the context of an OECD study, led me to the following conclusions.

'Research budgets range from less than £20,000 per annum in some of the smaller institutions to around £200,000 in some of the larger ones. Some departments, particularly in the social sciences, have no past tradition of research whatever. . . . By contrast, in some polytechnics it is not difficult to find departments (especially in the physical and engineering sciences) which differ scarcely at all from some university departments in the scope of their research activities. Thus, in many polytechnics research is concentrated in a limited number of departments. . . . Such situations may cause substantial internal strain.
'All the polytechnics seem anxious that the expansion of postgraduate work should figure prominently in their future development. They differ substantially, however, in how they feel this should be done, and in the extent to which they see their activities as clearly different from those of universities. But the point we wish to emphasise here is this: the polytechnics are thinking seriously about the role which research should play in the spectrum of their activities. Many are seeking to develop specific policies towards research. . . .'

(Blume 1974 p.43)

From patchy beginnings, then, the polytechnics were seeking to develop their research. Subsequently, the possibility of the establishment of readership posts — intended for individuals of high academic standing with the particular responsibility for developing research activity — gave a boost to this effort. But many in the polytechnics considered themselves disadvantaged by what they took to be the discriminatory policies practised by the research councils. The policy of 'selectivity and concentration' of the Science Research Council, in particular, was seen as a barrier to the realization of their aspirations.

TABLE 1.2
Number of students by type of establishment, mode of attendance and level, analysed by sex, 1966/7-1977/8 (thousands)

		Universities[1]								Advanced courses in establishments of further education[2] [3]				All students
		Full-time			Part-time				Full-time		Part-time	Evening only	
		Under-graduate level	Post-graduate level	Total	Under-graduate level	Post-graduate level	Total		Teacher training[5]	Other			
1966/67	Men	112.4	25.8	138.1	2.9	11.3	14.2		27.9	47.2	62.1	48.5	338.0
	Women	44.4	6.7	51.1	1.4	1.8	3.3		70.3	13.3	4.0	3.7	145.7
	Total	156.8	32.4	189.3	4.4	13.1	17.5		98.2	60.5	66.1	52.2	483.8
1967/68	Men	121.0	27.9	148.9	3.0	12.2	15.2		29.7	55.1	69.3	46.3	364.5
	Women	48.6	7.7	56.3	1.5	2.1	3.7		79.1	17.0	5.0	4.9	166.0
	Total	169.6	35.6	205.2	4.6	14.4	18.9		108.8	72.0	74.3	51.2	530.4
1968/69	Men	127.1	30.0	157.1	3.0	14.3	17.4		32.5	63.3	70.3	42.1	382.7
	Women	51.9	8.4	60.3	2.0	2.5	4.5		86.0	20.2	5.6	4.4	181.0
	Total	178.9	38.4	217.4	5.0	16.8	21.8		118.6	83.5	75.9	46.5	563.7
1969/70	Men	131.2	31.1	162.3	2.9	16.4	19.3		32.3	68.9	73.5	42.9	399.2
	Women	55.0	8.8	63.8	2.2	3.1	5.3		87.4	22.9	6.5	4.7	190.6
	Total	186.2	39.9	226.1	5.1	19.5	24.6		119.7	91.8	80.0	47.7	589.9
1970/71	Men	133.9	33.1	167.0	3.0	14.9	17.8		34.4	72.7	69.8	39.8	415.8
	Women	58.6	9.7	68.3	2.3	3.2	5.6		89.4	24.8	6.7	5.0	205.1
	Total	192.4	42.8	235.3	5.3	18.1	23.4		123.8	97.5	76.5	44.8	620.9
1971/72	Men	135.3	35.0	170.2	2.3	16.1	18.4		35.9	77.4	69.4	37.0	430.5
	Women	62.0	10.3	72.3	1.4	3.7	5.1		90.3	27.3	7.6	4.7	217.1
	Total	197.3	45.3	242.6	3.7	19.8	23.5		126.2	104.7	77.0	41.7	647.7

1972/73	Men	134.7	35.8	170.5	2.1	16.2	18.2	37.5	78.1	68.5	34.5	433.3
	Women	65.2	11.1	76.3	1.4	4.0	5.3	89.7	29.9	8.7	4.9	227.4
	Total	199.9	46.9	246.8	3.4	20.1	23.6	127.2	107.9	77.2	39.4	660.7
1973/74	Men	135.0	35.8	170.8	2.0	16.5	18.5	38.8	80.6	69.7	33.4	439.8
	Women	68.6	11.8	80.4	1.5	4.4	5.9	91.5	33.4	10.6	5.1	241.8
	Total	203.6	47.6	251.2	3.5	20.9	24.4	130.3	114.0	80.3	38.5	681.6
1974/75	Men	136.3	36.1	172.4	1.8	17.1	19.0	33.1	84.1	76.5	33.7	452.0
	Women	72.8	12.5	85.3	1.6	4.9	6.4	85.3	37.4	12.9	5.4	253.3
	Total	209.1	48.6	257.7	3.4	22.0	24.4	118.4	121.5	89.4	39.2	705.5
1975/76	Men	140.8	37.3	178.1	2.0	17.3	19.3	123.1		80.2	35.0	469.6
	Women	77.3	13.4	90.6	1.8	5.2	7.0	123.1		15.4	5.8	264.0
	Total	218.1	50.6	268.7	3.8	22.5	26.3	246.1[6]		95.7	40.9	733.7
1976/77	Men	146.6	37.1	183.7	1.9	17.9	19.9	126.8		82.5	33.9	483.0
	Women	81.6	13.9	95.6	1.9	5.6	7.5	118.8		17.2	6.2	270.3
	Total	228.3	51.1	279.3	3.8	23.5	27.3	245.6[6]		99.7	40.1	753.2
1977/78	Men	152.1	35.8	187.9	2.1	18.2	20.2	125.7		85.5	34.7	492.5
	Women	86.4	13.8	100.2	2.1	6.4	8.4	107.7		21.6	9.4	275.0
	Total	238.5	49.7	288.1	4.2	24.5	28.7	233.4[6]		107.1	44.0	767.4

1 From 1971-72 onwards students at universities on courses 'not of a university standard' are included in the figures for undergraduate level.
2 Public sector and assisted only.
3 Excluding students on courses not leading to a recognized qualification except for Northern Ireland (1975-76) and Scotland (1977-78).
4 All students including postgraduate students—556 in 1977-78.
5 Excluding departments of education in polytechnics for sessions up to and including 1974-75. The Northern Ireland component of college of education figures prior to the 1973-74 session includes students on teacher training courses at Ulster College (The Northern Ireland Polytechnic).
6 Because of the reorganization of teacher training institutions in England and Wales it would be misleading from 1975-76 to continue to show separate figures for colleges of education for the United Kingdom, even though colleges of education in Scotland and Northern Ireland remain as before. From 1975-76 figures for students in colleges of education have therefore been amalgamated with those for students on full-time courses in establishments of further education.

TABLE 1.3
Changing relationships between undergraduate, postgraduate and faculty numbers throughout the 1970s (universities only)

	1966/7-1970/1	1970/1-1977/8
	%	%
Average annual growth in full-time undergraduates	5·10	3·05
Average annual growth in full-time teaching and research staff financed from UGC funds	4·40	2·00

	1966/7	1969/70	1972/3	1975/6	1977/8	1978/9
Full-time postgraduates as % all full-time students	17·1	17·6	19·0	18·8	17·2	
Full-time students/staff	7·9	8·2	8·0	8·3	8·7	
Research students as % all full-time postgraduates		49·0	47·0	44·0		45·5

Source
Calculated from DES *Statistics of Education*

TABLE 1.4
Percentage share of 'fixed costs' in total current university expenditure

1958/9	1966/7	1970/1	1971/2	1972/3	1973/4	1974/5	1975/6	1976/7
64·6	56·0	54·4	55·1	54·9	54·8	68·3	68·2	67·8

Source
Calculated from DES *Statistics of Education*

For the universities too, science policy, the provision of research resources on a project basis by the research councils and (for the social sciences in particular) by government departments, was becoming an increasingly important determinant of research activity.

Science Policies
Through the 1960s, as we have seen, resources for research provided through the research councils grew rapidly: at about the same rate as the number of teaching staff and (almost certainly) somewhat more rapidly than the research element of university budgets. These resources, directed towards projects of 'timeliness and promise' proposed by academic scientists, had played an important role in supporting the expansion of research activity (other than in the humanities) through the 1960s. By 1970 the sum at the disposal of the councils (the 'science budget') was still growing at about 7 per cent per annum in real terms. But if this seems princely now, it did not seem so then. The scientific community had come to believe that in the natural sciences 'sophistication' required that real growth of 10 per cent was essential if British science was not to be left behind internationally. Nevertheless, from 1971 the rate of growth in the science budget declined, becoming finally less than the inflation rate in the middle 70s. Table 1.5 shows that in 1974/5 the real growth rate was -2.1 per cent, in 1975/6 -1.3 per cent. In the later years of the 1970s there was a slight improvement: over the period 1976/7-1979/80 there was real growth at an average of 2.6 per cent per annum (Expenditure White Paper 1980). But the uncertainties did not diminish: for example, extra funds were committed by government in December 1978, only to be taken back immediately by the new government in 1979.

These figures do not fully reflect the availability of research funds to academic investigators. For the fact is that for three of the research councils commitments to their own staff and facilities took an increasing share of resources. For the MRC, for example, this commitment to its research centres, units, and scientific staff amounted to 62.0 per cent in 1977/8 and 63.2 per cent in 1978/9. Moreover, as the CSP had pointed out, these cuts in resources necessarily hit in particular at new projects, since savings cannot be made on commitments to existing research. The consequences of this gradual squeeze on the research funds available to research councils, with almost no growth over the second half of the decade, were discussed by the ABRC in its *Third Report*. The ABRC points out that policy since 1974 had been to shift resources out of 'big science' (eg high energy physics, space science), but that the resources thereby freed had in fact been largely absorbed by salary increases and the need to replace obsolete equipment (ABRC 1979). Councils have thus

— been unable to develop new programmes in promising areas;
— been unable to offer postgraduate training for the rising number of well qualified graduates;
— had difficulty in keeping research facilities up to date;
— had to turn down an increasing number of good grant applications.

The ABRC, far from being the outspoken voice for science that the CSP had been, went on to argue that in view of this long period of deterioration, a period of sustained real growth of 4 per cent per annum 'must be regarded as a minimum'.

TABLE 1.5
Annual percentage growth of the science budget

	1966/67	1967/68	1968/69	1969/70	1970/71	1971/72	1972/73	1973/74	1974/75	1975/76	1976/77
ARC	7.3	12.2	7.3	3.2	7.0	3.1	3.7	4.0	−3.7	−0.6	3.3
MRC	11.6	14.9	5.1	6.9	8.1	3.6	3.6	2.7	−1.7	−1.0	2.7
NERC	17.8	20.6	3.5	20.4	10.4	5.3	4.9	4.4	−3.0	0.2	2.3
SRC	13.2	6.9	5.4	2.9	3.8	4.8	4.1	3.2	−2.2	−2.2	−1.6
SSRC	—	47.3	47.9	25.9	30.3	16.0	10.0	8.6	5.7	6.8	2.0
NHM	1.3	—	6.0	9.7	41.4	−9.8	3.8	23.1	−2.1	1.0	—
S: G & S	41.2	30.5	24.6	3.8	10.2	16.8	2.3	3.5	2.3	—	−1.7
TOTAL	13.3	11.2	7.4	6.1	7.1	4.7	4.2	3.9	−2.1	−1.3	1.7

Source
Second Report of the ABRC (1976)

The increasing inability of the research councils fully to respond to to requests for research support is shown by the example of the SRC (Table 1.6).

TABLE 1.6
SRC (SERC): Relationship between applications received and grants awarded 1967/8 to 1978/9

	Applications considered		Grants made		%	
	Number	Value (£m)	Number	Value (£m)	By number	By Value
1967/8	1,777	22·6	1,126	9·4	63·4	41·7
1968/9	1,791	23·3	1,128	11·2	63·0	48·2
1969/70	2,208	29·9	1,388	14·0	62·9	46·7
1976/7	2,841	69·8	1,670	29·8	58·8	42·7
1977/8	3,040	80·2	1,812	43·9	59·6	54·7
1978/9	4,414	142·9	2,242	58·0	50·8	40·6

Source
SRC Annual Reports

But developments in science policy bearing upon the performance of academic research are not to be accounted for purely in terms of the declining availability of financial resources. For as resources declined the research councils began increasingly to concern themselves with the uses to which funds were put. In common with their counterparts in other countries, the councils began to ensure that funds were used to the best advantage. The old 'responsive' tradition was being abandoned in favour of a more 'interventionist' or 'dirigiste' approach to the funding of research in universities and polytechnics.

One aspect of this was a greater emphasis upon efficiency in the use of resources, expressed in the SRC's policy of 'selectivity and concentration', expounded in 1970.

'The Council is convinced that it must make its support of research, whether pure or applied, more selective, both in relation to particular fields of science meriting concentrated attention and in the choice of scientists responsible and the laboratories where they work. . . . Given its limited resources, the Council must, in order to sustain viable research groups endowed with adequate equipment and ancillary staff of appropriate expertise, concentrate its support in any one field at a limited number of universities.'

(SRC 1970)

It is this doctrine, with its implied emphasis upon support of a limited number of centres of established reputation, which the polytechnics saw as standing in the way of the development of their research.[2]

A second aspect was the earmarking of funds for designated areas of research felt to be of particular scientific and economic importance, and thus meriting additional effort. SRC began to work in this way, on a limited scale, from about 1970, with funds earmarked for (inter alia) polymer and enzyme chemistry and technology. But whereas at that time considerations both of scientific potential and of likely economic advantage carried considerable weight, gradually economic (or in the case of SSRC, policy) considerations came to predominate.

The attempt to make research more 'useful' received a particular stimulus from the Rothschild Report and the White Paper (Cmnd 5046) which followed it in 1972. The aim of the developments announced was to ensure that research and development made a more effective contribution to the formulation and discharge of government policies. This objective included the intention

> 'to make it easier to make Research Councils aware of the policy problems of Departments and to persuade Councils, where this made scientific sense, to adjust programmes so as to make them more relevant to these problems.'
>
> (Review of Cmnd 5046 1979)

As is well known, three of the councils (ARC, MRC, NERC) were required to 'earn' substantial proportions of their existing budget by securing commissions from government departments. This arrangement was not supposed to cover the SRC or the social sciences (SSRC), nor was any mention made (attention paid?) to the effect upon the universities. Indeed there was no direct effect. But the government's own (disquietingly bland) review of the operation of the arrangements acknowledges that there have indeed been effects.

> 'First, the change in the climate of opinion which was embodied in Cmnd 5046 has doubtless affected the attitudes of many university and polytechnic scientists who have responded in various, and generally unquantifiable, ways to the government's desire to relate research, wherever that is appropriate, more closely to national needs in the longer term. A stimulus in this direction has come from the Research Councils, particularly the SRC, who have modified the pattern of support for research projects and post-graduate research training to give greater emphasis to such areas as engineering which are especially relevant to the Government's industrial policy.
>
> 'Second, Departments are placing more commissions with the universities and polytechnics where these have particular skills not found elesewhere.'
>
> (Review of Cmnd 5046 1979 pp.14-15)

Thus the extent to which the ideas underlying the Rothschild doctrine had (been) diffused is illustrated by this Review's singling out SRC — which had been excluded from the transfer arrangements — for special mention. In the social sciences, not considered by Lord Rothschild, a similar attempt was made to initiate research in areas deemed of interest to government departments. The idea that the social sciences might have some special character, or that their usefulness was of a different order or quality from that of the natural sciences, had now long vanished. But so, of course, had the notion of 'utility' articulated by Ben-David in the 1960s. It was no longer a question of doing good research and ensuring that potential users were aware of it. By the middle seventies it had become a question of industrial representatives and officials together (in the industrial field), or officials and scientists together (in the health field), or middle-ranking civil servants alone (in many other fields of government activity) themselves deciding what research needed to be done, and looking for someone to do it.

Useful research now was what such committees thought they wanted, in some cases (it must be said) irrespective of its scientific merit, interest, feasibility, or indeed of the scope for making use of the research results.

Increasingly, then, the funds available for the support of research in higher education became earmarked for research areas, or even specific topics, judged to be useful to industry or government departments. Influences of this kind have been exercised on the one hand through the direct allocation of the research budgets of government departments (although, with the exception of research in the health field and in the social sciences, such commissions have largely not been placed in higher educational institutions, as Table 1.7 shows). On the other hand, and less directly, they have been exercised through the research councils' attempts increasingly to establish priorities in the light of such interests.

In the field covered by the SRC (now SERC) attempts of a variety of kinds have been made to relate academic research more closely to the requirements of industry. For some time a growing share of a static or declining total budget has been set aside for the field of engineering. Within this engineering allocation, an increasing proportion of funds has been earmarked for topics felt by the Engineering Board (and generally by the Department of Industry too) to require more attention. By 1979 these 'specially promoted programmes' took up about 25 per cent of the Engineering Board's allocation. Within the field of postgraduate training the SRC has made considerable efforts over many years, for example through the initiation of schemes of training involving collaboration between a university department and a firm, as in the 'CASE' awards for research training; or more recently in the Teaching Company scheme, financed jointly with the Department of Industry.

In the case of SSRC there has been a more gradually developing concern to orient at least part of the council's research support to areas identified as of interest to a government department. This attempt to step closer to Whitehall has recently gathered momentum. Moreover, as I have indicated, there are special circumstances obtaining in the social sciences, since departments themselves spend more on social research commissioned of academic institutions (and independent research institutes sometimes allied with universities) than is available to SSRC. Steering of the research effort in the social sciences, then, under the influence of current policy preoccupations, is therefore a more extreme phenomenon than is encountered in other fields. In the SERC steering has generally been towards engineering, whereas the MRC has been able to formulate its own priorities within biomedicine, and to seek to implement them largely through its own units and centre.

Naturally, the two sets of policies which have been discussed — those covering higher education, and science policies — have interacted in their effects upon research in higher education. So far as the universities are concerned, we have seen that the 1970s witnessed a relative decline in postgraduate rersearch; an immobile and ageing faculty, with little recruitment; and a declining share of university funds available for research purposes. External funds came to have increasing importance, and research grant applications in science and technology increasingly included requests for salaries and provision of basic scientific equipment. But these funds too had ceased to grow. Lack of growth, the imposition of sudden budgetary cuts, the virtual impossibility of planning, and the extent of existing commitments, took their toll on the research councils. The funds available for *new* research within the academic institutions were not large: an increasing proportion of applications for support had to be turned down. But at the same time the councils were becoming more dirigiste in their deployment of resources: increasingly seeking to earmark their resources for areas of research identified as of interest to industry or government. It is clear that within academic institutions it was becoming more difficult to engage in research for which no such immediate utility was apparent. It is worth reiterating the way in which the concept of utility had changed, and now depended upon the attempt to satisfy the request of an identifiable 'customer'.

The situation which I have tried to characterize, and to put into sharp contrast with the decade which had gone before, was not unique to the United Kingdom.

International Comparisons
A recent OECD report (OECD 1981a) enables us to set the situation which emerged in the British higher education system over the 1970s into an international context. In almost all OECD countries the rate of growth in enrolments diminished greatly in the early years of the 1970s, compared with the previous decade. As the 70s advanced growth fell virtually to zero: in the later years there was almost no growth at all in student numbers in the universities. The implications of this for university research are seen as deriving from three distinct types of linkage: institutional budgets, faculty

TABLE 1.7
Government expenditure on R&D by department and sector of performance 1977/78 (provisional out-turn £m)

Department	In-house £m	In-house %	Institutions of higher education £m	%	Research councils £m	%	Research associations £m	%	Industry £m	%	Other govt. depts, & public agencies £m	%	Other £m	%	Total £m	In-house[1] receipts
Department of Industry	31.3	28.0	0.8	0.7	3.0	2.7	7.8	7.0	48.6	43.4	18.0	16.1	2.4	2.1	111.9	13.2
Department of Energy	—	—	0.2	1.2	7.5	44.6	0.7	4.2	3.9	23.2	2.6	15.5	1.9	11.3	16.8	—
Department of the Environment	11.0	40.5	1.7	6.2	5.0	18.4	2.4	8.8	2.1	7.7	1.5	5.5	3.5	12.9	27.2	2.5
Department of Transport	7.7	54.3	0.9	6.3	—	—	0.5	3.5	4.6	32.4	0.3	2.1	0.2	1.4	14.2	0.8
Department of Health and Social Security	5.8[2]	25.7	4.1	18.1	9.3	41.1	0.2	0.9	1.1	4.9	0.9	4.0	1.2	5.3	22.6	—
Scottish Office–Health	—	—	0.7	31.8	1.1	50.0	—	—	—	—	—	—	0.4	18.2	2.2	—
Ministry of Agriculture and Fisheries	16.5	36.6	0.3	0.7	26.1	57.9	1.0	2.2	—	—	—	—	1.2	2.6	45.1	—
Scottish Office–Agriculture and Fisheries	3.6	20.1	4.4	24.6	—	—	—	—	—	—	9.9	55.3	—	—	17.9	—
Home Office	3.4	64.1	0.3	5.7	—	—	—	—	1.1	20.7	0.4	7.6	0.1	1.9	5.3	—
Scottish Office–Social and Environmental	0.8	72.7	0.1	9.1	—	—	—	—	—	—	0.1	9.1	0.1	9.1	1.1	—
Department of Employment	0.3	37.5	0.2	25.0	0.2	25.0	0.1	12.5	—	—	—	—	—	—	0.8	—
Health and Safety Executive	2.9	67.5	0.3	7.0	0.7	16.3	0.1	2.3	0.1	2.3	—	—	0.1	2.3	4.3	—
Welsh Office	—	—	0.5	83.3	—	—	—	—	—	—	—	—	0.1	16.7	0.6	—
Ministry of Overseas Development	2.1	17.4	2.0	16.5	1.1	9.1	0.1	0.8	—	—	1.4	11.6	5.4	44.6	12.1	—
Department of Education and Science	0.1	3.3	0.6	20.0	—	—	0.2	6.7	—	—	—	—	2.1	70.0	3.0	—
Scottish Office–Education	—	—	0.1	25.0	—	—	0.1	25.0	—	—	—	—	0.2	50.0	0.4	—
Total: Civil Departments	85.5	—	17.2	—	54.0	—	13.2	—	61.5	—	35.2	—	18.9	—	285.5	16.5
Ministry of Defence	215.0	26.8	2.9	0.4	—	—	1.0	0.1	582.2	72.6	0.5	0.1	0.4	—	802.0[3]	23.0
	300.5	—	20.1	—	54.0	—	14.2	—	643.7	—	35.7	—	19.3	—	1087.5	39.5

1 These sums are received for work done in internal research establishments for customers other than the parent Department.
2 Includes (a) Commissions with the National Health Service;
   (b) A sum of £2m for capital expenditure.
3 Excludes expenditure on Headquarters staff costs and on capital investment in establishments.

Source
Review of Cmnd 5046

recruitment, and postgraduate education. In most countries university budgets did not quite keep up, in real terms, with the slight growth in student numbers of the 70s. It has been generally true that salaries have come to take up a growing portion of funds available. Lack of recruitment over the 70s has also been a general phenomenon, and there is widespread concern over the collective ageing of university faculties. The third link, through recruitment of postgraduate (research) students from the (static or declining) pool of new graduates, could not be quantified owing to lack of up-to-date international statistics. However, it appeared that, for reasons which almost certainly differed from one country to another, there was decline in postgraduate studies (most precipitously in Sweden, but also in Germany, where it seems to have been the *best* graduates who took other work). The OECD report comments on this as follows.

'Declining doctoral level work has a number of implications. First, for the health of the national R&D system, since highly trained scientists will be crucial to any future expansion or change of direction. Second, for the well-being of the research potential of the universities themselves since, particularly in the natural sciences, postgraduate students, as part of their research training, have traditionally . . . carried out much of the routine work involved in research.'

(OECD 1981a p.18)

The resource problem, too, has been common to most OECD countries, and is shown to have borne especially heavily upon the provision of capital equipment for research in the natural sciences. This is considered in terms of capital expenditure *per* research scientist and engineer, and this indicator shows a sharp decline through most of the 1970s. On this, the report comments:

(This problem of obsolescence) 'is a source of concern within the universities of nearly all OECD countries. Not only are research scientists unable to re-equip their laboratories, but undergraduates in science and engineering are now frequently being trained on scientific apparatus no longer being used in some government or industrial research establishments.'

(Ibid p.26)

Similar to the British situation also is the general tendency to give an increasingly important role to external or project funding of research. Whilst statistical evidence does not, in fact, generally show an increasing weight of such funds within academic research, there appear to be trends in the structure *of* this external funding: 'it seems to be the case that funds deriving from research councils are typically growing less rapidly than funds deriving from industry and (above all) mission-oriented government departments' (p.29). Moreover, the share which external funds appear to have in total research expenditure by academic institutions actually much underestimates their importance for the performance of research. This is because much of the share attributed to internal funds is taken up by salaries, which are not

— of course — resources available to meet the needs of new research projects. 'Thus', the report argues, 'the funds received from outside may represent a very much greater proportion of the resources available for distribution according to the needs of research' than aggregate statistics suggest.

Given this importance, it is significant to note that in many — but not all — OECD countries it is not only the research funds of government ministries which are being used to stimulate research on topics judged economically or socially important. The tendency of research councils to at least partly abandon traditional 'responsive' policies of research funding, identified in the British case, is characteristic also of many of the larger OECD countries. The attempt increasingly to steer the research work of academic institutions (or, put differently, to seek to mobilize this major research resource in concerted attack on pressing economic and social questions) is thus not unique to the United Kingdom.

Broadly sketched in this way, then, the situation of university research seen as generally obtaining in OECD countries corresponds to that which has emerged in the UK. Or to be more precise, the *pressures* which have emerged over the 1970s have been similar. It will therefore be useful to follow the OECD analysis a little further, and consider the relevance of the diagnosis provided for the situation we face in Britain.

Before doing so, however, it is necessary to point to two facts which have to be borne in mind in making comparisons between the United Kingdom and other comparable OECD countries. These are illustrated by Tables 1.8 and 1.9. Table 1.8 shows that in relation to the total national effort in research and development the higher educational sector in the UK is much smaller than in most countries. It follows that in, say, Sweden government (which has chosen not to build up a network of government research establishments) *cannot but* turn to the universities for the bulk of the research which it considers to be in the national interest to require. It is clear that the situation in this respect is quite different in Britain where, in statistical terms at least, the universities do not dominate in the same way. Second, and despite the well-established belief to the contrary, it is hard to say that in Britain we do too much basic research and too little applied. Indeed, though the indicator is a somewhat different one, Table 1.9 suggests that we do very little basic research by international standards.

THE CRISIS OF RESEARCH
It will be useful now to follow the OECD analysis a little further, bearing these two particularities of the British situation in mind. For though its precise application remains to be considered, this analysis attempts what we must also attempt here. That is, it addresses itself to the questions: what, in the 1980s, should be *expected* of the universities in research? and what must be done in order to enable them to respond effectively to the demands made of them? So far as the second question is concerned, what is minimally

necessary is that steps be taken to surmount some of the difficulties which arose in the 1970s. But clearly the two questions are related: different notions of what it is that higher educational institutions *should* contribute in research will necessarily lead to different analyses of the policy initiatives necessary.

TABLE 1.8
Research in the higher education sector as % of all R&D expenditure

	Business enterprises[1]		Government		PNP		Higher education	
	Expend- iture	Man power	Expend- iture	Man power	Expend- iture	Man power	Expend- iture	Man power
United States	66·8	68·5[2]	15·2	11·3[2]	3·3	4·8[2]	14·7	15·4[2]
Japan	57·8	54·1	12·1	9·3	2·4	1·6	27·7	35·0
Germany	65·0	61·9	16·1	16·5	0·4	0·3	18·6	21·2
France	60·3	54·3	22·8	24·3	1·4	1·7	15·5	19·6
United Kingdom (1975/76)	60·3	n.a.	25·9	n.a.	3·3	n.a.	10·4	n.a.
Netherlands	51·7	50·1	20·8	23·3	2·5	2·6	25·0	23·9
Canada	41·9	38·4	30·5	36·0	0·8	0·4	26·8	4·7
Italy	53·6	41·0	24·6	19·3	n.a.	n.a.	21·8	39·7
Sweden	71·0	66·8	8·6	9·8	–	–	20·5	23·4
Switzerland	75·7	74·9	6·8	5·7	1·2	0·9	16·3	18·4
Belgium	67·9	61·6	11·4	9·5	0·8	0·8	19·9	28·1
Australia (1976/77)	24·8	21·0	50·9	42·6	1·3	1·3	23·0	35·1
Norway	47·1	44·8	18·4	21·3	0·5	0·8	33·9	33·1
Denmark (1976/77)	49·1	52·5	21·7	21·5	0·6	0·8	28·6	25·2
Finland	51·9	45·8	26·3	30·4	0·8	1·0	20·9	22·7
New Zealand	18·0	23·0	61·2	58·7	1·7	1·8	19·1	16·5
Ireland	32·2	24·2	46·8	44·6	4·1	3·7	16·8	27·5
Portugal (1978)	13·1	10·8	66·7	58·0	2·4	1·6	17·8	29·6
Iceland	4·8	1·8	65·7	63·6	3·8	4·9	25·7	29·7

1 SSH wholly or partly excluded.
2 Scientists and engineers only.

Source
OECD 1981b

For present purposes I wish to pursue the discussion of the previous section, and consider (following the OECD report) the implications for research performance of the trends in structure and finance which characterized the 1970s. But because of the dependence of interpretation of

TABLE 1.9
'Advancement of knowledge' as share of public R&D expenditure

	1975	1976	1977	1978	1979	1980
Australia	—	32·3	—	—	—	—
Belgium	52·2	42·8	42·9	29·3	30·2	31·8
Canada	18·0	17·8	18·8	19·3	20·0	—
Denmark	39·7	40·2	39·3	38·0	38·2	39·1
Finland	49·9	49·7	47·8	46·9	43·6	41·3
France	24·1	24·7	25·2	24·5	23·6	22·7
Germany	51·0	51·5	47·2	44·7	42·9	42·8
Greece	—	—	34·9	—	—	—
Ireland	12·5	13·4	19·7	19·0	—	—
Italy	50·8	44·5	41·6	39·3	35·2	35·7
Japan	54·7	54·1	54·2	53·6	53·1	—
Netherlands	60·0	59·7	57·1	55·9	56·0	55·3
New Zealand	15·6	15·4	15·9	16·3	15·3	—
Norway	—	—	48·4	45·5	43·8	42·4
Portugal	—	14·8	—	—	—	—
Spain	—	23·6	22·5	23·0	—	—
Sweden	38·0	—	38·5	38·1	39·3	39·3
Switzerland	42·1	37·1	37·8	38·9	—	—
Turkey	—	—	7·2	—	9·7	—
United Kingdom	20·3	21·9	21·2	21·7	20·5	20·5
United States	4·3	4·1	4·1	4·0	3·9	3·9

Source
Science and Technology Indicators Unit, OECD

these trends upon a view of what it is that higher educational institutions should contribute, the view which will underpin my considerations ought to be made clear. In what must for the moment stand as a purely subjective view (though I hope to support it later) I would in this respect also follow the OECD study. This is most appropriately expressed through the following quotation.

'It is of course perfectly legitimate for governments to seek to secure the assistance of university scientists in developing, through research, means of dealing with pressing national problems. University research systems . . . are too expensive, and too valuable as resources of expertise, to be ignored in any mobilisation of national resources. The fact that it may prove impossible to find academic scientists prepared to develop research programmes in, say, the field of energy . . . is not to the credit of the academic community. On the other hand, it is also the case that government have sometimes been too little aware *both* of the fact that some pressing issues cannot be directly "solved" through the injection of massive resources alone (but require considerable basic research first) and of the need to take some account of the scientific commitments which all good researchers have. . . . Society, and governments, have a valid claim upon the expertise in the university, but to turn the university into a centre primarily of applied research is an abuse and a misuse of that expertise.'

(OECD 1981a p.35)

In the light of this we may consider now the analysis of the implications for the research-performing capabilities of higher educational institutions of the trends of recent years.

Decreasing Flexibility

The OECD report suggests that a number of factors have now come together which serve to render the higher education system less 'flexible' in its research activities: less able to respond to new opportunities in research, whether deriving from developments in scientific disciplines or from external challenges. One of these has been the employment protection legislation passed in a number of countries, which has made temporary employment of project-financed research personnel and technicians a risky undertaking for universities. The other two factors may have more relevance to the British situation. One is the view that as academic institutions become more specialized in their research (research in a given field being increasingly limited to a small number of institutions) so cross-fertilization of ideas between fields will be attenuated. The truth and the implications of this must remain at the level of speculation at the moment. On the final factor adduced it is possible to say rather more. This concerns the implications for research of an ageing faculty, the result of the virtual end to recruitment in the late 1970s. That this is true of the British universities is hardly in doubt, although it may be less true of the polytechnics. It is almost certain that the rapid recruitment of the 1960s, and the period of 'consolidation' which followed, have resulted in a generally ageing faculty in British universities. Table 1.1, which showed a clear 'grade drift' in the structure of faculties, provides indirect evidence.

Sufficient work has now been done for some assessment of the implications of this for research to be possible. The argument does not depend upon the controversial matter of the potential relationship between age and individual creativity or achievement: it is rather more sociological than that. Partly the issue is one of the internal dynamics of research groups: the effects of groups collectively ageing in the absence of recruitment or mobility. Stankiewicz carried out a study of the effects of ageing in this sense upon the productivity of research groups in natural science and technology within Swedish universities (Stankiewicz 1979). He found a curvilinear relationship between group age and output of research papers, such that performance increased over a period of about ten years, and then either stabilized or declined. It seems possible that a certain necessary tension vanishes from the interactions of long-term colleagues. Walford has provided empirical data relating to a physical science department of one of the 'new' British universities (Walford 197?). In this department, which the author indicates is not atypical, 'not only has the number of academics remained very nearly constant for the past 10-12 years but the actual personnel have remained constant . . . 34 of the present 35 members of academic staff have now been in the department for 10 years or more.' The department was initially very successful in building up 'a nationally, if not internationally, recognized reputation for research'. Walford then goes on to examine the department's record in publication. Now it is true, as the author recognizes, that there are dangers in making too much of this particular indicator. Nevertheless, especially since people have been working in more or less the same research specialisms over the time considered, it is certainly of *some* significance. Figure 1.1 shows the total number of publications by members of the department over the period 1967-77.

FIGURE 1.1
Count of publications for 34 tenured members of academic staff

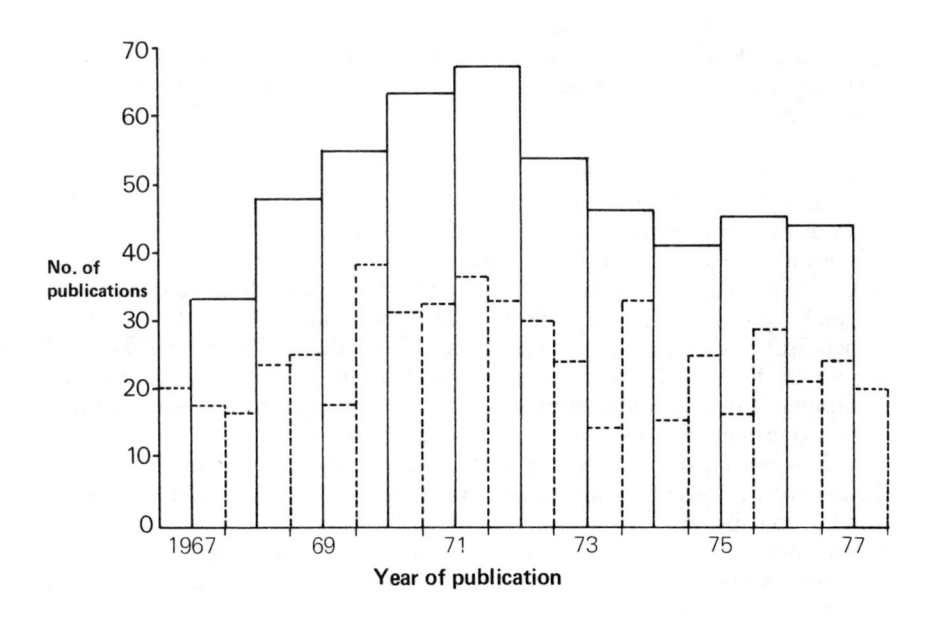

It is clear that there was a significant decline in output in the later 1970s: publications in 1976/7 amounted only to some two-thirds of those of 1971/2. After considering a number of possible explanations, Walford concludes.

> 'It is most probable that the decrease in publications in this case can be attributed to some members of the academic staff gradually moving out of active scientific research altogether, and to a general decline in the level of morale and research commitment within the department.'

This conclusion fits, all too well, with that reached on quite different evidence by Halsey and Trow, which I quoted earlier. Their study, it will be recalled, led them to the conclusion that with advancing age 'the motivation to do a good deal of research grows weaker. . . .'

There is one final point to be made here, although I can provide no empirical evidence with which to support it.[3] It seems to me likely that as scientists (or indeed scholars of any kind) age the likelihood of their being willing significantly to change their field of research will diminish. Of course there are eminent exceptions, but the commitments made, and other things, militate against any such a change appearing attractive to the older scientist. There is reason to believe that, at least in some fields of natural science, significant new areas tend to be opened up by younger men (see Mullins 1980). It may be, then, that an ageing university faculty will, on the whole, be less equipped to respond to new challenges and opportunities, at least in certain disciplines.

Put together, evidence of this kind seems to me both to support the contention of the OECD study — that there is declining flexibility — and to suggest that it may be having serious implications for British academic institutions.

Obsolescence of Equipment

The OECD study refers to the fact that 'universities are increasingly unable to provide an adequate base of research equipment from their normal operating budgets'. Research councils in many countries are now being asked to provide for facilities which would until recently have come from normal operating funds. The OECD report also shows that capital expenditure per scientist declined sharply in the 1970s, in virtually all countries for which data were available. The conclusion is that the equipment upon which scientists must train new researchers, and conduct their experiments, is becoming increasingly obsolescent.

It is not clear that, were a more detailed analysis of the situation in British institutions of higher education to be carried out, it would give rise to similar conclusions. The UGC's scientific equipment grant to universities, which must include elements both for teaching and for research, provides only the roughest of indicators. Table 1.10, which shows the total allocation in current terms, is at least indicative.

On this indicator there has in fact been sustained growth, although from this sum must be provided teaching equipment for a still slightly growing student body. Nevertheless the SERC, in annual reports, has frequently in recent years alluded to the problem of obsolescence of routine scientific equipment. The council's policy has recently tended to be that more advanced and expensive equipment could be provided to an applicant research group only on condition that the facility would be shared with other groups.

TABLE 1.10
UGC scientific equipment grant (GB universities): at £m current prices

1970/1	1971/2	1972/3	1973/4	1974/5	1975/6	1976/7	1977/8	1978/9	1979/80
20·9	23·0	28·4	37·4	21·2	45·5	30·4	35·1	41·6	52·8

Source
DES statistics

It is increasingly claimed that the difficulties in meeting the needs of research groups for the more and more sophisiticated equipment necessary for scientific progress is 'closing off' important lines of research (eg Association of American Universities 1980). The argument is that without the most advanced equipment it is simply not possible to tackle significant problems in a number of fields of research. My own view is that, whilst this may indeed be the case in some fields, a less visible but more insidious process is likely more widely to be occurring. This is that research will simply become less efficient. Waiting one's turn for access to a facility; sending samples away for analysis; delays because apparatus cannot be kept running round the clock, or indeed adequately maintained (service contracts are expensive, technicians in short supply): all these things will be combining to slow down, render less efficient the process of conducting research.

Decline in Postgraduate Research Training
A third aspect of the 'crisis' documented by the OECD report reflects a decline in postgraduate research training. As I have already pointed out, international evidence here is sketchy: nevertheless there is evidence from a number of countries of a decline in the number of new doctorates being awarded.

> 'Although there are many complications involved in interpreting such output data, it seems reasonable to argue that the number of doctorates awarded per year gives an indication of the amount of research being carried out in the universities ... and, in addition, of the number of scientists available to industry, government, and the university itself.'

As this quotation indicates, postgraduate research has a double aspect, of which any judgement of the adequacy of its scale must take account. On the one hand it may be regarded as the production of the research-trained manpower required by industry and other research-performing institutions. In this sense the scale of such training has been seen as potentially subject to manpower planning. On the other hand, the stock of students undergoing such training represents a major part of the research capacity of the academic system. Thus, any significant reduction in the scale of training — whether or not the result of assessments of manpower demand — cannot but impact upon the ability of the academic system to respond to new research opportunities and requirements. Of course, in fields in which manpower demand is minimal, or in which it is not really possible to speak of the existence of a labour market at all, this second consideration stands alone. In the humanities, for example, it will be the scale of academic research alone which will be at issue when we are forced to depart from a pure consumption approach to postgraduate study.

Tables 1.2 and 1.3 showed that in Britain there was a small rise in the number of postgraduates over the 1970s, although their share in the total student body declined over this period. It appeared also that within postgraduate study there was some movement from research towards advanced training, and also a gradual shift to part-time studies. (In connection with this tendency for postgraduate work to become part-time, we may briefly note Rudd's finding that those working part-time for a higher degree are considerably less likely than those working full-time successfully to complete their studies (Rudd and Hatch 1968).) Part-time study is very much more common in the humanities and social sciences than in the natural sciences. Table 1.11 gives further information, on output by field.

TABLE 1.11
Higher degrees awarded in certain subjects 1970-1978 (UK)

	1970		1972		1975		1978	
	PhD	Other	PhD	Other	PhD	Other	PhD	Other
Engineering/ technology	945	1613	681	1587	1043	2092	1020	2890
Science	2548	1525	1765	1457	2241	1719	2378	2315
Social science	394	1738	309	2041	546	2765	671	3314
Other	1243	2217	790	2402	1426	4064	1450	4094
Total	5130	7093	3545	7505	5256	10640	5519	12613

Source
DES Statistics

It is not possible on the basis of these figures to reach any major conclusions. Clearly the shift from research training to advanced course work, indicated by enrolment figures, is substantiated. The growth in the social sciences at PhD level is striking, not least when contrasted with the lack of growth in doctorates awarded in other sciences. This must, however, largely reflect SSRC policy (at a time when its budget was growing): a policy which has always reserved a vastly greater share of finance for student stipends. This situation must certainly be now changing.

Clearly it is not accurate to speak of a serious decline in numbers being trained in research, as it is in certain other OECD countries. However it has to be recognized that these PhD figures reflect decisions made at least three years earlier, when graduates embarked upon their research training. That is, they largely predate the decline in resources for research which, as we have seen, has been particularly sharp since the mid-1970s. Moreover, in so far as decisions by graduates to enter research training are also a reflection of perceived opportunities for a career in research, it would seem likely that any decline in output is yet to appear.

The question then is Would such a decline matter? I have suggested that so far as the laboratory sciences are concerned, numbers have to be judged in their dual aspect. It is perfectly possible to conceive of economic demand (for trained researchers) implying a level of training which would render much academic research activity scarcely viable. But there is also the question of the validity of market demand. Many believe that the demands of the labour market have a major role to play in the planning of the proper scale of research training (perhaps in contrast to undergraduate education, where until recently student demands were thought a proper determinant). Economists have tended to write off the emphasis upon 'need' in many science policy documents as being an economically meaningless concept, and representing no more than special pleading on behalf of science. Yet, of course, from the point of view of science policy (as distinct from educational policy) precisely the *creation* of demand, through for example the stimulation of industrial research, may be a major objective of policy.

Once more we are thrown up against the potential conflict between science policy and higher education policy where expansion is not a shared objective. But this time the dilemma presents itself at a more fundamental level: that of the assumptions which should guide policy. I shall return presently to this question of the proper basis for a university research policy fitted to the exigencies of the 1980s.

First, however, to recapitulate. Evidence does point to the applicability of the OECD analysis to the British situation. The efficiency, the viability, of the academic research system has been in decline since the mid-70s: the consequence of lack of recruitment, ageing faculty, declining resources for research, the particular problem of instrumentation in experimental sciences, and perhaps growing demoralization. Of this system increasing demands have then been made: above all for *demonstrable* usefulness, and for research responses to Britain's industrial (and to a lesser extent social) problems. The pressures have intensified as the system has been rendered less and less fit to respond. It follows logically that the academic research system cannot reasonably have been expected adequately to have met all the demands made of it. But aside from the conclusion that steps must be taken to increase the research capacity of the system, or its effectiveness, there is a second possible line of criticism. As I tentatively indicated earlier, it is possible to argue that the pressure for 'relevance' which has built up is too extreme: that the demands made of the universities take too little account of their strengths and their weaknesses as a component of the national research system. This was the implication of the quotation from the OECD report given on page 31ff. If it applied at all, then it applies a fortiori to the British case where, as I have shown, universities represent a distinctly smaller proportion of the total research effort than in almost any comparable OECD country.

I have already made clear that I personally accept this argument, according to which the demands made of the university system in research are themselves called into question. In other words, whilst it is perfectly legitimate — indeed essential — to seek to mobilize the talents contained in universities and polytechnics in a research attack on national problems, it is necessary also to take account of their inherent institutional structures and values. These values, it should be added, are not of a purely national kind, but are to some degree shared with academic institutions everywhere.

We must then finally turn to two related sets of issues, with which any policy for the future must be fundamentally concerned. The first involves the steps which must be taken to compensate for the decline in recent years in research effectiveness and capacity. But the priority to be attached by government to such an initiative will necessarily depend upon the importance attached to research within public policy as a whole. The second, and related, set of issues revolves around the question: what exactly *should* be expected of universities and polytechnics?

A STRATEGY FOR THE FUTURE

I hope to have shown that a continuation of past trends leaves much to be desired if research is to form any significant part of the nation's response to the challenges of the 1980s. The question of whether research *should* be seen as particularly relevant at this difficult time, as meriting investment when economies must everywhere be sought, is a matter seemingly beyond the confines of this chapter. Yet we cannot pass on without attending to it. For, as I have argued, this broad question of political strategy has profound implications for what is both reasonable and desirable in regard to the future of research in the universities and polytechnics.

In Britain we have not been much concerned, in policy-making circles, by the experiences or initiatives of other countries, at least within the areas of policy now under discussion. The intentions of other countries (and, in so far as we are concerned with technological innovation, of competitors) are not in practice likely much to influence policy. Nevertheless, what such comparison shows is that OECD countries are increasingly agreed that research and development — designed to foster the growth and deployment of radically new technologies — should form a central plank of policies for the 1980s (OECD 1981b). Some examples perhaps provide useful illustration. In Japan, for example, the Industrial Structure Council (which advises the Minister for International Trade and Industry) offered a vision of Japan as a 'technology based nation'. A report published in 1980 argued that Japan would have to depend increasingly upon technological progress as the motor of her economic and social progress and economic security. Great importance is attached to training researchers capable of making significant technological breakthroughs, and Japan is planning significantly to increase investment in basic research. In France in July 1980, even before the change of government, a major political commitment was made considerably to increase investment in research. The priority accorded to science and technology has nevertheless been much enhanced by the new administration in Paris, where the lines of policy have been determined by a national colloquium (involving 2,000 scientists), and will be embodied in forthcoming legislation. Sweden is another example of a country planning a significant offensive in selected areas of technology, following reports on the nation's future prepared by the Royal Academy of Engineering Sciences and by the Board for Technical Development. A parliamentary bill is in course of preparation in Sweden too, and there is much interest in developing a more co-ordinated approach to the formulation of government research priorities. These examples could be multiplied over and again.

In Britain only the Advisory Council for Applied Research and Development (ACARD) has consistently — in a series of reports — put forward a similar view. In their 1978 report on *Industrial Innovation* ACARD argued for a number of steps which needed to be taken in order to stimulate innovation (ACARD 1978). These included additional money for the SRC (now SERC) to build up its support for programmes relevant to manufacturing technologies; further support for schemes designed to encourage more better qualified graduates to enter productive industry; additional attempts to improve university/industry relations, for example by offering tax incentives to firms lacking research facilities and making use of those available in universities. Although the views expressed by ACARD mirror those of comparable advisory bodies abroad (such as those quoted), they have not been translated into policy commitments to the extent that they have in Japan, France, Sweden, etc.

There is no doubt that any such commitment on the part of the British government would have significant implications for academic research and for the policies and funding mechanisms necessary to sustain it. This may be illustrated by the case of biotechnology: a field which in almost all industrialized Western nations is seen as offering particular potential for industrial development. A joint working group of ACARD, the Royal Society, and the Advisory Board for the Research Councils reported in March 1980 on the initiatives necessary for stimulation of this field in Britain (ACARD/RS/ABRC 1980). Lacking established industry, the field is seen as requiring 'technology push' for its development, 'reflected in a firm commitment to strategic applied research'. The analysis and recommendations show clearly the importance attached by the working group to academic research in the generation of ideas and the production of skilled manpower necessary for the development of industrial biotechnology.

> 'Biotechnology lacks university centres specifically for it and this results in a shortage of new ideas for industry and of suitably trained manpower.' (p.8)

In relation to this manpower requirement

> '... expertise must be built up in universities, and ... this will best be done by expanding the research and teaching capability in a limited number of existing centres of excellence and ensuring their close interaction with industry.' (p.25)

Moreover, the development of these centres should not be restricted to research and postgraduate studies: the group argue that 'it is not too early to envisage undergraduate courses in biotechnology'.

The group is much concerned, as was ACARD in the earlier report cited, by the poor relations existing in Britain between universities and industry:

> 'Co-operation between British universities and industry seems particularly poor in the biological sciences and traditional attitudes of indifference or mistrust are prevalent on both sides. Even where the commercial potential of a new scientific discovery is recognized and there is a desire to establish contacts, there is much uncertainty about how to improve the situation. . . .

> 'The ignorance of most academic scientists about the complexities of patenting, industrial markets, profitability and cash-flow problems limits their immediate usefulness to industry. Many would, however, be happy to devote part of their time to applied problems, but they seldom know what these are. British industry lags behind that of most other countries in the extent to which it uses academic consultants.' (p.24-5)

Thus the analysis implies the crucial important of building up university research and teaching, and of improving links with industry, for the development of British biotechnology. Beyond this, an important weakness in the structure of public funding is identified.

> '... the present structure of public and private support for R. and D. is not well suited to the development of a subject like biotechnology which, at the moment, straddles the divisions of responsibility both among Government departments and among Research Councils and the arbitrarily defined fields of fundamental and applied research. Strategic applied research is in general ill-served by our research funding

mechanisms. . . .' (p.8)

Now, were there in Britain to be a major national commitment to technological innovation, involving not only biotechnology but a number of other fields (including micro-electronics and its many possible areas of development) as well, it seems to follow that the kinds of initiatives proposed by the Biotechnology Working Group would need to be equivalently multiplied. The group speak of the need to build up centres of expertise by the creation, over five years, of twenty new teaching and research posts 'with a capital investment of around £2 million to provide adequate laboratory facilities'. There is tacit recognition of the virtual impossibility of achieving anything really new within existing resources: a view which fits all too well with our own earlier conclusion as to the 'inflexibility' borne of ageing and shortage.

But perhaps the most significant conclusion, with implications well beyond the biotechnology field, is that relating to the structure of funding (see above, p.40). The doctrine enunciated by Lord Rothschild — the 'customer-contractor principle' — which has come to govern so much of British research policy, is based upon a simple dichotomy. Either research is 'fundamental', or else it must be of discernible use to a clearly identifiable customer. The doctrine does not admit of the possibility of utility in the absence of an existing customer. The concept of utility, of applied research, which has dictated the allocation of government research funds (and a significant share of research council funds too) is therefore logically dependent upon the *existing* structure of industry, and the *existing* structure of public administration. There can be no 'need' for applied research not expressed as customer 'demand'. The conservative effects of this view, militating against the initiation of 'strategic applied research' (and radically new technology), were pointed out by the Biotechnology Working Group. Relatively speaking, the pernicious effects of this conservatism are more serious by far in the social sciences. For here, as I indicated earlier, funds allocated on this basis have come increasingly to dominate research: and will do so all the more as the SSRC seeks to step closer to Whitehall. In other words social science research has been pushed increasingly to respond to the identifiable current interests of existing administrative structures. This has inevitably led to a relative undervaluing of research which would, for example, have relevance only within the context of a more integrated approach to social policy, planned within a longer-term perspective.

By raising the special problems of the social sciences I have not intended to depart from my general theme at this point: the implications for research of a major commitment to technological innovation. As has been widely recognized abroad any such commitment carries with it an important role for the social sciences. This is bound up with the problems of securing the acceptance within society of technological change, and of planning the social policy initiatives necessary to mitigate its worst effects. In the Netherlands, for example, a programme of research on the social and cultural implications micro-electronics (going beyond identifiable employment effects) is one plank in current policy towards their introduction. In other words social research must provide the means of assessing the implications of technological change (which will frequently transcend financial and labour market effects) and of helping society better understand the implications of such change. It must also be the means by which social and educational policies can be designed in order to alleviate the costs which will fall, as they always do, upon those least able to bear them. But if this is to be done — and indeed if the necessary technological opportunities are to be identified — *long-term* thinking and planning is essential. Despite some ill-fated initiatives taken in the early 70s the culture of British public administration is opposed to such strategic thinking and planning. It is precisely the fate of these initiatives (PAR, the initially strategic role of the CPRS, many proposals of the Fulton Committee) which cannot strictly be attributed to the exigencies of inflation, which is indicative. Perhaps at this point I might refer back to an earlier conclusion: that it was the breakdown of planning, and the financial uncertainties transmitted by the UGC and the research councils, which has posed one of the major problems for academic research since the mid-70s.

It is now possible to begin to consider the kinds of steps which need to be taken if the academic research system is to make an adequate contribution to the economic and social well-being of the nation, proceeding on the view that technological change must play an important part in any such revitalization.

I shall not dwell upon the initiatives necessary to restore the research capacity of the system. There is no doubt that significant investment in new scientific instruments will be necessary. Equally, ways must be found of bringing new blood into the system: of ensuring that the most talented of the rising generation of research scientists are not denied the possibility of a career spent at least partly in academic research. This will require radical rethinking of the availability of research fellowships; the creation of temporary posts (perhaps guaranteed for ten years — though to the institution not to the individual); steps to encourage greater mobility of research personnel between government, industry and the academic world, and so on. This is an international problem upon which, it must be said, little action has as yet been taken. Clearly there is room for a much more effective exchange of ideas.

Though the precise details of policy initiatives of these two kinds have not been worked out — and in the absence of any political will they are unlikely to be — their significance as *areas* for initiative-taking are clear. But much beyond this, there is need for significant rethinking on what exactly it is that universities and polytechnics should be contributing, and still more fundamentally on how this rethinking should take place. There has been a tendency in Britain for research priorities to be established — in a research council committee, or in a departmental research committee of one kind or another — in considerable isolation from the views of the scientific community. Moreover, such priorities have tended to be developed in isolation too from the parallel priorities of other bodies with possibly overlapping interests. The lesson that it is almost impossible truly to *impose* research priorities — especially where these have little in the way of scientific interest to commend them — has never been learned. Research priorities established by the public bodies which allocate funds for academic research — research councils and government departments varying in relative importance from field to field — must be established in a much wider context. They must take account of the existing commitments of scientists working in a field and win their co-operation, which is obviously crucial. They must take account of the priorities and research activities of other organizations both public and private, including industry. I do not propose that the attempt be made to derive them from a National Colloquium on the scale of that soon to take place in France. (Nevertheless the extent to which the French colloquium has engaged, excited, re-moralized, inspired the French scientific community cannot be underestimated. In so far as demoralization, borne in part of a seeming denial by society of the fundamental worth of academic research, is a crucial aspect of the problem, there is something to be learned from current events in France.) Perhaps a more appropriate initiative, worthy of consideration, is the Dutch idea of sector councils. Broad strategic research goals for fields of application could be established by representatives of the variety of organizations with an interest in the field, including the universities, and on the basis of wide consultation. Such plans would then have an indicative function in regard to programmes of research support. Potential users of research (conceived broadly), as well as a wide spectrum of the scientists who would have to be involved, would have the opportunity of making their views known.

Related to this is the question of planning by bodies with financial responsibility for supporting research: the UGC, the research councils, and so on. If the Council for Scientific Policy was correct in its view that 'the chief danger for science . . . arises from a failure to plan: the sudden imposition of a financial ceiling . . . would strike most at new men and new projects', then this can be no less true today, even if more difficult to implement. Research support cannot be seen as providing scope for short-term economies if research is to be successful. Means must somehow be found of re-injecting an element of financial (and thereby psychological) stability into mechanisms for the support of research: we must at least strive to return to the days of meaningful multi-year funding commitments.

There will of course be a natural tendency, especially on the part of government departments, to seek to respond to changing political priorities and emergent concerns. Academic institutions are likely at such times to have the Queen's shilling thrust upon them. There is much to be said for their enlisting in a more considered fashion: for they themselves to seek to determine the extent of the response which they can make without danger to their principal missions in fundamental and strategic research. To this end the developing interest on the part of a number of European universities in formulating their own research policies (at the level of the department and of the faculty) merits consideration. Universities such as Leiden (Netherlands), Konstanz and Bremen (Germany), Leuven (Belgium), the Technological University in Zurich (Switzerland) are all, in their different ways, taking steps in this direction. Mechanisms being established permit not only the determination of priority fields for development, but also continuous review of the balance between different kinds of research activities proceeding within the different disciplines. In Germany the Wissenschaftsrat has for some time been urging universities to make efforts to establish such mechanisms: a similar initiative should be considered here.

A second counterweight to the tendency for short-term research demands to drive out longer-term work also merits consideration. In Sweden an official committee looking into university relations with industry and public bodies sponsoring applied research (sector agencies, in Swedish terminology) has proposed recently that these public bodies be required to reserve a proportion of their research budgets for support of strategic research within their areas of interest. There is in my view a case for government departments here acting in the same way. As I have indicated it is especially in the social sciences that their funds have come entirely to dominate in some research fields. This carries great risks at a time when the traditional concern of many departments to support relevant strategic research has largely been stripped away. The Swedish committee argues also that ways might usefully be sought of encouraging industry partly to support academic research in this way. In Germany this is already the case, through for example industrial contributions to the Stifterverband für die Deutsche Wissenschaft. In a number of places industrial enterprises are beginning to think anew as to *how* they can best make use of academic skills and facilities. In the USA, for example, Exxon has recently chosen to consolidate its research contracts with MIT into a multi-year 'strategic' agreement. In Japan the industrial view is that universities should be doing fundamental research in fields generally of interest to industry: not applied research, which the firms consider they can do more effectively themselves.

I am by no means arguing that the variety of higher educational institutions which we still enjoy should have identical commitments to research, with similar balances between theoretical work, contractual work for industry, and so on. This indeed is the danger, and I have already referred to an historic tendency to a single model. Diversity must be encouraged. There is plenty of room for short-term problem solving for local industry, for applied studies by social scientists on behalf of a local social services department. But such work must not be at the expense of the research activities which in the longer term are likely to contribute most to Britain's economic, social and cultural development.

To reiterate, the higher education system composes only 10 per cent of the research and development activity of the United Kingdom. Given some determination to overcome the deterioration of the late 70s (and the demoralization brought about by more recent events) there is a major contribution to be made. But it must be widely recognized that this 10 per cent is not simply available, to be drawn on at will, but that it has certain strengths, certain weaknesses, not shared by the other 90 per cent: that it has a *particular* role to play. Universities and polytechnics, together with senior representatives of industry and government, must at last begin to *think* about precisely how the special talents contained in higher education can best contribute to the nation's need for research. A debate of this kind, a modest version perhaps of the French colloquium, will be essential when science (taking the word now in the broad sense it has in most European languages) becomes something more than a source of financial savings. After the experiences of the 1960s and 1970s, shared with most industrialized OECD countries, Britain stumbles alone into the 1980s.

NOTES

1   I have dealt with this issue in two unpublished papers: 'Elite institutions in post-secondary education systems: France, United Kingdom, United States' (OECD paper SME/ET/78.32) and 'Structures and values as barriers to innovation-oriented research in Britain' (1979).
2   Farina and Gibbons have in fact shown that no such concentration has in fact taken place, although this does not affect the social consequences of the belief referred to. But see Farina and Gibbons (1979).
3   A current SERC-financed project of Beverton and Ziman may cast light on this.
4   University/industry relations are being seen as increasingly problematic in a wide range of countries, including those (such as German, Netherlands, Switzerland) where they have traditionally been seen as effective. A current OECD inquiry is investigating the issue.

REFERENCES

AAU (1980) Assocation of American Universities *The Scientific Instrumentation Needs of Research Universities* Washington DC: AAU

ABRC (1979) Advisory Board for the Research Councils *Third Report* Cmnd 7467. London: HMSO

ACARD (1978) Advisory Council for Applied Research and Development *Industrial Innovation* London: HMSO

ACARD/RS/ABRC (1980) *Biotechnology* Report of a Joint Working Party. London: HMSO

Ben-David, J. (1968) *Fundamental Research and the Universities* Paris: OECD

Blume, S. (1974) New teaching-research relationships in mass post-secondary education. In *Structure of Studies and Place of Research in Mass Higher Education* Paris: OECD

Burgess, T. and Pratt, J. (1971) *Technical Education in the United Kingdom* Innovation in Higher Education series. Paris: OECD

Cohen, A.V. and Ivins, L. (1967) *The Sophistication Factor in Science Expenditure* Science Policy Studies No 1. London: HMSO

CSP (1966) Council for Scientific Policy *Report on Science Policy* Cmnd 3007. London: HMSO

CSP (1967) Council for Scientific Policy *Second Report on Science Policy* Cmnd 3420. London: HMSO

Farina, C. and Gibbons, M. (1979) A quantitative analysis of the Science Research Council's policy of 'selectivity and concentration' *Research Policy* 8, 306

Halsey, A.M. and Trow, M. (1973) *The British Academics* London: Faber

Heyworth (1965) *Report of the Committee on Social Studies* (Heyworth Report) Cmnd 2660. London: HMSO

Layard, R., King, J. and Moser, L. (1969) *The Impact of Robbins* Harmondsworth: Penguin

Leavis, F.R. (1972) *Nor Shall My Sword* London: Chatto and Windus

Mullins, N.C., Hargens, L. and Hecht, P.K. Research areas and stratification processes in science *Soc. Stud. Science* 10

Nisbet, R. (1971) *The Degradation of the Academic Dogma* London: Heinemann

OECD (1981a) Organization for Economic Cooperation and Development *The Future of University Research* Paris: OECD

OECD (1981b) Organization for Economic Cooperation and Development *Science and Technology Policy for the 1980s* Paris: OECD

Review of Cmnd 5046 (1979) *Review of the Framework for Government Research and Development (Cmnd 5046)* Cmnd 7499. London: HMSO

Robinson, E. (1968) *The New Polytechnics* Harmondsworth: Penguin

Rudd, E. and Hatch, S. (1968) *Graduate Study and After* London: Wiedenfeld and Nicholson

Stankiewicz, R. (1979) The size and age of Swedish academic research groups and their scientific performance. In Andrews, F. (Editor) *Scientific Productivity* Cambridge/Paris: Cambridge University Press/Unesco

SRC (1970) Science Research Council *Selectivity and Concentration in Support of Research* London: SRC

Swann Committee (1968) Committee on Manpower Resources for Science and Technology *The Flow into Employment of Scientists, Engineers, and Technologists* Cmnd 3760. London: HMSO

Trend (1963) *Committee of Enquiry into the Organisation of Civil Science* (Trend Report) Cmnd 2171. London: HMSO

Truscot, B. (1951) *Red Brick University* Harmondsworth: Penguin

UGC (1968) University Grants Committee *University Development 1962-1967* Cmnd 3820. London: HMSO

Walford, G. (1979) Spontaneous creation: study of a university department
Chemistry in Britain 15, 447-453

SEMINAR DISCUSSION

Much of the seminar discussion on Blume's contribution focused around his call for a national forum to define research priorities. In his introduction Dr Blume stressed the need for improving morale among academic researchers. Such improved morale had certainly occurred recently in France following the national colloquium. Several people agreed that a rejuvenation was also required in Britain and supported the suggestion of a forum. Others were more sceptical and felt the present system of 'muddling through' to be the best in the circumstances. It was also pointed out that ultimately the forumulation of national priorities for research was a political initiative. There had been as much fervour about science and technology in Britain in 1964 as there is in France today.

Some participants also pointed out that national priorities *are* in fact determined in Britain. ACARD had made a number of proposals for major British research efforts (eg biotechnology), and the research councils and the ABRC also determine priorities for the science budget. The UGC is also beginning to establish priorities. However, most participants felt that a new system was required, which should be more open and permit greater involvement of both the scientific community and potential research users. This would promote a wider dialogue and lead to improved morale.

Problems with the present Research System
Dr Blume identified a number of problems which needed resolution. The discussion amplified the nature of the problems but did little to identify solutions.

The decline in funds was the major problem; this in turn had led to the decline in recruitment to academic posts, which had led to an ageing of faculty. This was common to most OECD countries and would be a problem for many years. There were no obvious solutions. In addition, there was a fall off in the number of postgraduates and postdoctoral students, and in some branches of science this decline in the number of 'front line troops' would have serious implications for the research output in those disciplines. A lack of academic research opportunities might prove to be to industry's advantage if it was thereby able to recruit the better quality graduates who would in better times have gone into academic jobs.

Polytechnics
Since the local education authorities support only teaching in the polytechnics, it is left to individual faculty initiatives to develop research. This has led to an enormous variation in the amount of research carried out in polytechnics.

When it was agreed in the early days of the polytechnics that they would be encouraged to do research, it was suggested that they should be directed to solving local problems. The implication was that local industry would pay. This has not worked out in practice since industry sees no greater advantage in turning to its closest polytechnic. It is interested in turning to whoever, nationally, has the best research record and capability in the topic in question.

Those polytechnics which have managed to build up a substantial research programme have found that this has helped them to attain a much higher degree of autonomy.

2

THE FUNCTIONS OF RESEARCH

by Michael Gibbons

INTRODUCTION
This chapter is concerned with the policy issues surrounding the function of research in institutions of higher education in Britain. It will be primarily concerned with the question 'What is to be done? if research is to be maintained as a central activity within the nation's universities and polytechnics. As will become clear the answers are, in large measure, conditioned by what already is accomplished and by perceptions by vice-chancellors and principals, among others, of what can realistically be accomplished in the current turbulent environment.

To attempt to write on this theme is a daunting task. So much has already been said about the function of research in universities and polytechnics. 'Is there any point to repeating the conventional wisdom which is not necessarily less true for all its familiarity?' Some argue that the institutions of higher education have not been effective in explaining their activities to the wider public and, therefore, that there is always a need for polemical writing which tries to communicate to an increasingly sceptical public what does go on. Happily, the Society for Research in Higher Education (SRHE) is aiming at something quite different: 'a relatively neutral, even expert, forum in which strategic choices can be identified, illuminated and discussed' (THES 8.5.81, p.27) Although there is always a need for increasing public awareness about the function of higher education, there is, currently, a much greater need to formulate and discuss policy alternatives. Policy research is about identifying, illuminating and promoting discussion of alternatives — choices which will have to be faced by central governments, local authorities, vice-chancellors and principals, or even academics themselves, especially if a policy of contraction for the higher education sector continues to be pursued. The primary task of this chapter will be to identify some of the strategic choices that face institutions of higher education in relation to their research function in the 1980s and 1990s.

In order to do this it will be necessary to outline the context in which higher education will develop. It might be a useful preliminary, however, to mention the main factors underlying the policy alternatives to be discussed later in the chapter. The first, and perhaps most general issue regards the relationship of institutions of higher education to central and local government. The universities and polytechnics are currently engaged in defending their autonomy against further encroachment by various forms of bureaucratic control. In effect, they are renegotiating their positions vis à vis government. Professor M. Kogan, in the SRHE Leverhulme seminar on institutional change (L. Wagner (editor) *Agenda for Institutional Change in Higher Education* SRHE 1982) identified four basic models for promoting or facilitating change: centralist-managerial, oligarchic, political and market. He makes the point that higher education is coming increasingly under a centralist-managerial style of bureaucratic control. As will become clear, research in universities and polytechnics is characterized more by an oligarchic style of management and, therefore, the management of education generally is likely to conflict with the currently practised style of managing research in academic institutions. There is little that is more feared by academics than the bureaucratic planning of research (see for example, P. Gummett and G. Price (1977) An approach to the central planning of British science *Minerva* 15, 141) and, as a consequence, in renegotiating their position vis à vis central and local governments, universities and polytechnics will be required to specify more clearly the types of research they wish to promote.

It seems likely that the process of further clarifying the functions of research will lead to the setting up of a more diversified system of higher education institutions. As Professor Clarke has pointed out in the SRHE Leverhulme seminar on institutional change, 'a single sector of nationalized public universities cannot zig-zag in all the many directions called for by the increasing heterogeneity of functions. The form becomes overloaded. It does not adapt well to new types of students, new connections to labour markets, new academic fields' (THES 2.10.81, p.10). Such 'zig-zagging' will also be necessary if universities and polytechnics are to orient their research activities more toward social and industrial needs. In responding to social needs, generally, what is required is not so much a once and for all redirection of research programmes but building into the universities and polytechnics an increased capacity to respond to continuously changing market signals.

One of the principal problems facing the higher education sector, then, will be concerned with functional clarification. The traditional functions — teaching, scholarship and research — have emerged historically and at different times. The research function, in particular, is of relatively recent vintage. Moreover, it was added before the dynamics of scientific specialization had become clear. Science itself has become differentiated into pure and applied research, into curiosity-oriented and mission-oriented research, into strategic and short-term research. Teaching, too, has differentiated into natural science and social science, into science and engineering, into non-vocational and professional training, into postgraduate and undergraduate studies. Such is the fragmentation of research and teaching in the temporary context that Lord Flowers has recently questioned whether the function of scholarship is not being seriously undermined (*Fundamental Research and the Universities of Europe* Council of Europe, Helsinki 1981). Each of these differentiations of research and teaching was appended to the institutions of higher education. Teaching and research are now said to be essential constituents of the higher education sector. But, what kinds of teaching, for whom, to what purpose? What kinds of research are appropriate? What kinds of scholarship are possible in an age of specialization? Are universities and polytechnics to teach all comers; to carry out all types of research? If so, is there not a danger of functional over-load? What are the choices to be made? Who will make them?

It is a question of strategic choice to clarify what kinds of teaching and research are to be carried out in the higher education sector. It is a strategic choice to resist pressures to acquire functions which are either inappropriate or which the universities and polytechnics cannot fill in addition to existing functions without more or different types of resources.

CONTEXT

The Re-organization of Research
Any discussion of the functions of research in institutions of higher education for the late 1980s and 1990s must take account of the reorganization of all government research and development activities which took place as a result of the Rothschild reforms put forward in the government White Paper of 1971 (Cmnd 4814). Although the implementation of the Rothschild proposals over the past decade has encountered many difficulties and some set-backs, the customer-contractor principle embodied notions about the nature of government in the United Kingdom in general and the need for control over all public expenditures in particular which are as much in evidence now as then. In the case of the former, the principle of functional government still dominates such current thinking about structure: ministers are in charge of departments whose function it is to work towards certain objectives or be responsible for certain areas of activity: for example, industry, health or the environment. It is partly because scientific research figures as an element in each government department that Britain has so vigorously resisted establishing a Ministry of Science; such a ministry, it is argued, would cut across the responsibilities of the various departments.

Responsibility for public expenditure generally is often referred to as public accountability. Public accountability requires that ministers justify not only how much money has been spent but why resources were allocated in the ways that they were. Lord Rothschild tried to meet both the demands of functional government and the need for public accountability in research by setting up in each ministry a Chief Scientist's Organization which would ensure that research was related to departmental objectives. The selection of a departmental research portfolio was to be guided by the customer-contractor principle by which the department as customer would invite or receive proposals from government laboratories or any other research organization and contract with them for its research needs. In this way, not only was the principle of functional government maintained but via the Chief Scientist's Organization, operating within the customer-contractor principle, the need for public accountability with regard to research expenditures would also be met.

From the point of view of this chapter, it is necessary to take note of the fact that in the first round of implementing the Rothschild reforms it was decided to leave the research councils under the DES and to re-orient parts of the research programmes of the Medical Research Council (MRC), the Natural Environment Research Council (NERC) and the Agriculture Research Council (ARC) and effect cash transfers to the appropriate departments. It was also decided to leave the resources of the Science and Engineering Research Council (SERC) and the Social Science Research Council (SSRC) untouched 'for the time being'. This was logical enough — each of the research councils has responsibility for university research and postgraduate training which, under the Rothschild re-organization, was the responsibility of the Department of Education and Science (DES).

Government Policy
More recently, the whole question of the rate of growth of public spending has come in for closer scrutiny. At stake here is neither the principle of functional government nor public accountability. For the present government, control of the money supply is seen as the principal means of controlling inflation. Money supply is reduced by cutting outlays on public expenditure and, thereby, reducing the need for public sector borrowing. Cutting expenditure has, therefore, been an imperative for all government departments and it is now clear that the universities are not going to be exempt from it; though the research councils, so far at least, have suffered relatively less from these cuts than might have been expected.

Indeed, the need for government to control all aspects of public expenditure cannot be contested. What can be debated is the appropriate management style through which this control is exercised. As Professor Kogan has pointed out, the DES generally has tended to opt for a mixture of systems but there remains, nonetheless, a strong pre-disposition for the centralist-managerial type of control. It is worth remembering that there is an abundance of evidence to the effect that centralized forms of organization are not at their most effective when technical or social change is rapid. On the other hand, the decentralization that is necessary during times of rapid change is to some extent catered for as far as research is concerned in the currently predominant monetarist economic philosophy; for example, in industrial research and development it is part of government policy to devolve, where possible, responsibility to industry itself for supporting research.

Social Factors
In addition to these developments, policy for research in the higher education sector cannot ignore questions of national need. To re-equip British industry with a range of new technologies and supply graduates and postgraduates to

operate them cannot be done without the assistance of the universities and polytechnics. A mitigating factor in matching supply and demand in highly qualified manpower in the creation of new industries is the demographic trend whereby the numbers of 18-year-olds will fall after the mid-1980s: a trend which, if not looked at closely, gives the impression that the universities and polytechnics will be overstaffed until the 1990s when once again expansion is expected to occur. So far at least, there has been more concern about overstaffing than with ensuring that the appropriate scientific capabilities are maintained and developed.

THE HIGHER EDUCATION SECTOR IN THE UK

To deal with the strategic choices which will face the higher education sector through the 1990s, a framework or model is necessary to guide deliberations. This must be able to identify the main links between universities and polytechnics and the wider society and be able to offer some guidance as to how the different relationships are likely to be influenced by trends arising from within or without the higher education sector. To provide such a framework is a tall order; the universities and polytechnics are complex institutions and as such have histories which effectively delimit the sorts of changes that are concretely possible.

An approach which casts some light on the strategic choices facing the higher education sector can be had by recourse to a relatively simple model in which functions, structures and roles are interrelated. At an elementary level, it is possible to regard the institutions of higher education as being set up to fulfill a number of functions; for example, teaching, scholarship and research. Whether by accident or design, such institutions de facto comprise the structures whereby these functions are achieved; for example, society's requirement for a capability in basic research is filled, in part, by research carried out in universities — though, it should be remembered that other institutions also carry out basic research.

Finally, it should be noted that structures provide a framework within which individual academics fulfill their roles, say as teachers or researchers or, increasingly, in a wide range of academically-related administrative activities. Within the institutions of higher education in Britain, the number of functions, the kinds of structures and the types of roles as well as their mutual inter-relationships are historical. By this is meant not only that they are contingent but that the values embodied in a given disposition of functions, structures and roles may change and require a more or less complete revision of the status quo.

Functions
Originally the university was conceived as a teaching institution and a centre for the preservation of scholarship. Now it has acquired a number of additional functions with respect to the society which maintains it (see Figure 2.1).

FIGURE 2.1
University functions in relation to national sub-systems

University functions in respect of:	
1 The national research system	Maintaining the scientific infrastructure across all fields of science. Maintaining the capacity to develop potential in new fields of science. Sustaining national centres of expertise in selected areas. Stimulating emergence of new conjunctions of ideas and hence the development of pluri-disciplinary research. Maintenance of scientific standards.
2 The education system	Production of future generations of scientists through training in research methods.
	Maintaining the quality of undergraduate teaching and introducing them to research methods.
3 Economic and social	Carrying out the basic work necessary to underpin future innovation. Contributing to innovation in public policy areas through 'strategic' research. Promoting applied research for industry, community, government.
	Providing consultants for industry, Government departments and the Community.
4 The cultural system	Advancing knowledge. Fostering individual, communal and national self-awareness. Interpreting the national culture, heritage: the national identity.

Source
OECD (1981) *The Future of University Research* Paris

1 Higher education fulfills certain functions with respect to the broader national research system, which includes both government and industrial laboratories. The universities and polytechnics are expected to maintain the scientific infra-structure across all fields of science and engineering; to maintain the capacity to move into and develop new areas of science; to sustain national centres of expertise in selected areas; to contribute towards the solution of multi-disciplinary problems; and to maintain scientific standards.

In fulfilling these functions the universities and polytechnics are connected to a larger number of other institutions by both formal and informal arrangements.

2 The higher education sector has, in addition, the function of training future generations of scientists and engineers in the techniques and methods of research, and through undergraduate teaching diffuses the latest ideas in both the sciences and the social sciences to the many who will not do research but will fulfill a variety of educational and managerial roles in society.

3 As recent government have been all too aware, the higher education sector has a function in respect of the economic and social system. It must not only discharge its function with regard to the research system but also carry out the basic research necessary to underpin future technological innovation. This includes applied research in both the natural and social sciences for industry and government. Again, this can be provided in a variety of ways, both formal and informal.

4 Finally, the universities and polytechnics have a function in relation to the general advancement of knowledge through scholarship whereby the individual, communal and national self-awareness is continually refurbished and handed on as tradition. This tradition embodies the values with which we identify most closely and through which it becomes possible to interpret national culture. (*The Future of University Research* OECD 1981, p.8).

There is, perhaps, no other single instituion in society that is called upon to perform such a diverse range of functions. Some are by now well established, as for example those in respect to education and culture. On the other hand, others are quite new: for example, the function of universities and polytechnics in relation to the national research system dates from the early years of the twentieth century when the first elements of the system were being put in place. But, it was not until the end of World War II that the complex and diversified network emerged of government and industrial laboratories which now exist, and that the higher education sector acquired a specific function in relation to the maintenance of the system. Similarly, the relationship of science to industry has a history which goes back to the Industrial Revolution, if not before, but the industries of that revolution are no longer with us and, subsequently, the development of university-industry relations has brought forth a complex array of schemes aimed at involving the institutions of higher education more closely with the new industries.

The balance between these four functions has changed over time. In particular, it should be noted that the expansion of the universities and the polytechnics during the 1960s, inspired by the Robbins report, was conceived primarily, but not solely, in relation to their educational function. The expansion of the system to admit all those in a position to benefit from higher education was intended not only to increase the general level of education of those destined for careers in government and industry but also to train highly qualified graduates who would possess advanced scientific and technological training and thereby help towards building a technically stronger and ultimately more competitive industry. Latterly, Robbins is in retreat and the higher education sector as a whole is likely to contract but, paradoxically, the need for this sector to provide scientific and technical manpower for industry has not lessened, indeed the pressure on universities and polytechnics to orient research and teaching toward social needs has very much increased. One of the questions which will be addressed below is the extent to which emphasis on this function of the higher education sector can be increased without modifying fundamentally the structure of university and polytechnic institutions.

Structures
The network of functions which the higher education sector is supposed to fulfil is maintained through a three-tier structure whereby financial resources are allocated. Although the relationship between structure and function is imperfect, the four functions can be related to three flows of funds into universities and polytechnics (*The Future of University Research* OECD 1981, passim).

Flow I is of funds from central or local government which have the principal purpose of supporting Functions 1, 2 and 4: ie the education and cultural function. This flow corresponds to general university funds and these are used to purchase buildings, stock laboratories and pay academic and administrative salaries. In so far as academics spend their time doing research, a part of these funds may be deemed to be an expenditure on research.

Flow II is of funds intended to fulfil Function 1: ie the maintainance of Britain's scientific capability across all fields of science and social science. In the main this flow comes from the research councils.

Flow III is of funds from all other sources, but in the main flows of money into universities and polytechnics from industry and government departments, with a small amount coming from private foundations. Functionally this flow of funds is directed at supporting the research needs of the economic and social system.

It is possible to express the financial structure of the higher education sectors of most countries in terms of these three flows. For Britain, the combination of Flows I and II comprises the 'dual support system'. The problem is that Flow I contains an element which is intended to provide the 'well-found laboratory', to which Flow II is expected to be added to provide special pieces of equipment needed by academics in pursuit of research. It is widely known that the precise amount of Flow I going towards research cannot be determined accurately and, therefore, an estimate of the amounts of money spent by government on research in higher education is correspondingly difficult to determine. Further, when one speaks of the dual support system it is usually implied that either Flow I or Flow II (or perhaps both) are declining and, therefore, either the basis for the well-found laboratory or the availability of research grants is preventing the universities and polytechnics from effectively pursuing their research function. The basic soundness of the dual support system in higher education in Britain is well established and even in these times of extreme financial stringency, it is seldom questioned. For example, the most recent re-evaluation of the dual support system by the Merrison Committee seems likely to state that the principle is sound but that means must be found to make it work better.

As might be expected, Flow III is much smaller than the other two. This flow represents the successes of individual academics in attracting resources for research or consultancy from sources which are primarily interested in the *results of research*. It is sometimes used as a measure, albeit a crude one, of the amount of socially relevant research being performed by a given university or polytechnic. It should be noted that most universities have no policy about such research activities and the amount they directly receive in overheads from it is most unlikely to be in excess of 40 per cent of the total funds received. In its current form it cannot really be counted as making a significant addition to general university funds, though of course it does enable universities and polytechnics to carry out research which in all probability would not otherwise be done.

A final point. As might be expected, the bulk of Flow III can be attributed to research carried out in the physical and engineering sciences. It remains to be seen what the prospects are for increasing Flow III resources from the social sciences. Ralf Dahrendorf has recently stressed that the social sciences are in his view a long way from being able to contribute to society's need for problem solving in the manner carried out by the natural sciences (see *Universities and Industry* Proceedings of the conference at Imperial College, November 1981). Nonetheless a full assessment of the capability of the social sciences in this regard will have to await the results of the current re-organization of the SSRC and its policy of pursuing more policy-oriented research (*A Changing Structure for Changing Circumstances* SSRC 1981).

Roles
Within this financial structure sustaining the universities and the polytechnics as institutions, academics live and work. In terms of the framework being presented here, they fulfill a variety of roles. For most academics the two major roles are those of teacher and researcher. Some may also play a role in the administration of their institution and commonly enough this implies that their involvement in research be attenuated or stopped altogether. On the other hand, determined academics may avoid or minimize their administrative activities for the purpose of getting more involved in research. Not infrequently, this means that their teaching function is differentiated into undergraduate teaching, postgraduate teaching and research supervision, each of which requires a different type of

skill. Although there are a few academics who manage to keep all these roles going at the same time, it is much more common for academics to concentrate on one or two at a time, the particular role combination depending on the stage of their careers.

In anticipation of what is to follow, it is perhaps worth noting that if it should ever be necessary for universities and polytechnics to maintain their research function by trying to increase Flow III resources, the effect will be to create a new kind of academic role: a researcher oriented towards and motivated by a desire to make his way forward in his career by becoming involved with industry or some other government agency. Although there are already a certain number of such individuals in the higher education sector, they are probably not present in sufficient numbers to require any changes in the criteria for appointments and promotion. On the other hand, the prospects for higher education of raising significant resources by increasing Flow III resources is consequently seriously limited.

THE ORGANIZATION OF THE SCIENTIFIC COMMUNITY

To some extent an academic researcher lives a schizophrenic life. As an academic he plays his role within the university or polytechnic and, through this, the institution is enabled to fulfill its many functions with respect to society at large. As a researcher however, the academic is connected to the scientific community generally and to one or other specialist groups in particular. The other members of a specialist group may be employed by a variety of organizations other than universities or polytechnics, and in this regard the specialist group transcends the institutions of higher education, having aims and objectives related to the development of the specialization as such. Almost every specialist group finds it necessary to institutionalize its activities and to band together to form a professional group. The purpose of this is both to identify the group and to distinguish its research activities from other, similar groups. The result is the spread of institutional as well as cognitive specialization. Scientists, particularly those with new specializations, are often required to devote as much time to developing their subject professionally as they do in developing it cognitively; though, once again, the balance of effort depends on the age of the scientist and the career opportunities involved.

This is an important development and, in some of its higher forms such as the engineering professions, these institutions have an additional profound influence on what is taught to undergraduates as well as on what post-experience work is required before one can be admitted to the profession. Most academics have to go through some 'rites of passage' even though they may not be as clearly articulated as they are in the case of engineering.

One function of the institutionalized specialism is that it provides a forum for the evaluation of research work; or, in more traditional terms, it constitutes a peer group. To it all aspiring researchers must appeal for support if they expect to make their way in their speciality or profession. It is the peer group that will read the academics' papers, pass judgement on their research proposals and make recommendations for their promotion to senior lecturer or professor. To be successful, then, an academic must be strongly bound to some peer group and it is arguable that this group exerts as strong a hold on them as does the university or polytechnic which in fact supports them.

The reason for referring here to the institutionalization of science is to draw attention to the fact that the dynamics of the research community are essentially the dynamics of specialization. Within both science and social science specialisms are continually being created and, as Belver Griffith has pointed out, dissolved (H. Small and B. Griffith (1974) The structure of scientific literatures I *Science Studies* 4, 17-40). The nucleus of the specialism is much smaller than the academic discipline to which these specialisms are frequently appended and the direction in which each specialism develops is determined by both cognitive and social considerations that are particular to it. And, if the path of development should also correspond to a perceived social need all well and good, but it need not, or it need not do so all the time. Indeed, it is one of the challenges of research policy to try to discover the sorts of factors which influence the formation and direction taken by a speciality. From the perspective of this chapter it is important to note that the university (or polytechnic) as such exerts little direct control over this aspect of scientific life. From the perspective of research, the university or polytechnic has become a *holding company* for a diversity of scientific operations; as such, university research policy is little more than the aggregate of these activities. In so far as it wishes to change the balance of these activities, it must take into account the dynamics of the professional aspects of specialization, whose essential direction is determined neither by the institutions of higher education nor by the research councils but by the scientific community itself. The point is that each academic in fulfilling his research role must align himself with specialist interests which may or may not coincide with those of the university or polytechnic. Although the research councils are to some extent the agents of scientific specialisms, in that they must react to research proposals presented to it, research councils have in recent years become increasingly interested in trying to influence the direction of science not only in government laboratories but in the universities also.

THE RESEARCH COUNCILS

In relation to the universities and polytechnics, the research councils form part of the 'national research system' referred to above. The councils have a statutory responsibility to maintain Britain's scientific capability in agriculture via the ARC; in medicine via the MRC; in relation to the natural environment via the NERC; in the natural sciences and engineering via the SERC; and in the social sciences via the SSRC. In the reorganization of government research and development under Lord Rothschild, an attempt was made to make research councils more accountable for their expenditures by relating research programmes more closely to the objectives of the appropriate departments. Thus, ARC, NERC and MRC experienced not only a general exhortation to this end but found parts of their budgets transferred to the Chief Scientist's Organization of the Ministry of Agriculture, the Department of the Environment and the Department of Health and Social Security respectively.

In part, because of their general responsibility for research and postgraduate training in the universities and polytechnics, the SERC and SSRC were left more or less untouched during the initial phases of the administrative reorganization that followed the 1971 White Paper; though it was stated that the situation of these two councils would be reviewed at a later time. The SERC and SSRC constitute the principal sources of research grants and postgraduate training awards for the higher education sector. These funds make up the main component of Flow II and as such constitute the 'other half' of the dual support system.

The idea behind the dual support system is well known; part of the general university fund via Flow I is intended to provide academic salaries as well as the basic requirements for a 'well-found laboratory' while the research councils, particularly the SERC and SSRC, are intended to provide research grants with which to purchase special items of equipment and to employ the necessary support staff to operate it. In addition, through postgraduate training awards, the SERC and SSRC provide an opportunity for graduates to acquire research training in the latest, most advanced techniques of scientific research. The dual support system, it will be evident, is a very complex system whose successful functioning depends on a delicate complementarity between the base of support supplied along Flow I by the DES and the resources for additional, specialized equipment supplied by the research councils. In particular, it should be noted, the relationship of complementarity is different between subject areas and because of this it is difficult to specify an appropriate ratio of support between the two halves of the system. One thing is clear, however, and that is that as the growth rates in general university funds have declined, investments in research and development capital expenditure per research worker as well as total research and development expenditure per research worker have begun to drop. As indicated in Figures 2.2 and 2.3, the changes that have taken place, internationally, in capital expenditures per research worker since 1966 have been dramatic; for the UK they dropped by 160 per cent between 1967 and 1975. Although these data refer to the government's total research and development expenditure, there is no reason to believe that the higher education sector has exhibited a counter tendency, particularly in view of the fact that the growth of research council funds has been slowing during this period. When the growth in Flow I resources is decreasing there is a tendency to place the burden of capital expenditure for research on the research

FIGURE 2.2
Capital R&D expenditures for RSE Index 1975 = 100

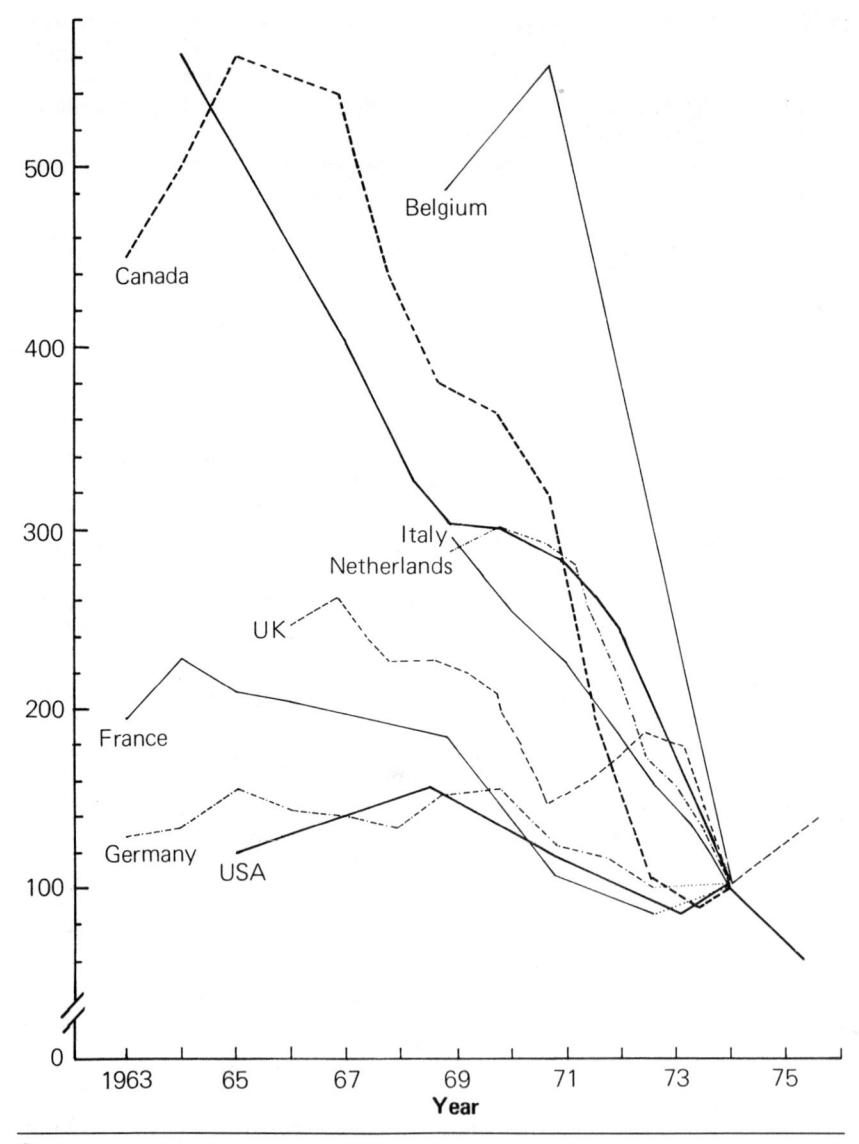

Source
The Future of University Research
OECD Paris 1981

FIGURE 2.3
Total R&D expenditures for RSE Index 1975 = 100

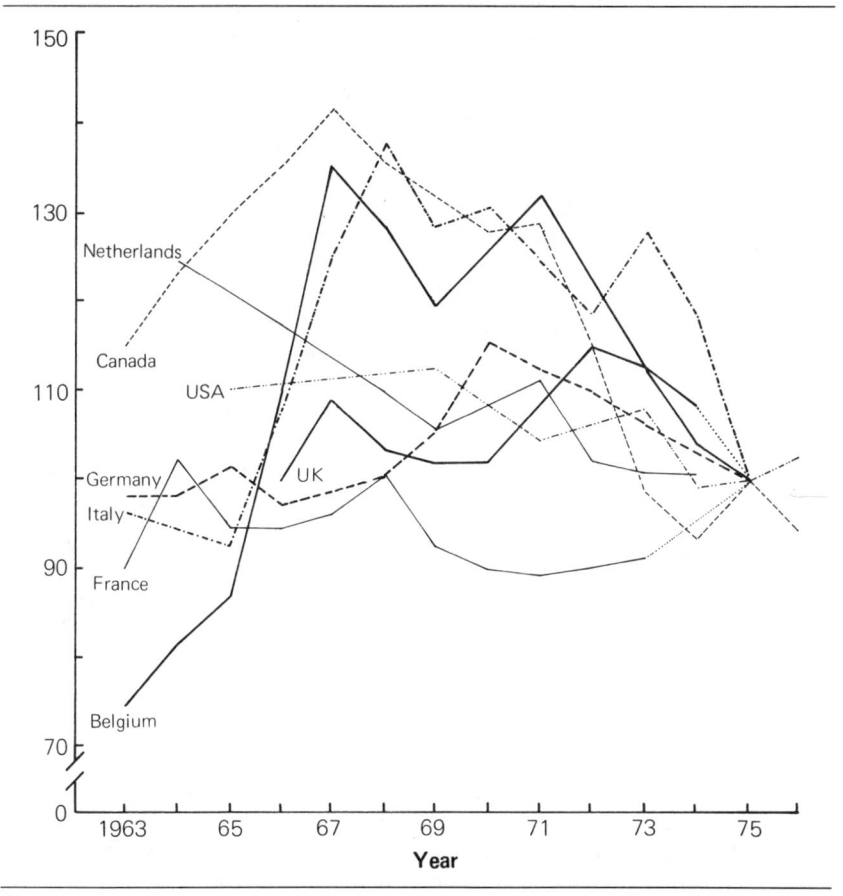

Source
The Future of University Research
OECD Paris 1981

councils; when the resources from Flow II are also slowing the councils are increasingly unable to bear this burden. As a result research activities begin to decline and, if prolonged, the principle of dual support is undermined altogether. Although precise data on the level of the resources available for *research* via Flow I is not available, the volume of testimony from academics in universities and polytechnics as well as programme directors in the SERC certainly gives good grounds for believing that the dual support system is creaking badly. Nonetheless, it is expected that the Merrison Committee will, when it completes its deliberations, endorse the principle of dual support. One will have to wait to see the evidence adduced in support of this conclusion but if it is not overwhelming then chronic shortage of resources may face some universities and polytechnics and they will have to consider the strategic question of whether they will be able to continue to carry out effective research within the system.

There is, however, a further development within the research councils generally which bears upon the question of the viability of the dual support system. This concerns the amount of research being carried out in the council's own laboratories. As far as the ARC and NERC are concerned, the bulk of their research activities is located in their own institutions; between 5 per cent and 10 per cent of it is carried out in the higher education sector. It is arguable that this is as it should be, because these laboratories are intended to provide both basic and applied research relevant to departmental objectives. In the case of the MRC, the situation is more complex. While it is true that the MRC makes extensive use of units as well as project and programme grants in supporting research, these are often attached in some way to universities. This allows not only a variety of forms of contact with academics generally but also provides a limited number of opportunities for graduates to receive special training in selected areas. The larger question of whether the MRC is providing a research capability relevant to the needs of the DHSS is far from clear, as the recent 'de-Rothschildization' of the MRC appears to give evidence. (For a clear statement of some of the difficulties involved, see M. Henkel and M. Kogan (1981) *The DHSS Funded Research Units: The Process of Review* Brunel University 1981.)

National Facilities
As with other councils, the SERC and the SSRC also operate their own laboratories and units attached more or less closely to the higher education sector, but unlike the MRC, and SERC and SSRC have an additional responsibility for maintaining the overall scientific capability of the universities and polytechnics in the natural and social sciences. In the case of SERC specifically, it is useful to identify four principle flows of resources to this end:
    1   Flow of resources to international facilities
    2   Flow of resources to national establishments and units
    3   Flow of resources to research grants for academics
    4   Flow of resources for postgraduate training

As far as Flows 1 and 2 are concerned, they constitute around 50 per cent of SERC's annual expenditure (see Table 2.1) and to a large extent, represent a continuing commitment. It is, of course always possible to terminate a treaty or run down a national facility but experience shows that this is a difficult task which can be accomplished only over an extended period. The reason for mentioning it here is that these facilities — both national and international — require staff in order to operate and although the facilities are intended to be available for academics as well, there is a tendency for them to acquire an independent research programme and the staff appropriate to execute it. In this case, the university staff who participate in the programme constitute only one element in the overall research programme. Although relationships between universities and national facilities can be difficult, this can usually be overcome with a little good will on both sides. What is much more difficult to control is the tendency for a bureaucracy to grow, and with it, the annual costs of the establishment. On the other hand, because so much of contemporary science is based around expensive pieces of capital equipment, it is clearly good economic sense to set up central facilities and invite universities to make use of them. But there is the further question about whether, in terms of good science — science which is competitive internationally — national laboratories might tend to ossify rather too quickly and, in the end, come to impede the further development of good science.

TABLE 2.1

Payments to	1978/79		1979/80		1980/81	
	£m	%	£m	%	£m	%
Flow 1 International organizations	45·3	28·73	43·0	23·8	41·52	20·0
Flow 2 SERC facilities	49·52	31·4	61·0	33·7	70·78	34·0
Flow 3 Research grants	30·93	19·62	43·6	24·0	56·6	27·2
Flow 4 Postgraduate awards	22·18	14·1	25·0	13·8	29·8	14·3
Other (including administration)	9·74	6·2	8·4	4·6	9·55	4·6
TOTAL[+]	157·67	100·1	181·0	99·9	208·3	100·1

+ Errors due to rounding

There does not seem to be much evidence, one way or another, to show whether the growth of national and international commitments has affected the growth of Flow 3 and Flow 4 — the resources available for academics in terms of research grants and postgraduate training awards. In the case of the SERC the balance has remained approximately constant. But, whereas the research programme of a national facility may be expected to come forth on a recurrent basis, expenditures via Flows 3 and 4 require scientists, through their research proposals, to apply to the council for the funds they need. As the growth rate of SERC's annual budget has begun to slow down during the 1970s many academics have expressed concern at the apparently sharp increase in the rejection rates for research grant applications. It was perhaps to be expected that some academics would begin to attack the SERC-funded laboratories in terms of the quality of the science being carried out in them. There is some evidence to support this view. See for example J. Irvine and B. Martin, A methodology for assessing the scientific performance of research groups *Scientia Yogoslavia* 6 (1-4) 83-95. Although this research is not yet completed, it seems clear at least in the cases of medium-sized optical astronomy and high energy physics, that the position of the UK national facilities is not strong by comparison with other, similar faculties abroad. But, as with university departments, national facilities can be expected to have their ups and downs and it is still very much an open question whether the UK can play a fuller part in science internationally through specially funded national facilities rather than through the more conventional method of funding of university departments. If this question were to be resolved in favour of national facilities, it would have serious implications for the future of the dual support system in general and for the practice of research in many universities and polytechnics in particular.

Research Grants
Although it is certainly true that national facilities such as the Rutherford and the Daresbury laboratories have been used by many academic researchers, much of this is supported in the same way that all SERC (and SSRC) research *in* universities and polytechnics is supported — via research grants (Flow 3). Research grants are allocated by the peer review process and for this reason are sometimes referred to as 'peer-adjudicated grants'. It is in the process of allocating these that universities and polytechnics come into close contact with the research councils: the councils depending as they do on applications from the universities to set their decision-making processes in motion. While it is possible, for example, for the SERC to try to stimulate applications in specific areas, in the final analysis academics must prepare research grant applications, and, whether stimulated by the council or not, submit them to the peer review process. As a result it is possible to argue that the outcome of the annual research grant allocation cycle represents in some sense an optimum of the *available* research ideas. No doubt the various committees of the SERC are influenced in their choices by the range of work that is on-going. Because they cannot begin each year ab initio, a certain inertia or pattern of allocations year by year is to be expected. But, at present, there is no other way of making the decisions required and, though it is easy enough to talk, as some academics do, about the biases of the SERC committee members, it would be difficult to sustain this charge in any

concrete case.

Through the late 1960s and the 1970s the SERC, along with the other research councils, began to experience a decline in its annual growth rate of resources. In addition, there was within the scientific community as a whole a growing concern about the proportion of resources going to 'big science', especially to nuclear physics. In this situation, the SERC, advised firstly by the Council for Scientific Policy and later by the Advisory Board of the Research Councils, had to re-consider the overall balance of its funding between various areas of science and between science and engineering. The SERC reaffirmed its intention of supporting projects which showed 'timeliness and promise' in any field but also accepted the need to select certain areas or disciplines for special support and to concentrate resources in specific university departments — sometimes referred to as centres of excellence. The policy of 'selectivity and concentration', as it is sometimes called, represents, on the whole, a rational attempt by SERC to use its resources as efficiently as possible. While it was true that there was concern that too much money was being spent, for example on nuclear physics, there was also worry that resources in general were being spread too thinly over the range of sciences and that perhaps there were some areas of science which were being supported at sub-critical levels. Clearly something had to be done. In the end, it was decided

i   To reduce support for nuclear physics below its current level of 40 per cent.
ii   To redirect resources to the generality of science.
iii To increase support for engineering within the envelope of current expenditure.
iv   To concentrate resources favourably in certain departments.

An analysis of the impact of these policy intentions would offer some important insights concerning the support of science in the universities and the polytechnic and about the possibility of its direction. In fact, a detailed study of the SERC's policy of 'selectivity and concentration', as it has affected peer adjudicated grants over the period 1965-1974, has been carried out, and while this is not the place for a discussion of the study as a whole, there are several conclusions which require careful consideration for the purpose of this paper.

In the first place, the authors have developed a numerical measure of concentration, L (called the Lorenz coefficient), which provides a unique indicator of how research grants of various sizes are distributed among the population of researchers, the population of university departments and the population of universities. An important finding is that these distributions do not appear to have changed over time. That is, the percentage of researchers who receive a given percentage of research grants is described by the log-normal distribution and does not appear to vary.

Similarly, the concentration indexes for departments and universities has remained static over the period investigated. Thus, at the highest level of aggregation, that of the universities, a pattern of allocation seems to have been established which has been quite resistent to change (C. Farina and M. Gibbons (1979) A quantitative analysis of the Science Research Council's policy of 'Selectivity and Concentration' *Research Policy* 8, 306-338).

The results at the highest level of aggregation — that of the universities and polytechnics — are presented in Table 2.2. For example, the resources allocated by the Biology Committee exhibited an average Lorenz coefficient, $(\bar{L}) = 0.568$. This is interpreted to mean that the proportion of universities and polytechnics below the mean value of awards to the group was 71 per cent and that that group received 29 per cent of the resources available. Another way to express this concentration ratio is to note that the top 10 per cent of the universities and polytechnics receiving grants from the Biology Committee received 43 per cent of all the funds it awarded. Similarly, the average concentration index for the Astronomy Committee was $\bar{L} = 0.745$, which implies that 79 per cent of all the universities and polytechnics had total grant incomes below the mean for all universities and polytechnics; and the same 79 per cent received only 21 per cent of all the funds awarded by the committee in an average year. The top 10 per cent of this group received 65 per cent of all the funds allocated by the committee. The concentration indexes for the remaining committees fall between these two extremes and the concentration of resources may be interpreted accordingly. These findings lend support to the view which originated the policy of selectivity in concentration in the first place: that is that the majority of universities might be receiving support at sub-critical levels; that these resources may be being used inefficiently; and that better research could result by increasing the resources in already favoured departments. The results of this study suggest, on the one hand, that resources are *already* concentrated and, on the other hand, that the decision-making processes used by the SERC committees have not been conspicuously successful, at least up to 1974, in shifting the distribution of resources allocated via peer-adjudicated grants.

There is, of course, no criticism of SERC intended or implied here. The characteristics of the distribution reflect the nature of the peer review process in that it is decentralized and tends to be geared to the evaluation of past performance. The results suggest that if it is desirable to concentrate resources in selected areas, the SERC may have to play a more direct role in the decision-making process. What is more important is the implication of these findings for the quality of research being carried out in the majority of the universities and polytechnics. The study shows that the largest grants tend to be in the heavily funded departments of the universities which themselves receive the largest (proportionately) funding. And this suggests, though with some expections, that the small grants are spread around in the less well funded departments of the less well funded universities.

If resources from both the UGC and the research councils continue to decline, does it now follow that sooner or later in the majority of departments aggregate support will fall below the level at which effective research is possible? What can research funded at these levels be contributing to international science? What does this portend for the scholarship of teaching and research?

TABLE 2.2
Test (λH_1) for the equivalence of measures of dispersion for distributions by universities or polytechnics for grants awarded by committees of the SRC

Board	Committee	N*	No. of funded depts./no. of funded universities or polytechnics	$\chi^2(^\lambda H_1)$	Significance	$\bar{\sigma}$	$\bar{L}$
ASRB	A	158	1·184	8·34	0·501	1·610	0·745
	S	132	1·106	14·50	0·106	1·708	0·773
EB	ACE	189	1·439	5·11	0·529	1·182	0·597
	CET	270	1·444	8·92	0·445	1·141	0·580
	CS	128	1·195	3·90	0·918	1·263	0·628
	CE+	53	1·094	4·71	0·318	1·408	0·681
	ESE	313	1·147	8·28	0·506	1·179	0·595
	MPE	282	1·379	4·48	0·723	1·243	0·620
	MM	368	1·427	9·60	0·384	1·201	0·604
	PS+	139	1·230	4·26	0·372	1·264	0·629
NPB	NP	160	1·200	3·290	0·952	1·793	0·795
SB	B	501	2·431	6·65	0·674	1·112	0·568
	C	593	1·182	9·95	0·385	1·285	0·636
	EC+	105	1·238	1·04	0·904	0·906	0·498
	M	188	1·218	14·27	0·113	1·057	0·545
	P	491	1·346	8·52	0·483	1·175	0·594

* Total of all cases for years considered
+ First year's data not considered

The universities will have to come to grips with some of these questions because if, as seems likely, resources for research in the next decade are not going to grow there will be great pressure to extinguish research in some departments in some universities. It will not suffice to repeat that in universities teaching and research belong together.

University — Industry Collaboration
Another element of the analysis of concentration provides a convenient way

to make a transition to another aspect of SERC policy — its attempt to promote research activities which are useful to industry. Since the late 1960s, it has been SERC policy to encourage research in engineering. The level of such research support in the UK appears to be a recurrent problem because engineering, unlike some of the natural sciences, does not seem to have an in-built research growth mechanism. As is shown in Table 2.3, the engineering community responded to SERC intentions in a rather complicated way.

'Prior to 1969/70 the committees listed under the Engineering Board were the responsibility of the University Science and Technology Board. During this period, the funds allocated to engineering remained approximately *constant*, or perhaps declined slightly. However, in 1969/70, the year in which the Engineering Board was created, commitments rose by approximately 6% to 35% of all SRC allocations via peer adjudicated grants. This rise was followed by a further rise in the next year, but from that date on commitments *declined* so that in 1973/74 their level was approximately that of 1964/65. Thus, overall, the trend in commitments has been upward with time, but in the post 1968/69 period the trend has been *downwards*.' (Farina and Gibbons op. cit., p.317)

Although more recent evidence indicates that this trend has turned upwards again the problem of expanding engineering research in the universities and polytechnics has proved rather intractable by conventional means, so much so that one former chairman of the SRC once wondered whether there was not a 'natural level' of support for engineering in the United Kingdom. However, research grants are not the only dimension of SERC policy in relation to engineering. More extensive have been their specific efforts to stimulate the transfer of ideas and manpower between industry and the university and to involve industry more closely in postgraduate training. The gradual development of these activities has profound implications for the research function of universities but before examining these it would be useful to consider what is known about the *utilization of research results* produced in universities and polytechnics.

The context within which SERC policies aimed at promoting better university-industry collaboration should be viewed is the context of technological innovation, for it is principally via the process of technological innovation that Britain's industrial performance will be improved. While this is generally accepted, there is much debate about the sources of innovation — that is about whether it originates in new scientific ideas and techniques or whether it arises out of previous technological achievements or perhaps a combination of both. Not surprisingly, many in the universities tend to see technological innovations as being critically dependent on previous scientific work and they tend to assume that if universities have worked with industry on a problem then their contribution was decisive in the eventual commercial success of the project.

TABLE 2.3
The proportion of SRC commitments allocated by committees and boards of the SRC

Board	Committee	1964/65	1965/66	1966/67	1967/68	1968/69	1969/70* % of Total Comm.	1970/71	1971/72	1972/73	1973/74	All years	& 1969/70 on
ASRB	A	-4·05	4·16	2·56	4·71	5·48	2·10	1·70	2·05	2·68	3·78	0·288	0·972
	S	-7·14	-0·99	-1·82	2·68	-2·73	8·37	-2·84	-2·20	-4·14	-2·30	0·041	-0·623
Total (ASRB)	—	-3·43	2·96	0·55	7·15	2·51	10·88	-1·33	-0·32	-1·52	1·36	-0·128	-0·345
EB	ACE	0·92	2·03	-0·06	-0·85	0·48	3·45	0·13				-0·501	—
	AME	—	—	—	—	—	—	—	3·73+	0·97	1·66	—	0·995
	CTE	—	—	—	—	—	—	—	—	2·27+	1·31	—	—
	CET	0·63	-0·39	0·31	0·64	-0·11	3·17	-0·40	0·65	0·00	0·35	-0·050	-0·437
	CS	-3·26	-4·76	-3·76	-2·39	-3·33	6·91	-3·51	-4·29	-2·40	-4·31	0·59	-0·660
	CE	—	—	—	—	-1·14	2·33	-5·22	-0·60	-0·86	-0·97	-0·164	-0·482
	ESE	2·73	2·30	3·67	1·83	0·01	3·06	2·64	0·11	2·99	1·19	-0·322	-0·310
	MT	—	—	—	—	—	—	—	—	1·90+	0·47	—	—
	MPE	0·61	-1·78	-2·12	-1·17	-0·58	7·12	-0·62	-0·17	0·13	-0·63	0·232	-0·101
	MM	1·75	1·00	1·52	-0·45	2·54	5·77	-0·70	0·96	-0·10	0·24	0·555	0·449
	PS	—	—	—	—	-3·11	3·39	-0·44	0·27			0·709	—
	T	—	—	—	—	—	—	0·58+	2·80			—	—
Total (EB)	—	-2·34	-7·32	-6·18	-8·11	-6·21	35·20	3·05	0·99	-1·27	-2·56	0·559	-0·695
NPB	NP	-2·42	-1·16	0·29	-3·98	0·34	20·01	-1·39	2·99	-0·22	3·18	0·649	0·580
Total (NPB)	—	-1·24	0·03	0·04	-3·11	0·16	20·26	-1·64	2·74	-0·47	2·92	0·518	0·547
SB	B	0·48	2·61	2·33	0·38	0·73	9·09	-1·04	-1·58	0·78	-2·00	-0·724	-0·301
	C	8·21	5·03	4·44	6·56	2·51	12·97	-1·58	-1·63	-1·58	-1·08	-0·914	-0·492
	EC	—	—	—	—	0·08	1·55	0·36	-0·01	0·84	0·50	0·673	0·653
	M	-1·24	-1·22	-0·90	-0·43	-0·44	1·91	1·06	-0·02	1·24	-0·25	0·768	-0·073
	P	1·52	-0·12	1·69	-0·48	1·07	7·72	0·53	-0·11	1·95	1·40	0·132	0·744
	—	7·01	4·33	5·59	4·07	3·54	33·66	-0·08	-3·41	3·28	-1·54	-0·796	0·018
Total (SB)		0·00	0·00	0·00	0·00	0·00	100·00	0·00	0·00	0·00	0·00		—
Total all Boards													

* In cases where this figure is not available because the committee did not allocate grants in this year the figure for the first year in which the committee did allocate grants is used. This percentage is recorded in the column for the appropriate year and is marked by a cross. For example, the changes in percentages for the AME grants are calculated using the percentage of total SRC commitments in 1971/72 (ie 3.73%).

However, the process of technological innovation is too complex to be explained by the simple causality implied by a linear- or science push-model. In a research project carried out some years ago, into the interaction of science and technology in the process of technological innovation, it was shown that in the complex and manifold range of problems that face any innovating team, much recourse was had to science as reported in the literature and to scientists in the universities and polytechnics. Further, it was shown that the 'impact' of this information in solving the problems in question was frequently decisive, not necessarily in the sense that it solved the problem but in that it pointed the way to its eventual solution. Although the study was limited in the range of industries covered, there seems little doubt that in concrete problem solving university research results are used frequently, albeit in an indirect way (M. Gibbons and R. Johnston (1974) The roles of science and technological innovation *Research Policy* 3, 220-242). A further interesting finding of this research was that the sources of information which were sought in solving a particular problem were closely correlated with the educational backgrounds of the engineers and scientists working in industry. For example, it was discovered that engineers and scientists who were educated in polytechnics via the HND or HNC schemes instinctively made use of different sources of information when stuck on a problem than did scientists trained in the universities. Now, while it was not possible to distinguish the 'adequacy' of the solutions achieved by various routes, it was clear that the utilization of research results produced in universities is critically dependent upon the presence in industry of people familiar with universities, their libraries and modes of research. Based on an admittedly small sample of innovations, it would appear that by encouraging a diversity of schemes which involve universities and industry in joint problem-solving activities, SERC is moving in the right direction. For example, the co-operative Awards in Science and Engineering Scheme (CASE) provides research training opportunities in pure science and engineering at the problem-solving level between specific supervisors and specific firms. This scheme has flourished since it was started in 1967 and, with students becoming increasingly concerned about employment, may well come under pressure to expand.

In a similar vein the Teaching Company Scheme seeks to establish close, more permanent links between specific university departments and companies. It is an extension of the CASE scheme to a higher organizational level and is jointly supported by SERC and DOI. In this scheme, companies and university departments develop an on-going relationship in which problem solving and research training take place in certain areas of manufacturing technology. Again, the idea is the same, to encourage flows of ideas and information, techniques and methods between universities and industry while at the same time providing an opportunity for graduate students to experience problem solving as it arises in and is carried out by industry. The scheme has grown rapidly over the past five years and is likely to continue.

In terms of what is known about the innovation process, both the CASE scheme and the Teaching Company Scheme would appear to be stimulating interaction between university and industry at the right levels. In these cases, the orientation of research work, if indeed any occurs, takes place in an unco-ordinated way in the context of on-going work with industry. Much more ambitious in this regard are the SERC-sponsored Directorate schemes. In these cases, a high level decision is taken within the SERC about a national need and the function of the director is to establish (or create) a research capability relevant to the need. For example, SERC funds directorates in polymer engineering, marine technology and, most recently, biotechnology. The directorates may be established with some industrial support, but it remains the responsibility of the director to stimulate academics to work in areas of basic and applied research deemed relevant to a specific capability. Although the funding of this academic work comes initially from the SERC, the objective is to use it to seed university-industry collaboration so that in the fullness of time the SERC contribution can be much reduced or phased out altogether.

The Directorate schemes if successful contain considerable potential for transforming the environment in which university research is carried out. The directorates are intended to change academics' perceptions about their research activities. At present, as we have tried to indicate, the orientation of academic research is linked by the peer view process to the development of science internationally. Academic advancement, in turn, is related to successful performance within one or other of the micro-specialisms that make up contemporary science; and successful performance is evaluated in terms of a contribution to the understanding of a particular set of phenomena. In addition to this role within his speciality, however, an academic may be more or less involved with industry and government on a variety of levels as consultant. But, it is important to realize that the current research programmes of academics may be only loosely connected to the advice they provide to the groups for which they act as consultants. (After all, why should one expect the contribution one makes to an academic speciality to be exactly what industry requires? It may be so, but consultants draw upon a wider range of knowledge and experience than that of their current academic preoccupations.)

The Directorate schemes are trying neither to provide more academic research per se nor to increase the range of contacts within industry or government per se. They are trying to promote what has been called in other contexts 'strategic research': that is fundamental or basic research which is related to national needs or problems. The Directorate schemes aim to break down the conventional division of research into short- and long-term in which short-term research is regarded as applied research and long-term as pure research. It is a mistake to think that all socially relevant research must be short-term in nature.

'The issue is not about whether the university should be engaged in short term socially relevant research as opposed to long term blue sky research but whether the university should be engaged (or is best equipped to perform) socially relevant strategic research or socially relevant short term research. By distinguishing between short term and strategic research, the objective of that research — its social relevance — is not called into question, only the framework in which it is performed. For by strategic research is meant research related to social and industrial objectives.... What seems to be required is a substantial investment in strategic research: that is to say research addressed neither to the problems of immediate short term relevance nor to problems which derive their interest solely from scientific theory but having as a background a practical orientation. It is via the performance of such research that the universities could make a significant contribution to the economy.' (*The Future of University Research* op. cit., p.72)

The performance of academic research with such an orientation is the aim of the various Directorate schemes and the principal problem of the director is to establish an ethos of research with a practical orientation. To be successful, something close to a 'change of heart' on the part of academics is required. For while it is necessary for the director in the early stages of a programme to gather support from several areas of science and engineering, it is possible for academics to use the directorate as a further source for attending to essentially discipline-oriented problems. But as the general notion of national need is transformed into a set of research problems, it becomes increasingly difficult to get away with a strictly discipline-oriented approach and, if the director has been successful, the set of problems that have been identified as requiring strategic research will involve a degree of joint funding with industry or government departments. Ideally, as outside funding begins to grow, the directorate's role as the primary source of funds should decline and the initiative be left to academics or groups of academics to build upon the relationships that have been established.

One of the key aspects of the Directorate schemes is that by reorienting university research under a national objective, a different type of research will be carried out. Implied in this is a loosening of the bonds which attach the academic to the international scientific community; or possibly a reduction of the quantity — though perhaps not the quality — of the research judged solely by reference to discipline-oriented peer groups. Further, because problems so identified tend to be multidisciplinary, a form of collaborative research not familiar to academics is required and if the research is to be really effective some commitment from universities or groups of universities is often required. (But here, we meet again the problem of the lack of a university research policy.)

POLICY ALTERNATIVES

As stated earlier, the objective of this chapter is to clarify certain of the strategic choices facing universities and polytechnics in the UK in relation to their research functions. To this end, it has been necessary to dwell on a number of factors. In the first place, the university in carrying out research contributes to the objectives of several other social sub-systems: principally the national research sub-system, the educational sub-system, the economic/industrial sub-system and the cultural sub-system. The institutions of higher education in carrying out their research function contribute directly or indirectly to each of these sub-systems and, at any given time, a balance is struck in terms of effort devoted to each. In this way, the role of the universities or polytechnics is established. It is suggested here that a combination of a number of external factors is having the effect of changing the balance among the various functions and that in arriving at a new balance the universities and polytechnics will be required to consider seriously what sort of institutions they want to become. In sum, the institutions of higher education are faced with making strategic choices.

To highlight the context in which choices will be made, we have focused on a structural model of university/polytechnic funding in which three flows are involved: general university funds from the DES or local governments; funds for research grants and postgraduate education from the research councils, and funds from other sources. We have tried to indicate that if the existing balance of higher education research functions is to be maintained then there are certain relationships between the level of the three flows which must also be maintained. In particular, the operation of the dual support system requires that Flow I and Flow II complement one another and, if the current situation makes this difficult or in some cases impossible, then some hard choices may have to be made. To insist on the theoretical validity of the principle of dual support in the full awareness that the basic conditions for its successful operation cannot be fulfilled seems an odd way to develop an effective higher education sector.

A third element in the analysis is related to the emergence of the international scientific community. This community (or properly, communities) is now fully professionalized and institutionalized in nearly every country in the developed world and within it research schools are established, scientists trained, journals founded and paper published, and conferences and meetings organized; in so doing the scientific community exercises major force on the rate and direction of scientific activity. In so far as the objectives of these activities are primarily concerned with the advance of specific scientific specialisms they lie outside the direct control of the universities and, as long as evaluation by peer review is maintained, may, by adhering strictly to the internal criteria of what constitutes good science, override the policy intentions of the research councils.

For their part, the research councils are committed to developing and maintaining Britain's national capability in scientific research and, as we have seen, by far the largest part of this research is going on outside the universities and polytechnics, in council-funded units or establishments. The question must at least be asked whether, given the structure of contemporary science, units or institutions or other forms of peri-university organizations are not better adapted to the goal of maintaining the position of UK science internationally. Mention has also been made of the recent efforts, particularly in the SERC, to orient research and postgraduate training specifically towards the needs of industry. In a time of decreasing budgetary growth rates, these efforts are bound to constrain further the proportion of resources available for activities whose sole aim is to do good science as dictated by the specialist group. About the effects on the peer review process of large numbers of industrially-related scientists and managers little is known, but what evidence there is suggests that partly as a result of this 'enlarged' peer review process academics who are involved with the Directorate schemes, for example, are re-thinking the sorts of research they wish to undertake. Is it likely that the SERC (or for that matter, SSRC), in pursuing relevance in research, will want to push further the idea that units or research institutions devoted to particular — albeit long-term — objectives may be a more efficient way to proceed than by trying to wean academics away from their attachment to the norms and values of the international scientific community? Academic scientists like other professional groups seek to advance their careers, and there is some evidence to show the scientists are well able to adjust their norms and values to the ethos of the institutions in which they work (S.B. Barnes (1971) Making out in industrial research *Science Studies* 1, 157-75).

Each of these elements, the economic effect of decreasing resources, the desire to improve UK industrial performance, the need, particularly from the point of view of the research councils, to keep pace with developments in science internationally, have their implications for future research in the higher education sector. Universities and polytechnics are, however, not in a strong position to determine this future because they have no research policy. For the most part, the institutions of higher education act as a kind of holding company for a diverse range of research activities; though perhaps in this regard Cranfield Institute of Technology is a significant exception. Such research activities are the immediate result of the entrepreneurship of professors and other academic staff who are little influenced by the university or polytechnic in the research choices they make. Each university, it appears, is content to bask in the glory of its most energetic professors and to cream off when possible some financial contribution to overheads.

In the current context of contraction in the higher education sector, universities and polytechnics are faced with serious strategic choices as to what research is to be carried out; how much research is to be carried out; by whom and for whom? At the moment, however, there are no frameworks within which they can examine the options before them. In what follows three *possible* scenarios are considered: the development of a triple support system; the development of a single support system; and a version of the status quo

Presuppositions
The discussion presented below is based upon a number of presuppositions about the existing situation in the higher education sector, the scientific community and the research councils and about the likely impact on it of social and economic trends.

Firstly, it is assumed that the universities and polytechnics will continue into the 1990s to function *primarily* as teaching institutions. It is in relation to supply and demand projections for post-secondary education and training that the budgets in the institutions in the higher education sector will be determined. The principle social trend affecting this would appear to be the 'demographic shift': the drop in the numbers of 18-year-olds who could put themselves forward for registration in courses in the universities and polytechnics. It is perhaps worth mentioning here, briefly, that there are differences of opinion as to how much the demographic shift will, in itself, affect enrolments.

Secondly, it is presumed that economic pressure will continue to make it necessary for any UK government to exercise tight control over the growth of public sector borrowing. While it is agreed that universities and polytechnics play a vitally important role nationally, they will *not* receive special treatment and will consequently be required to trim their operations in line with the cuts imposed on other areas of public spending. It is further assumed that the current round of cuts is but the first in a much larger programme cutting the higher education system down to a more economically efficient size.

Thirdly, the contraction of higher education will be such as to force on the universities and polytechnics some degree of specialization. This will be necessary *if* the traditional solidarity of teaching and research is to be maintained.

Fourthly, specialization within and between universities will be severely hampered because the universities qua universities have no research policy and are not directly involved in the national deliberations about priorities for research. In addition, science within the DES enjoys a relatively low prority in a department devoted primarily to education. The department's support for university science will be carried out via the research councils, particularly the SERC and SSRC, who will continue to support research in the national interest; the funding of university departments will be only one element in this. Coupled with a perception of universities and polytechnics as primarily teaching institutions and a declining resource base this provides some of the ingredients for a recipe for the decline of the research function of the higher education sector. Note that it is because the research function is not sufficiently differentiated institutionally within the higher education sector that it is likely to suffer most when resources are declining. Academics have to respond to the more insistent pressures of teaching: the students are there, they must be taught. (Possibly the polytechnics with their Institutes of Advanced Study provide a useful institutional focus to research activities.)

We conclude, then, that universities and polytechnics must begin to develop their own research policies to protect not only research but also teaching and scholarship. There are a variety of ways in which this might be done and the scenarios outlined below are but three possibilities which might be considered.

Scenario One
Given the likelihood of prolonged research constraints, universities and polytechnics might set about building a third leg of financial support — that is, they might develop a triple support system. In terms of the discussion presented in this paper, this would be accomplished by increasing the level of Flow III resources and this, in turn, implies seeking funds more systematically from industry and government departments. There are two ways to build up resources, the one more radical than the other.
(i) In the first case, the purpose of increasing Flow III is to enable universities and polytechnics to carry out research and to enable them to recruit new staff, neither of which would be possible by relying on resources from conventional sources along Flow II. The object is to produce research papers and at the same time to satisfy the needs of some customer. In this case, the basic principle of the dual support system remains: Flow III is added to Flow II, but Flow I continues to provide the basis of the well-found laboratory. To some extent this describes the status quo. As the recent report of the CVCP, *The Universities and Industry*, makes abundantly clear, many universities and polytechnics have established companies, contract research organizations or consultancies in a variety of socially and industrially relevant areas. Although it is difficult to establish precise data, there is no doubt that some of the resources received through these activities contribute to the institution and pay for the time of academics, the use of facilities and equipment, heat light and telephone, etc. These items represent the real costs of carrying out the research and consequently enter the university and polytechnic accounts as 'self-balancing' items (*Universities and Industry* CVCP 1981).
(ii) The more radical alternative within this scenario is to transform these self-balancing items into income-generating activities. This means putting contract research activities on a *commercial basis* within the *university as a whole*. The reason for doing this is clear: universities and polytechnics are experiencing a severe cut in Flow I resources to offset which they must identify new activities that not only maintain research output but also generate sufficient income to support general funds. In other words, part of Flow III is intended to contribute directly to the maintenance of the well-found laboratory.

It is far from clear, however, whether sufficient opportunities exist to generate income at significant levels, or whether the universities and polytechnics possess the right balance of skills to exploit them if, indeed, they do exist. The problem is that in order to find out, an administrative structure capable of mediating between these activities and a wide range of organizations and agencies would have to be put in place. Mediation would be a crucial function of the structure because the idea is to make use of the existing skills, not to establish an independent, parallel organization. Unless the skills of academics are utilized more fully there is the ever present danger that, over the university as a whole, Flow III resources will revert from income-generating activities to self-balancing ones. For example, the CVCP booklet referred to above cites many examples of university-industry collaboration but what it does not make clear is the extent to which these activities generate positive flows of resources overall and, if so, whether these are sufficient both to offset other activities which do not make a positive contribution and to provide sufficient resources to make new developments possible. This is largely an empirical question but it is not unrelated to the question of whether it is at all realistic for universities and polytechnics to expect to generate significant income by expanding the range of their connections with industry and government.

(iii) The SERC has, over the past decade, been in the forefront of trying to promote university-industry relations through a side variety of schemes (see above, p.70). As a result, the possibilities of developing these into commercially successful activities are very much improved over what they were a decade ago. It remains to be seen which universities will be able to develop further the opportunities created for them in part by the SERC.

Scenario Two
The second alternative adds to the current financial situation of contraction the observations made above about the concentration of resources in universities and polytechnics and the departments thereof. The apparently static nature of the Concentration Indexes raises the possibility that for the majority (ie greater than 50 per cent) of the institutions of the higher education sector there will simply not be enough funds to carry out work that can compete internationally. This has been recognized for some time and is among the reasons why the SERC sought to concentrate resources in favoured departments. One conclusion which can be drawn from this is that while it may be possible for a small number of universities to pursue research across a wide spectrum of fields, for most there will be a real need to specialize: to select some areas of teaching and research and perhaps to cut out whole areas of science or social science altogether.

To do this the institutions of higher education would have to play a fuller part in developing their individual capabilities. In particular, there would have to be greater clarification of the flows of general university funds into teaching and research respectively. This would involve working out with the UGC (or the DES) an appropriate research budget, not necessarily independently of the peer review process but independently of the granting processes of the SERC and the SSRC. Because the institution itself takes over responsibility for the direction of its research activities, this scenario could be referred to as the development of a single support system. Although the main thrust of this scenario is to give specific universities and polytechnics the option of developing their own research capability independently of the programme of work being funded by the research councils, it does not necessarily follow that institutional links with them need to be broken altogether. Universities and polytechnics could still bid for research grants or contracts, but a single support system would not make it imperative for them to do so. In addition, the research councils, particularly the SSRC and the SERC, could continue to provide higher education institutions with access to both national and international facilities and thereby reduce some of the cost of duplicating facilities in university or polytechnic departments.

At stake in this system is the development of specialization among the institutions of the higher education sector. Although this specialization is mainly concerned with research, it is bound to affect undergraduate and postgraduate teaching as well. It is almost axiomatic in higher education today to insist upon the inseparability of teaching and research. If the universities specialize in certain areas of research, this principle of solidarity implies that some universities will be able to offer a much more restricted range of courses at the undergraduate level than heretofore. Some would argue that to restrict the range of teaching and research in this way attacks the very notion of a university as a centre where students can be exposed to a wide range of intellectual influences and methods. For a start, one could suggest that the breadth of university activities overall is not being tampered with; it remains a property of the system as a whole. It may, of course, be that if the institutions of higher education have to specialize then it will be necessary to cater for the smooth movement of students between the elements of the system.

Scenario Three
This alternative intends more than a patching up of the existing dual support system. It is, rather, a development of Scenario Two. It assumes that pressure of resources will make it necessary for SERC and SSRC to provide more in the way of national facilities and laboratories and, by means of a complex array of programmes and international agreements, etc., allow British academics access to the instruments of first-class research. It is further assumed that both SERC and SSRC will continue to build their links with industry and government and that both councils will, in the future, become more concerned with promoting strategic research. Because the development of strategic research in, say, marine technology, bio-technology or polymer science, is a large undertaking linking both postgraduate teaching and research, it should be negotiated with each university or polytechnic (or group of them) concerned. In other words, it should involve more direct contact between the universities and the councils. The SERC in

particular, through its Directorate schemes, has evolved one way of linking academics to long-term national needs and in this it appears to have been successful.

CONCLUSION

The scenarios outlined above are three options within which research in higher education can be maintained and, hopefully, improved. Each presupposes an institution's greater involvement in directing its own development. A key aspect of this is that most universities will have to specialize their research activities if a reasonable standard is to be achieved.

Each scenario involves some change in the relationship of the university to the research councils — particularly the SERC and the SSRC. In the first the growth of Flow III funds is increased largely on the initiative of the institution concerned and while it does not suggest that universities opt out of the research grant scheme, it stresses the role of the SERC in providing a wide range of university-industry schemes upon which further, commercially based, ventures might be built. In the second scenario, the universities select their own research priorities and concentrate resources in departments accordingly. Here, the research councils are looked to less for specialized equipment and more as a co-ordinating mechanism linking university departments to national and international facilities. Finally, in the third scenario, the universities and polytechnics are assumed to have followed Scenario Two and achieved some degree of specialization. The universities' relationship with the research councils is concerned with deciding upon areas where strategic research is necessary and working out their respective contributions to the development of the capability. To some extent, each of these scenarios takes cognizance of the fact that the research councils, too, are experiencing resource constraints, and to maintain their functions vis à vis the national research system they are seeking different relationships not only with government departments and industry but with the universities as well.

In a similar way, each of the scenarios affects the relationship between teaching and research in the institutions of higher education. In the first, the build up of Flow III resources carried with it the possibility of teaching and research becoming separated; this will be necessary if the levels of resources are to be achieved that will generate an income large enough to launch new academic developments. In the second scenario, specialization in research is seen to imply a similar specialization in teaching. Restricting the range of subjects taught within a university or polytechnic carried with it serious implications for the types of undergraduate study which a given institution will be able to offer. In the third scenario, both teaching and research are oriented broadly to areas of national need. A significant aspect of building a strategic research capability is that it also requires creating the conditions of supply for highly qualified manpower. The universities and polytechnics are in danger if, having committed resources to specific strategic areas, circumstances change and the area ceases to be important nationally. For this reason it is necessary, in this scenario, for the university to be more closely linked to the formation of national policy, taking in science and technology as well as the social sciences.

Finally, some mention should be made of the implications for the academics themselves of these three options. As has been indicated academics are used to developing their research interests independantly and to date they have been allowed to do so more or less unhindered by external constraints, subject only to the availability of resources and the favourable judgements of their peers. Each scenario implies some tighter degree of supervision by the university itself. This implies that in terms of promotion and career development broader criteria of performance than those offered by the peer review will have to be worked out and implemented. This, in turn, will affect the sorts of people who will aspire to be academics. In brief, the role of the academic must change and the direction of change will be in the direction of greater perceived utility to the society which supports their activities. In this, too, the universities must strive to take the lead.

SEMINAR DISCUSSION

Discussions on the Gibbons paper led to recognition that the word 'research' covered many different activities, and that it was difficult to make recommendations which would apply to them all equally. They include fundamental research, strategic research, applied research, scholarship and reflective inquiry. All such activities are important and all should be carried out in higher educational institutes. Unfortunately, a system of rewards and esteem has grown up which in the natural sciences gives greatest recognition to attainments in fundamental research and lowest to scholarship and reflective inquiry. There was general agreement that this system of rewards was wrong. Excellence in scholarship and applied work needs to be recognized just as much as excellence in fundamental science. There is also a need for people who can present the academic work in a way that society can absorb. There needs to be parity of esteem among all the different types of research activity.

In his paper Professor Gibbons asked whether funds for research from industry and government might grow to form a substantial third flow of resources to complement the UGC and the research councils. There was general agreement in the discussions that this was unlikely. Some parts of some universities and polytechnics might be able to earn substantial flows from industry, but it would be unrealistic to expect industry to become a major source of university and polytechnic income.

Several speakers from both academia and industry supported the notion that the universities' principal role should be to do fundamental and strategic research, not to try to solve industry's problems. It was up to industry to be alert to new research discoveries made in universities and polytechnics, and certainly it was largely industry's responsibility to exploit them. What was needed was more interchange and collaboration between institutes of higher education and industry, and this called for pluralism in the approaches used to foster the objective. High marks were given to the pioneering efforts of the SERC in this regard. The conflict between publishing, which is usually rapid, and patenting, which is usually slow, was pointed out as being a problem in university and industry collaboration.

Setting Priorities for Strategic Research
There was plenty of support for the view that there is a need for someone to determine research priorities at a national level. There was little agreement, however, as to who should do it. Some participants felt that if the potential users of research could be involved in the process of setting

priorities, then there would be a greater possibility of the results ultimately being applied. There was, however, a concern that too much planning and priority setting would stultify individual research initiatives. A balance had to be found between the extremes of too much and too little planning. The experience of planning for basic research in Japan was discussed, but their committee approach was discarded as inappropriate for the UK.

Management for Research in Universities
A number of suggestions were made for a more flexible approach to managing research in universities. Some of these could follow if the UGC were to separate their funding for research from that for teaching. Other suggestions follow from a move towards greater selectivity in research.

Suggestions made included:
— More UGC-funded research appointments for fixed (5-year?) terms.
— A system where university staff were able to spend blocks of time on research and blocks on teaching.
— A system where staff could teach in one university but have a research affiliation in another.

What many people stressed was the need for flexibility. These schemes should not replace the normal pattern whereby most faculty do both teaching and research. The new schemes should be additional. These and other changes are required if the productivity of research in the universities is to improve. There is too much UGC money being used to support second-rate research.

The call for flexible and pluralistic approaches to both staffing and patterns of funding research recurred throughout the seminar.

FUNDING AND POLICY FOR RESEARCH IN THE NATURAL SCIENCES

by R.J.H. Beverton and G.W.D Findlay

INTRODUCTION

The cuts in future funds for the universities, first announced in March 1981, have created a situation unparalleled in the peacetime history of higher education in the United Kingdom.* For the first time many universities are being required to reduce their teaching and research activities, and it is hardly surprising that the transition from the earlier period of growth following Robbins is raising fundamental issues of principle as well as causing serious practical difficulties. The future of the polytechnics is less clear, but some economies seem likely for them too.

The exceptional nature of recent events should not, however, be allowed to obscure the fact that the universities have been under increasing pressure for several years. Therefore, in attempting to analyse future policy options for the support of research, it is important to understand what those pressures were, how they arose and what consequences they have had for the present state of university research. To explore these questions is the aim of the first part of this chapter, using as source material statistical data and commentaries in the official reports of the various bodies that support research at the universities. We then offer broad outline of how university scientific research might best be supported in the future.

We are aware that the 'university system' is in no sense a tightly-knit entity that behaves in a unified way. The fifty individual universities, each an autonomous self-governing body, vary enormously in their size, character, traditions and financial circumstances. Generalizations about 'the university system' have to be interpreted with care, and ideally they ought to be built up in full awareness of individual universities' circumstances and responses. This, however, would have been an impossible task in the time available.

Even before the announcement of the recent cuts, mounting anxiety in official circles about the difficulties facing university research, and the functioning of the Dual Support System, caused the Advisory Board for the Research Councils (ABRC), jointly with the University Grants Committee (UGC), to set up in 1980 a working party under the chairmanship of Sir Alec

---

*The opinions expressed here are those of the authors, and do not necessarily represent the views of their present or previous employers.

Merrison on the Support of University Scientific Research.[1] At the time of writing, the report of this working party has not been published, but the issues it has been addressing are essentially those which are the subject of this chapter.

CONSTITUTIONAL BACKGROUND

Ultimate responsibility for determining policy on higher education and the total resources to be provided from public funds lies of course with the government. Since 1964 the responsible minister has been the Secretary of State for Education and Science. Neither that minister nor the officials at the Department of Education and Science concern themselves with the detailed allocation of funds to individual universities. That is delegated to the University Grants Committee, set up in 1919 by a Treasury minute to:

'enquire into the financial needs of university education in the United Kingdom and to advise the Government as to the application of any grants that may be made by Parliament towards meeting them.'

In 1964, when the Robbins expansion was at its height and funds for higher education and science were increasing at 10 per cent or more each year in real terms, the brief of the UGC was extended to enable it:

'to assist in consultation with other bodies concerned, the preparation and execution of such plans for the development of the universities as may from time to time be required in order to ensure that they are fully adequate to meet national needs.'

The Science and Technology Act of 1965 marks the other important constitutional development of that period. By this Act the former Department of Scientific and Industrial Research (DSIR) was dissolved and many of its responsibilities, including those for the financial support of research and postgraduate training at the universities, were placed under two new Research Councils — the Science Research Council (now renamed the Science and Engineering Research Council, SERC) and the Natural Environment Research Council (NERC). With the already existing Medical and Agricultural Research Councils (MRC and ARC) and the Social Science Research Council formed shortly after, there were by 1965 five research councils under the Department of Education and Science, all of which had responsibilities for the support of research at the universities and polytechnics.

The research councils are funded from the 'science budget', ie part of the DES overall vote set aside for the purpose. To advise the Secretary of State for Education and Science on the science budget and on how it should

---

[1] The ABRC, set up in 1972, is the successor to the Council for Scientific Policy (CSP). Although the chairman of the UGC is an ex officio member of the ABRC, this was the first time the two bodies had formally joined forces to investigate a matter of fundamental importance to both.

be allocated among the five research councils,[1] the former Advisory Council for Scientific Policy was reconstituted in 1965 as the Council for Scientific Policy (CSP) and given a wider and more explicit (though still formally advisory) remit. The only substantive change in the sixteen years since 1965 has been the introduction in 1972 of the Rothschild customer-contractor principle for research 'commissioned' by 'customer' departments from three of the five research councils.[2] The effect of this was to transfer proportions of the budgets of the ARC (55%), the MRC (25%) and the NERC (40%) to various 'customer' departments, but as discussed later (p.118) this has had no direct financial effect on the universities. At the same time the Council for Scientific Policy was replaced by the Advisory Board for the Research Councils (ABRC) whose functions were still basically the same as its predecessor (the CSP), but whose remit was extended so that it could take into account the research commissioned with the research councils by the customer departments. The heads of the five research councils, and the chief scientists of the five main customer departments[3] were made full members of the ABRC, as was the chairman of the UGC, on an ex officio basis.

The polytechnics were evolving at the same time, but quite independently. Many had their origins in local technical colleges concerned primarily with vocational and craft teaching of local, or at least regional, significance. During the 1960s and into the 1970s many of these institutions developed into colleges of advanced technology (CAT) and offered a more academic training. As part of the national policy of strengthening higher education, some were encouraged to take the further step of becoming fully-fledged polytechnics, offering education to graduate and postgraduate level and developing, in so doing, an explicit research function in their own right. Although the Department of Education and Science has an overall responsibility for policy for polytechnics (manifest, for example, in the recent proposals for centralizing policy for them), their financial support is still provided at the local level, through the local education authority (LEA). Their funds therefore come partly from the rates, but mainly from central funds via the rate support grant.

---

[1] The science budget also includes support for the Natural History Museum and the Royal Society, but the combined research council budgets make up by far the greater proportion.

[2] Profound though the effects of the Rothschild system were (announced in the White Paper *Framework for Government R&D*, Cmnd 5046), its introduction did not need an Act of Parliament and no strictly constitutional changes were involved.

[3] The five departments are DoI, DoE, MAFF, DEn, and DHSS. The R. and D. activities supported by the Ministry of Defence account for over half the total government expenditure on R. and D. (including the research councils), and some (eg the Meteorological Office) have significant non-military applications, but these do not come under the ABRC.

FUNDING AND POLICY IN THE NATURAL SCIENCES

Since 1965, therefore, ultimate responsibility for the universities, the research councils and, in part, the polytechnics, has come under one department of government and one Secretary of State.[1] In theory, the means have existed since 1965 which would have enabled the research carried out by these three groups of bodies to have been viewed as a whole, distinct from the educational function, and policies developed accordingly. In fact, so far as we are aware, no serious attempt has ever been made to take an overall view of policy for research in this way. The affairs of the UGC and of the research councils are dealt with by two separate branches of the DES, and only recently has a deputy secretary been appointed with responsibility covering both branches.

Since it may be argued that the role of government should be different in the future, it should not be overlooked that the high degree of delegation of responsibility to the UGC and the research councils has been based on the principle that they, and not ministers or departmental officials, are best able to decide how to use the grants made to them. This applies whether those funds are for the furtherance of higher education or for the advancement of scientific knowledge. Few would question the wisdom of this principle, but the extent to which it can be put into practice without some agreement on priorities depends to a degree on the availability of resources. What was satisfactory in the ample days of the sixties, or even the early seventies, may not be so nowadays when resources are being significantly reduced. How this difficulty can best be resolved without prejudicing the freedom of expression which is essential both to higher education and research, and to the atmosphere of scholarship which both need if they are to flourish, is one of the central issues for the future, and is discussed further on page 140ff.

SOURCES AND TREATMENT OF DATA

Sources of Data

Statistics of income and expenditure are submitted by the universities to the UGC who compile it for publication annually in Volume 6, *The Universities*, of the DES series on *Statistics of Education*. The latest published edition of Volume 6 is that for the year 1977/78, but the UGC kindly made available to us manuscript copies of data for 1978/79 and 1979/80. Statistics of staff and students are also published in Volume 6, and in the Annual Reviews of the UGC.[2]

---

[1] The two establishments of higher education that come under neither the UGC nor a local authority are the Open University and the Cranfield Institute of Technology. Both, however, receive their grant-in-aid from public funds via the DES.

[2] Both these sources of information are published by HMSO.

Apart from private assets and endowments, the universities derive their income from five primary sources:
1. Grants made to them for teaching and research on the recommendation of the University Grants Committee
2. Tuition and maintenance fees for students
3. Grants made by the research councils for approved research projects and programmes
4. Government departments and industry as contracts for specified requirements
5. Trusts, foundations and charities, for particular or general research and educational activities

The recurrent block grant to the universities from the UGC comprises about 60 per cent of their total income; it covers most of the costs of teaching, administration and general services and part of the expenditure on research. Until the present time (July 1981) the way in which the recurrent grant is used has been decided almost entirely by the universities themselves; only rarely has the UGC given any guidance. An earlier example was the reduced provision for agriculture, when the number of departments of agriculture was reduced and rationalized in the late 1960s. More recently, special allocations were made to certain universities so that they could play their part in major projects promoted by the SERC (eg polymer engineering and interactive computing). This degree of intervention in university affairs has hitherto been regarded by the UGC as quite exceptional and, indeed, undesirable, but the situation has changed dramatically in the past year.

In contrast, virtually all the funds provided by the research councils, most of those by trusts and foundations, and some of those by government departments, do not cover the general running costs or equipment of laboratories, or the salaries of permanent staff. These funds meet only the additional costs of carrying out the approved research project in question, such as the employment of extra short-term staff (eg research assistants), the purchase of special equipment and the provision of technical services and other costs peculiar to the project. In other words, funds from all these sources take the form of a 'research subsidy' on a 'floor' of support from the UGC. This is the well-known Dual Support System, the future of which in the context of the financial stringencies now facing the universities will be considered later in this chapter.

In addition to the recurrent grant, the UGC provides most of the capital funds for the universities for major categories of expenditure such as buildings and, of particular importance for the present study, scientific equipment.

The expenditure by each university each year is divided in the statistics into the following categories:
    a   Departmental expenditure for teaching and research.
          This is sub-divided into:
            i   UGC funds for salaries and departmental (laboratory) running

expenses, covering both teaching and research (not distinguished).
  ii Funds for specific research from the various outside sources listed as 3, 4 and 5 on page 86.
 b General (central) expenses for the university as a whole; these include both specialized services (computing, libraries, etc.) and general administration and running costs.
 c Capital expenditure; distinguishing buildings, scientific equipment and certain other capital assets.

Only the first of these three categories, departmental expenditure, is shown broken down by subject, eighteen being used to cover the whole academic sphere. Eleven of these, including mathematics, cover natural sciences, but for the present purposes we have combined them into six groups, as shown in Table 3.1.

TABLE 3.1
Grouping of subjects in the natural sciences

			As designated in Vol. 6 Universities
A	Medical sciences	(iii)	Clinical medicine
		(iv)	Clinical dentistry
		(v)	Studies allied to medicine and health
B	Biological sciences	(x)	Biological sciences
		(ii)	Pre-clinical medicine and dentistry
C	Applied biology	(viii)	Agriculture and forestry
		(ix)	Veterinary science
D	Physical sciences	(xii)	Physical sciences
E	Engineering	(vi)	Engineering
		(vii)	Other technologies
F	Mathematics	(xi)	Mathematics

These are natural groupings except for the combination of pre-clinical medicine and dentistry (category (ii) in the DES statistics) with biological sciences (category (x)), which needs explaining. Plotting the data for the biological subjects separately (Figure 3.1) showed that in all probability there had been a shift from 1970/71 onwards in the classification of staff from pre-clinical medicine and dentistry towards biological sciences. The former includes subjects such as physiology and biochemistry which are, of course, taken by some biology students who do not intend to proceed to a medical

FIGURE 3.1
Staff: biological sciences and medicine

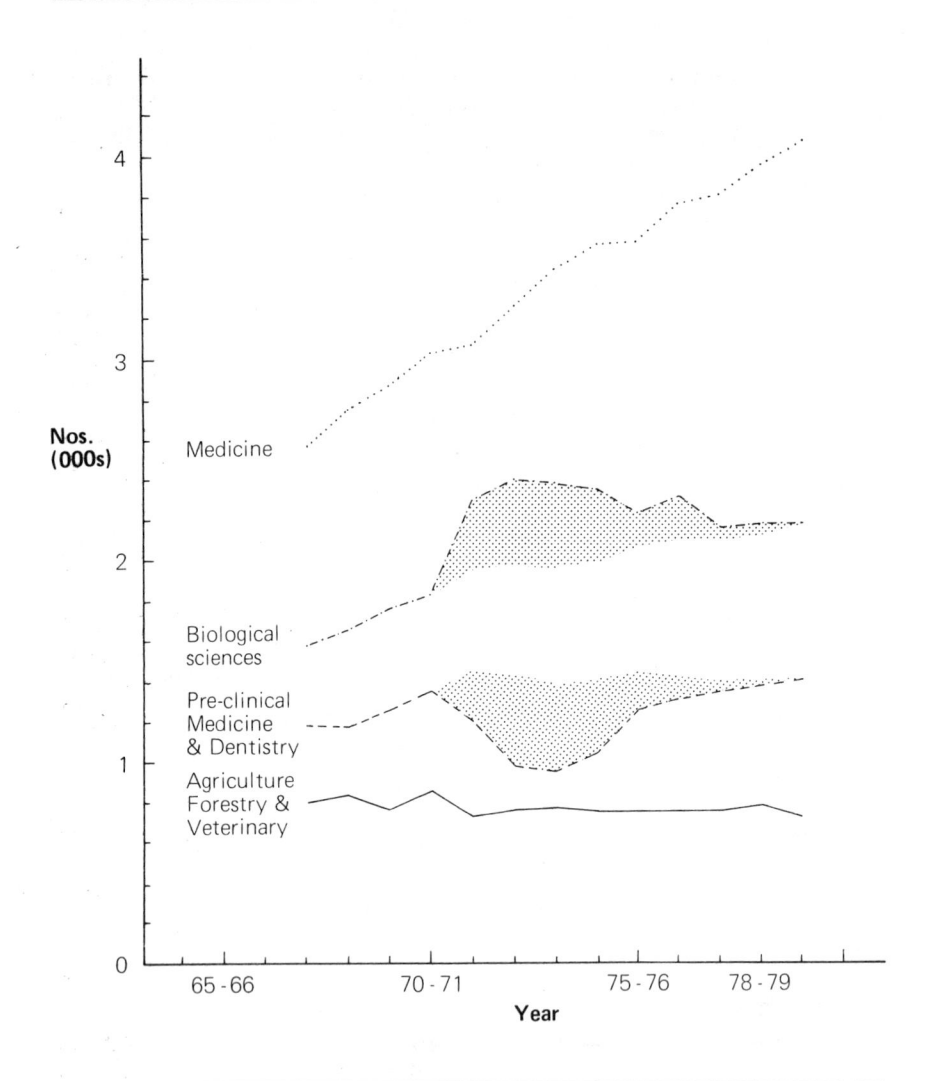

Trends in number of staff in the DES categories of medical and biological sciences. The shaded areas show what appears to have been a sudden re-classification in 1971/72 of about a third of the staff in pre-clinical medicine and dentistry (category ii of the DES statistics) and in biological sciences (category x).

degree. Each category taken alone is therefore suspect, but the bias can be avoided by combining them. There were no signs of any corresponding bias in the data for students or expenditure, but combining categories (ii) and (x) for staff made it obligatory to combine them for money and students also.[1]

The absence of such a manifest anomaly in the other subject areas does not, of course, mean that the classifications are unambiguous. This can hardly be expected with such broad subject areas, and the classification of subjects lying at the boundaries between, say, physical sciences and engineering, must depend to some extent on local convention. However, the pattern of the trends in other categories gives no reason to suppose that those classifications have remained other than reasonably consistent throughout the period under examination. Since neither the specialized central services (eg computing) nor scientific equipment are allocated to subjects in the official statistics, it will often be necessary to work with the aggregate of the six groups of Table 3.1, which we shall call the science sector.

Calculation of Expenditure on Research

The procedure used here is in principle the same as the Full Economic Cost (FEC) method used by government laboratories and the research councils, suitably modified to meet the limitations of the available data. Referring to the categories of expenditure listed above, let

$D_{int.}$ = expenditure on the science in question (teaching and research) at the departmental level with UGC funds

$D_{ext.}$ = expenditure on research in that field with funds deriving from outside sources

p_1, p_2 = proportions respectively of the internal and external funds that are spent on research, as determined by the proportions of the total working time spent on research by the staff concerned

Then the expenditure on that research at the departmental level (D_r), can be written as

$$D_r = p_1 D_{int.} + p_2 D_{ext.} \quad \ldots\ldots\ldots\ldots 1$$

Certain central university expenditure is on specialized support for research carried out in the departments. This should be assigned on the basis of the costs of the actual service to the research in question, where this is known. If the expenditure on a specialized service is designated as s. and the proportion p_3 of it is concerned with the research, then the cost of the various specialized services to be added to the research expenditure is

$$p_3 s = \Sigma\, p_3 s \quad \ldots\ldots\ldots\ldots 2$$

---

[1] We are grateful to the UGC for alerting us to the ambiguity which exists over the classification of subjects in these two categories. It is significant that statistics for staff, unlike those for students and expenditure, are collected for submission to the University Statistical Record (USR).

Next, there is the question of capital facilities and equipment used for research. Ideally, these should be charged to research on an annual 'rental' basis, the charge reflecting the replacement cost and length of life of the facility or equipment, suitably discounted. In the long term, the aggregated rental charges should equate to the mean capital spend over the period, but in the absence of the necessary data, capital in this analysis is confined to 'scientific equipment' and relates to the amount spent each year. On the advice of the UGC, 85 per cent of the money listed as 'scientific equipment' in Volume 6 was taken to be strictly for scientific research equipment. If the annual spend on scientific equipment is denoted by E, of which the proportion p_4 is used for research, the expenditure to be added to the costs of that research is

$$p_4 E \qquad \ldots\ldots\ldots 3$$

At this juncture it is convenient to identify the total money actually spent on research in a given year, which we call the total direct research expenditure, R_d as

$$R_d = p_1 D_{int.} + p_2 D_{ext.} + p_3 s + p_4 E \qquad \ldots\ldots\ldots 4$$

Lastly, a proportion of the general university expenses, such as maintenance of premises, heating, lighting and general administration, should be charged to the research costs as overheads, on the principle that without these central facilities and services the research activity would not, in the longer run, be viable. It is sufficient to make this allocation pro-rata on the ratio of the departmental expenditure on the research, D_r, to the total funds spent for all purposes in all subjects, including both teaching and research, at the departmental level ($=\Sigma D$). Thus, defining the general overheads to be allocated to the research in question as G, we have

$$G = \text{central expenses} \times \frac{D_r}{\Sigma D} \qquad \ldots\ldots\ldots 5$$

The grand total expenditure on research, R, in terms of the actual money spent in the year and with allocation of overheads, can now be obtained by summing equations 4 and 5 to give

$$R = p_1 D_{int.} + p_2 D_{ext.} + p_3 s + p_4 E + G \qquad \ldots\ldots\ldots 6$$

This formulation enables questions such as the relative contribution of the various kinds of expenditure to the costs of research in a given year to be examined, and how those proportions have changed with time. Comparison of the expenditure on research over a period of years in a way that reflects the true measure of research support it provided must, however, take inflation into account. Adjustment for inflation is a highly technical subject, but the limited information available to us precludes any sophisticated treatment. It is sufficient here to note that the 'research effectiveness' of each of the categories of expenditure in Equation 6 will have been influenced differently by inflation, and that this can be expressed by defining for each a 'revaluation index', $_v x$, applying to a given year, x. Thus, $_v x$ is the purchasing power of £1 for the activity or equipment in question in year x relative to a base year, which we have taken as 1978/79.[1] In real terms, relative to 1978/79, the grand total expenditure on research in year x can be written as

$$_x R = {_x v_1 p_1}\, D_{int.} + {_x v_2 p_2}\, D_{ext.} + {_x v_3 p_3}\, S + {_x v_4 p_4}\, E + {_x v_5}\, G \qquad \ldots\ldots\ldots 7$$

Allowance for Time spent on Research (p) and Inflation (v)
The requirement now is to assign values to the coefficients $p_1 \ldots p_5$ and $v_1 \ldots v_5$ of Equation 7. Taking first the p coefficients, the proportion of staff time spent on research (p_1) is the most critical in establishing the absolute magnitude of research expenditure. The only direct evidence on this question comes from an inquiry undertaken by the Committee of Vice-Chancellors and Principles (CVCP) in 1969/70 among all members of staff and eleven universities. Staff were asked to keep a special diary of how they spent their working time in three representative weeks; one a 'normal' teaching week, one a working week during university vacation, and one during examination time. In all, 7,995 responses were obtained from a total university community of 27,272. The findings were published in 1972 by the CVCP.[2]

The results showed that for university staff paid wholly or in part from university funds, the percentage of time spent on personal research ranged from 20 to 28 per cent according to subject, with a further 5 to 10 per cent on graduate course work or research time. For present purposes we have taken an overall figure of 30 per cent (ie $p_1 = 0.3$) for all subjects and, necessarily, have assumed that this percentage has not changed substantially in later years.[3] Expenditure deriving from external sources under the heading of 'Grants and Contracts' ($D_{ext.}$ of Equation 6) could be regarded as devoted wholly to research, in which case p_2 is unity, although the CVCP data suggested a figure nearer 70 per cent for the time of staff paid wholly from external sources. For our main calculations we have taken $p_1 =$ unity, but have also tested the effect of putting $p_1 = 0.7$.

In the case of computer services and equipment (p_3 and p_4) a proportion of the expenditure should be assigned to teaching rather than research. In the absence of specific information we have assumed for the main calculations that the whole of the expenditure is concerned with research, ie that p_3 and p_4 are unity but, as with p_1, we have also tested the

---

[1] The reasons for choosing 1978/79 as the base year rather than the latest year in which we have statistics, 1979/80, is that reliable revaluation indices for the latter year were not available.
[2] Report of an Enquiry into the Use of Academic Staff Time (CVCP 1972).
[3] One factor that might have caused this figure to change is a change in the teaching load per staff.

effect of putting $p_3 = p_4 = 0.7$.

Turning now to the allowance for inflation over the period (ie the v coefficients), our main source of information has again been the Committee of Vice-Chancellors and Principals, who arrange for the preparation at six-monthly intervals of an index of university recurrent costs, based on information received from a sample of universities and other published indices. The CVCP has kindly made available to us a weighted index for total recurrent expenditure for each year from 1965 to 1981. This covers funds received from all sources, including grants and contracts. In a more refined treatment it would be desirable to revalue the 'internal' and 'external' funds separately, since the proportion of staff costs and equipment costs in each is by no means the same. In the absence of this more detailed information we have used the same index for both, ie we have put $_xv_1 = {_xv_2}$ (except for 1979/80; see Table 3.2).

In the middle seventies, following the increase in oil prices, and again in

TABLE 3.2
Revaluation indices for university research expenditure

	A Tress-Brown indices	B RPI	C Capital equipment (DoI indices)
1965/66		3.47	(3.49)
66/67		3.35	(3.39)
67/68		3.28	(3.26)
68/69		3.13	(3.11)
69/70	2.97	2.91	(2.90)
70/71	2.63	2.72	(2.75)
71/72	2.44	2.48	(2.55)
72/73	2.20	2.30	2.30
73/74	2.01	2.09	2.17
74/75	1.66	1.79	1.74
75/76	1.32	1.42	1.41
76/77	1.21	1.23	1.23
77/78	1.09	1.09	1.06
78/79	1.00	1.00	1.00
79/80	(0.80 − 0.84)	(0.85)	0.89
80/81			0.78

1979-1981, the rate of inflation rose sharply to 20 per cent and more. Data for the latter period were further complicated as regards the salary element by the Clegg award and the exact timing of back payments. Marked perturbations of this kind are largely compensated for when occurring in the middle of a run, as in the years 1974/76, but not when at the end of a run, as in 1979/80. In fact, our estimates of the inflation increase applying to general recurrent expenditure for 1979/80 compared with 1978/79 varied from 18 to 25 per cent according to how the data were treated.[1]

In other circumstances it would have been preferable to exclude the year 1979/80 altogether, but this would have meant discarding a considerable amount of reliable data for that year and leaving a gap of three years between the end of our analysis and the present time. We therefore decided to make 1978/79 our reference year, but to include 1979/80 as the last year of our analysis, using the lower value shown in Table 3.2 for v_1 (0.80), and the higher value of 0.84 for external funds, since these are less affected by salary adjustments. Even so, our conclusions for 1979/80 that are sensitive to inflation must be treated with caution.

In view of these and other uncertainties, it is interesting to compare the Tress-Brown indices with the Retail Price Indices (RPI) over the same years,[2] which are given in column B of Table 3.2. The RPI is about 5 to 8 per cent higher in the years 1971-1976 when the inflation rate was changing most rapidly, but otherwise the two sets of figures are closely similar despite the rather dissimilar 'mix' of individual commodity indices.

In the case of scientific equipment, the UGC uses DoI indices for equipment purchased by universities for the years 1972/73 to 1979/80. These are shown in column C of Table 3.2 and are the values of the coefficient $_xv_4$ of Equation 7. A plot of the DoI against the Tress-Brown indices gave a reasonably consistent relationship, from which equipment indices for the years 1965/66 to 1971/72 were estimated; these are shown in parentheses in column C. The influence of 'sophistication' of scientific equipment, ie the greater research effectiveness of equipment due to technological advances, is of course a complication in attempting to relate the cost of equipment to its real research power over a period of years. In many fields, modern research

---

[1] When the rate of inflation is changing rapidly, the only satisfactory way of calculating an annual index is to sum the products of expenditure (φ_t) and corresponding inflation rate (v_t) over as short time intervals as possible. Thus, if monthly data are available, the annual index v_x is calculated as

$$v_x = \frac{\sum_{t=1}^{12} \varphi_t v_t}{\sum_{t=1}^{12} \varphi_t}$$

[2] Central Statistical Office *Annual Abstract of Statistics, 1981 and earlier years* HMSO.

technology is more costly to buy and to maintain, relative to research expenditure generally, than a decade or so ago, but it is also much more powerful as a research tool; indeed, many modern research fields could not exist without it. Attempts to identify and measure 'sophistication' and its variations with time have met with varying success. The best we can do is to note that in so far as sophistication applies it will tend to offset the extent of the change in the cost indices as measures of value of money for research.

Sophistication cannot, however, be disregarded in the case of computer services, since the cost of hardware per unit computing power has decreased by an order of magnitude or more over the period in question. On the other hand, the expenditure figures shown under 'Computing Services' include a substantial recurrent element (60 per cent on average, most of which is salaries) which has been subject to inflationary increase. For the present analysis we have assumed that the increasing 'research effectiveness' roughly counterbalanced inflation, so that expenditure on 'computing services' was effectively independent of inflation over the period in question. This means putting the coefficient v_3 to unity throughout.

To summarize, the values of the coefficients p and $_x$v of Equation 7 used in the calculation of trends over the period 1965-1980 are given in Table 3.3.

EXPENDITURE AND MANPOWER FOR UNIVERSITY SCIENTIFIC RESEARCH 1965-1980

Introduction
It will be recalled from the previous pages that three measures of research expenditure have been derived:
 Departmental expenditure D_r, comprising funds from internal and external sources but excluding the costs of specialized central services and capital
$$D_r = v_1 p_1 D_{int.} + v_2 p_2 D_{ext.} \quad \ldots\ldots\ldots\ldots 8$$

Total direct expenditure R_d, ie departmental expenditure plus the costs of specialized central services and capital equipment
$$R_d = D_r + v_3 p_3 S + v_4 p_4 E \quad \ldots\ldots\ldots\ldots 9$$

Grand total expenditure R, ie total direct expenditure plus a pro-rata allocation of general university expenditure
$$R = R_d + v_5 G \quad \ldots\ldots\ldots\ldots 10$$

One or other of these is needed according to the question to be examined; in particular, since neither specialized central services nor capital for equipment is broken down by subject in the statistics, analysis at the subject level has to be confined to departmental expenditure, D_r, (Equation 8).

TABLE 3.3
Coefficients p (allocation of expenditure to research and v (revaluation indices)

Category of expenditure		Proportion allocated to research	Revaluation indices
Departmental internal (D_{int})		$p_1 = 0.3$	$_xv_1$ = Column A of Table 3.2
Departmental grants and contracts (D_{ext})		$p_2 = 1.0$ ($\rightarrow 0.7$)	$_xv_2 = {_xv_1}$ (except for 1979/80)
Computing services	(S)	$p_3 = 1.0$ ($\rightarrow 0.7$)	$_xv_3 = 1.0$
Scientific equipment	(E)	$p_4 = 1.0$ ($\rightarrow 0.7$)	$_xv_4$ = Column C of Table 3.2
General overheads	(G)	$p = 1.0$ (by definition)	$_xv_5 = {_xv_2} = {_xv_1}$

Trends in Total Research Expenditure and its Composition

To establish the general picture, Figure 3.2 shows the total expenditure on research calculated from Equation 10, both in actual money (£m (actual)) and adjusted to the value of the £ in 1978/79 (£m (78/79)) by the indices of column A of Table 3.2. For comparison, Figure 3.2 also shows the overall expenditure by the universities, recurrent and capital combined, in both actual and revalued money. The effect of revaluation is, of course, marked. Without revaluation both trends would appear to be smooth upward sweeps continuing the Robbins expansion which began some years earlier. With revaluation, however, a quite different pattern emerges. Expenditure increases up to and including 1973/74, but on a concave instead of a convex curve; it drops significantly in 1974/75 and then steadies until 1978/79 when it increases again to about the 1973/74 level. Whether overall expenditure, in real terms, increased further in 1979/80 is impossible to ascertain in view of the uncertainties of the revaluation data. Our best assessment is that in real

FIGURE 3.2

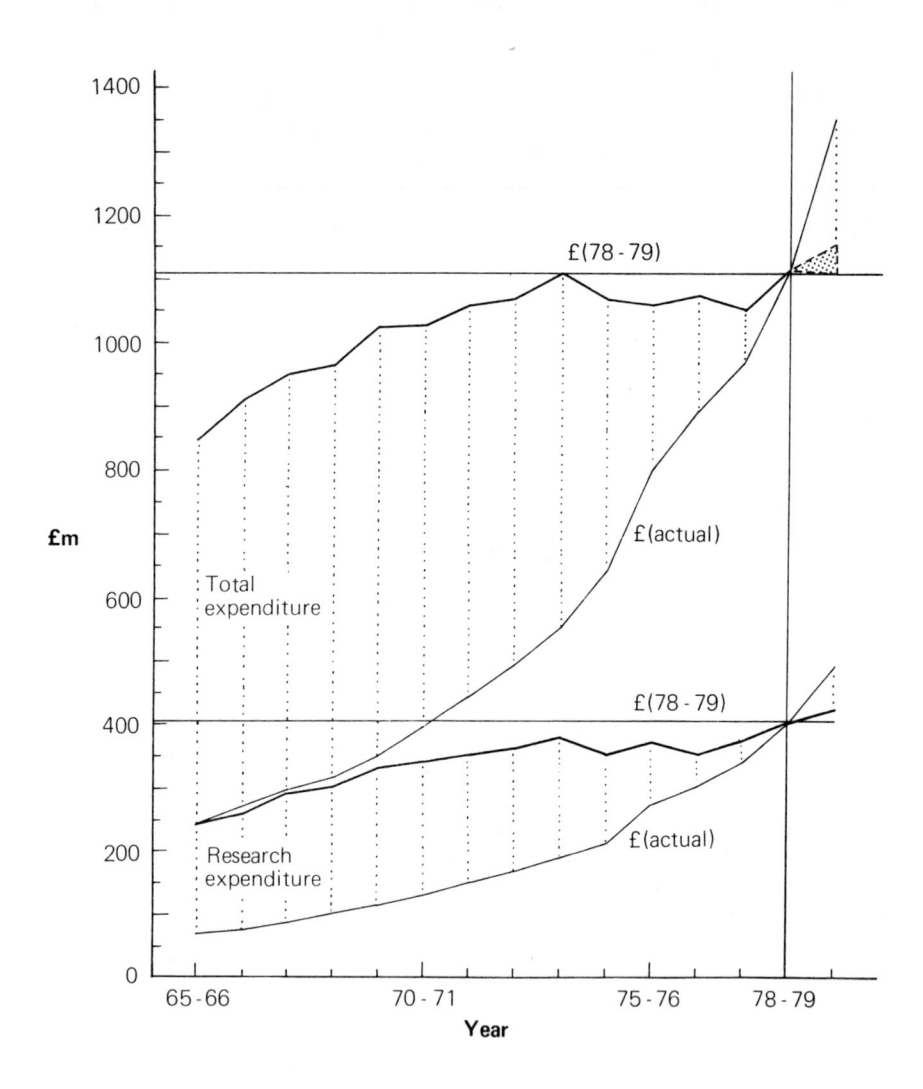

Overall expenditure and research expenditure (R) at the universities 1965-1980; actual expenditure (£m.) and revalued to 1978/79 prices (£m). The shaded area for 1979/80 in revalued total expenditure indicates the uncertainty due to rapid inflation.

terms overall expenditure for 1979/80 was in the range 0 per cent to + 3 per cent compared with 1978/79, as indicated by the shaded zone in Figure 3.2.

Figure 3.3a shows the trends in total research expenditure in more detail. The abruptness of the change after 1973/74 is now more apparent, as is the resumption of growth in 1978/79. In the case of research expenditure we can be reasonably confident that growth continued into 1979/80, probably by about 5 to 6 per cent in real terms. It would have required an inflation increase of nearly 30 per cent to cause research expenditure, in real terms, to be the same in the two years, and this is out of range of any inflation data available to us.

Figure 3.3a also shows the effect of some of the alternative assumptions referred to in the previous section. For example, if computing funds were to have been revalued on the CVCP indices instead of using actual £s, the resulting totals would be those shown thus - - - - -. If, in addition, RPI values of column B of Table 3.2 are used to revalue all recurrent expenditure instead of the CVCP indices of column A, the result is shown thus . . . . Both alternatives elevate the middle years of the decade, bringing the 1973/74 peak almost up to the 1978/79 level.

FIGURE 3.3a
Total research expenditure (R) 1965-1980

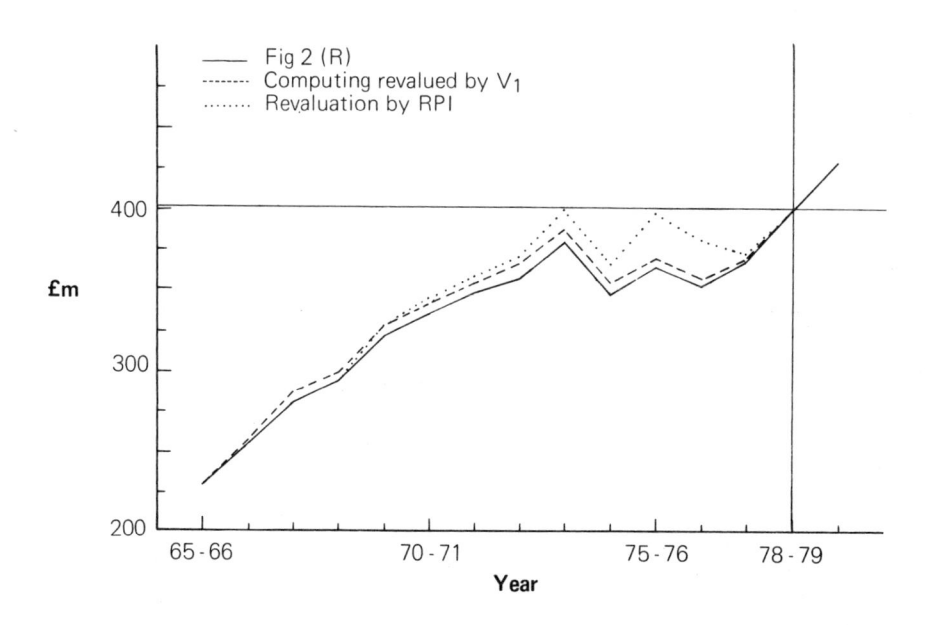

98   THE FUTURE OF RESEARCH

A question that can be asked at this stage is: What proportion is the expenditure on research of the total university expenditure, and how has it changed over the years? The answer is shown in Figure 3.3b, where total research expenditure (R, Equation 10) is plotted against total university expenditure less non-recurrent capital for buildings and associated costs.[1] Research expenditure has stayed within a narrow range of 35 to 40 per cent total expenditure throughout the period, though with evidence of a slight but sustained decline during the 1970s. Only in the last two years is this trend reversed and this is due largely, as we shall show later, to external funding.

FIGURE 3.3b
Total research expenditure (R) as percentage of overall expenditure 1965-1980

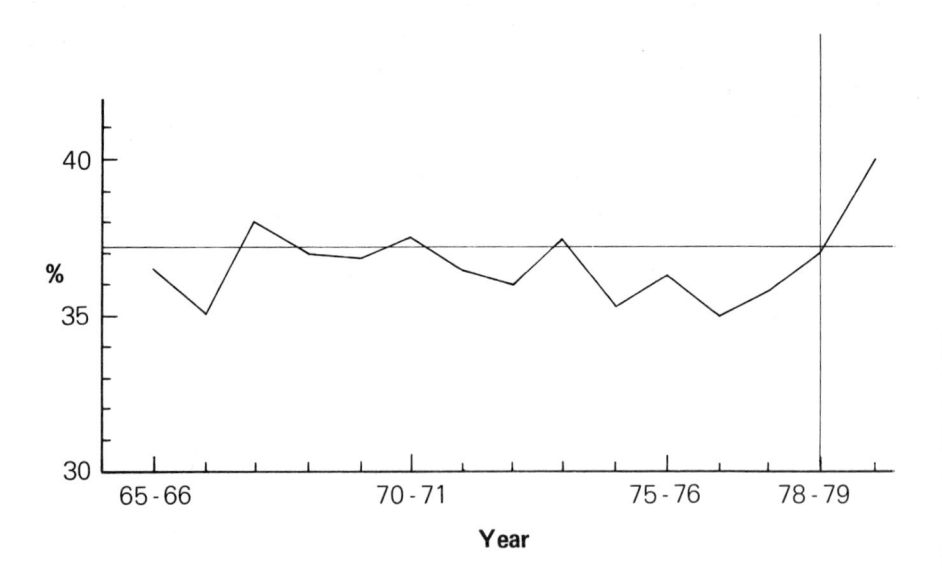

[1] Some of these buildings were for research laboratories, but to include expenditure on them with annual recurrent expenditure distorts the picture. If amortized on a, say, 100-year life-span, as should strictly be done, their effect, even with discounting, would be slight.

Estimates of total expenditure attributable to research are, of course, directly affected by the values of the coefficients p in Equation 8. Taking the lower set of values of Table 3.2 ($p_2=p_3=p_4=0.7$) gives the estimates of D_r, R_d and R for the reference year 1978/79 shown in Table 3.4.

TABLE 3.4
Estimates of research expenditure (£m 1978/79 prices) and as percentages of total expenditure 1978/79

	D_r		R_d		R	
	£m	%	£m	%	£m	%
$p_2 = p_3 = p_4 = 1.0$	213	19.7	273	25.2	403	37.2
$p_2 = p_3 = p_4 = 0.7$	181	16.7	222	20.5	332	30.7

On the other hand, using the lower values of p has an insignificant effect on the shape of the trends in expenditure since 1965.

We now look at the main components of total research expenditure (R), the relative proportions of which are shown in Figure 3.4. Taking first the change in external funding, ie in grants and contracts, which is shown in more detail in Figure 3.5a, this graph exhibits a sustained plateau starting in 1970/71, followed by a sharp upward movement in 1978/79 and 1979/80. It is important to ascertain how this expenditure changed relative to internal funding. Figure 3.5b shows grants and contracts as a percentage of total direct research expenditure, R_d, (Equation 9), and of departmental research expenditure, D_r, (Equation 8). Both graphs show an appreciable fall during the periods 1970/73, but thereafter external sources of funds for research have assumed increasing importance, especially in the last two years. We shall examine this question in more detail later (p.127).

It is instructive to see whether the gross statistics can throw further light on how the universities and the UGC responded to the abrupt cessation of growth after the peak year of 1973/74. We examine first departmental and laboratory maintenance. This provides for the day-to-day running of the department, including consumables and minor equipment — in other words, the basis of a 'well-found' department which, on the Dual Support System, would be expected to come from the UGC block grant to the university. Figure 3.6a shows departmental and laboratory maintenance from the first year in which it is recorded separately in the statistical record (1969/70). It hardly changes through the seventies, at between £9m and £10m (78/79 prices).[1] Figure 3.6b shows how this maintenance expenditure has changed

---

[1] This is, of course, the research share of this expenditure, as defined by Equation 1.

FIGURE 3.4
Composition of research expenditure 1965-80

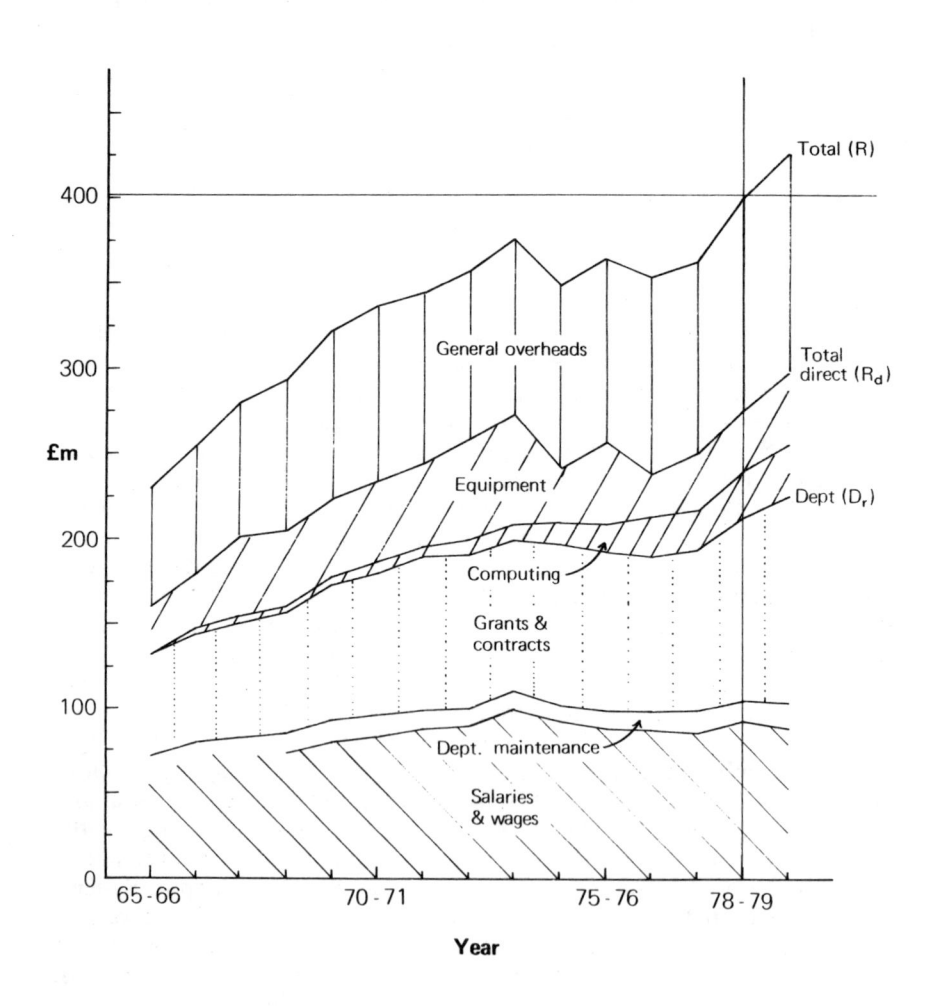

FIGURE 3.5a
Grants and contracts: 1978/79 prices (£m)

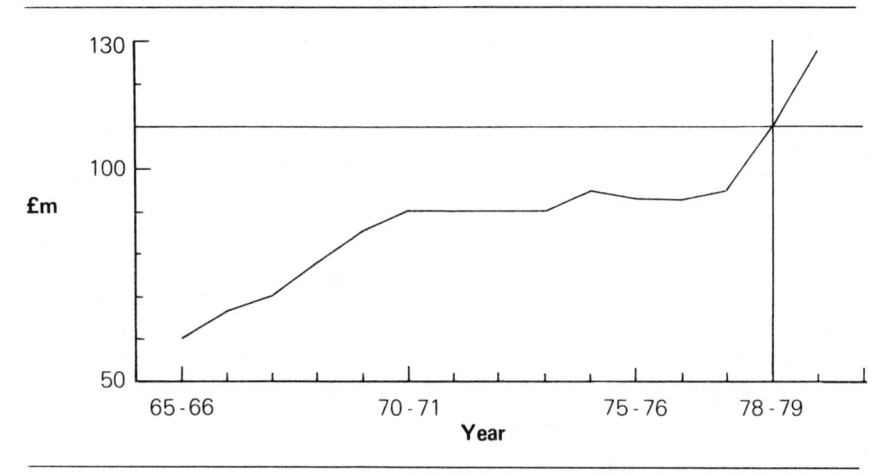

FIGURE 3.5b
Grants and contracts as percentage of total direct (R_d) and departmental research (D_r) expenditure

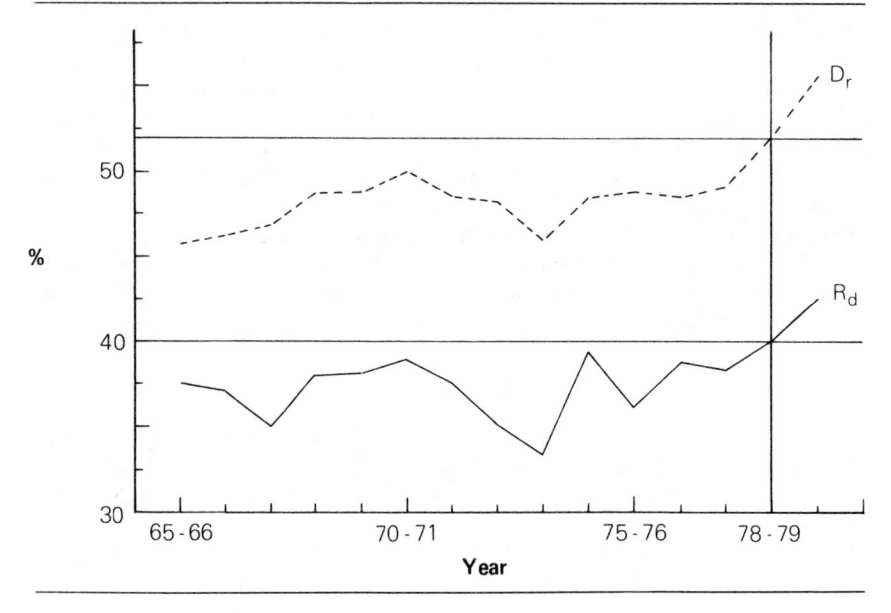

relative to the total direct research expenditure R_d, and departmental research expenditure D_r. A marked downward trend over the period, from 4½ to 3¼ per cent of total research expenditure, is evident.

The implication is that the resources for day-to-day departmental and laboratory activities declined by nearly one-third during the seventies, and continued to fall in 1979/80. Indeed, if the inflationary increase for this category of expenditure is higher than the average index for recurrent expenditure generally (as may be the case, eg through the steep rise in costs of petro-chemicals), then the implications are that much more serious.

Scientific equipment can also be examined separately. Unlike maintenance expenditure, this is provided centrally as earmarked capital to individual universities on the recommendation of the equipment sub-committee of the UGC. It does not, however, include specialized equipment needed to carry out a particular research project, which is normally provided by an outside funding body (usually a research council).[1] Figure 3.7a shows how this category of expenditure has changed during the period, both in actual money and revalued according to the indices given in column C of Table 3.2.[2] After increasing steadily up to 1973/74, expenditure dropped sharply in 1974/75; although in actual money the upward trend appears to have been resumed, albeit with much larger year-to-year fluctuations, the level of acquisition of equipment in real terms (1978/79 prices) has remained well below that of the peak year 1973/74. The transition after 1973/74 is seen in even sharper relief if expenditure on scientific equipment is expressed as percentages of the two measures of research expenditure, as in Figure 6b. It can now be seen that although equipment expenditure in real terms has been rising slowly since its lowest point in 1976/77, it has no more than kept pace with the most recent upturn in total research expenditure.

The third of the separate items, central computer services, presents a different situation. It has already been noted that the actual money spent on central computing increased from less than £1m in 1965/66 to £30m in 1979/80 (see Figure 3.4). Whether or not this expenditure is revalued, or expressed as a percentage of research as overall expenditure, the trend is rapidly upward throughout the period, as shown in Figure 3.8a and 3.8b. When it is remembered that most external grants and contracts, particularly from the SERC, also include provision for computing, it is evident that this aspect of research support has, uniquely, increased substantially throughout the period.

---

[1] This element of capital expenditure is included in 'Grants and Contracts' and is not distinguished either in the statistics published by the DES or by the research councils.
[2] The first two points, for 1965/66 and 1966/67, are estimated from general equipment funds, and are of uncertain reliability.

FIGURE 3.6a
Departmental and laboratory maintenance 1965-80 (£m 1978/79)

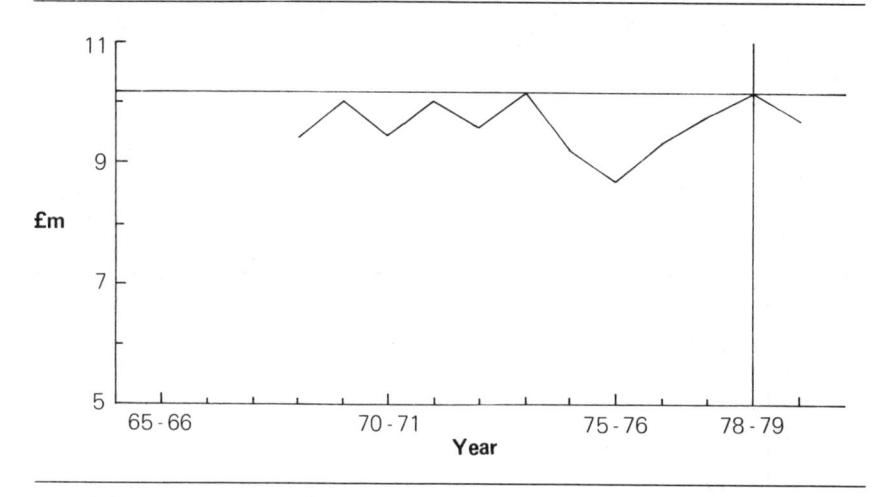

FIGURE 3.6b
Departmental and laboratory maintenance 1965-80 as percentage of total direct (R_d) and departmental (D_r) research expenditure

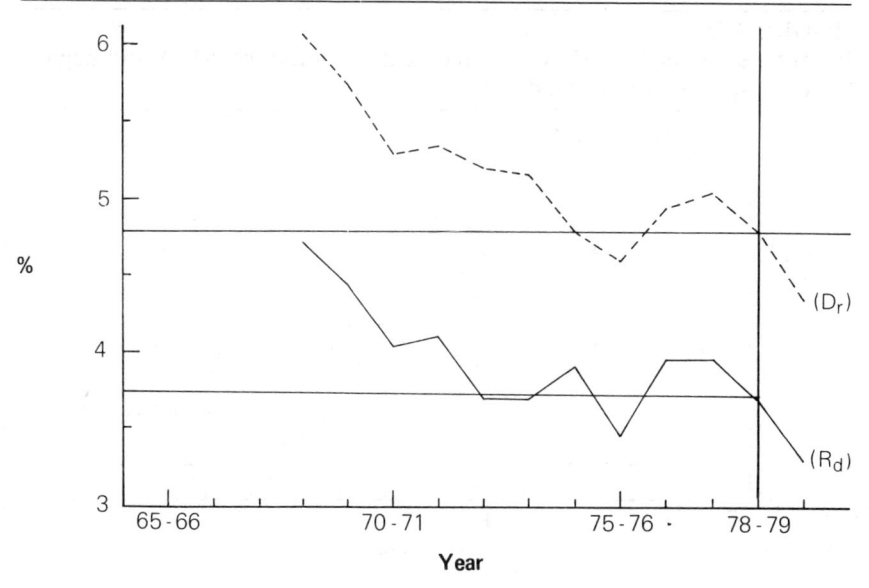

104   THE FUTURE OF RESEARCH

FIGURE 3.7a
Scientific equipment 1965-80 (£m actual and £m 1978/79)

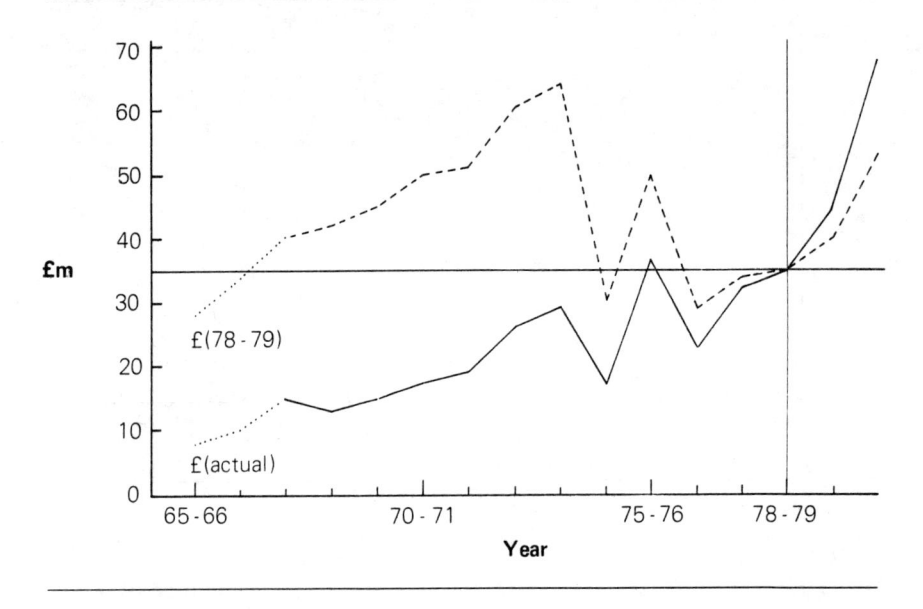

FIGURE 3.7b
Scientific equipment 1965-80 as percentage of total direct (R_d) and departmental (D_r) research expenditure

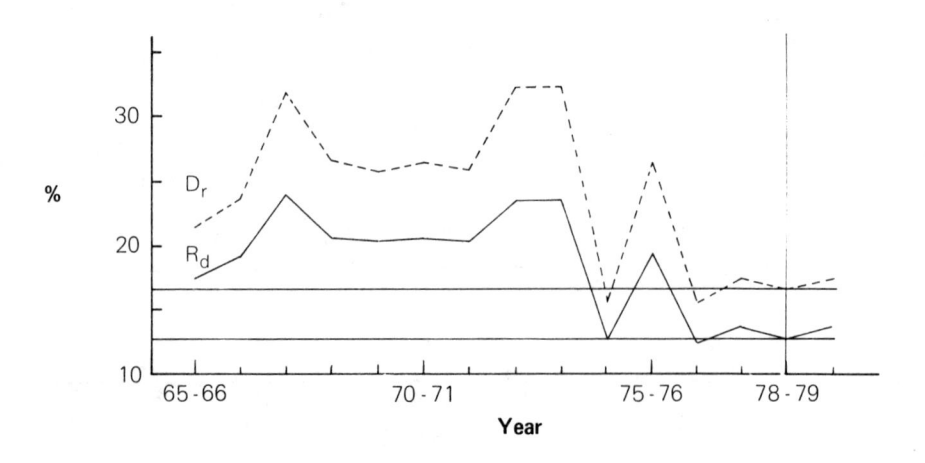

FIGURE 3.8a
Computing services 1965-80 (£m actual)

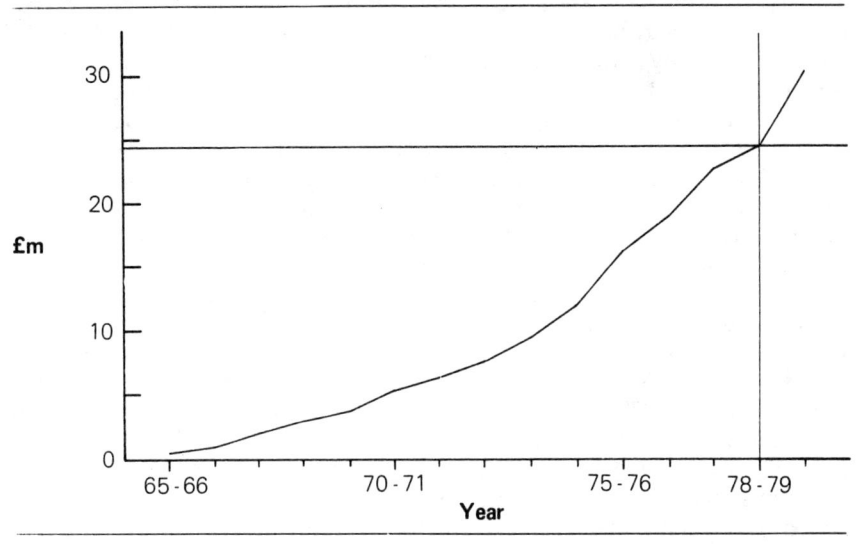

FIGURE 3.8b
Computing services 1965-80 as percentage of total (R_d) and departmental (D_r) expenditure

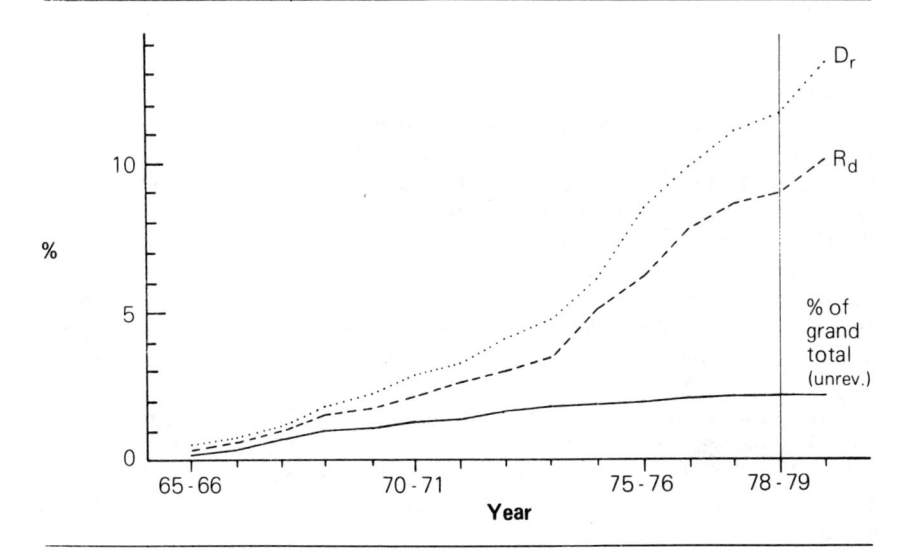

Staff and Students

Figure 3.9 shows the number of full-time university staff engaged on teaching and research in the science sector over the period 1965/80, together with undergraduate and postgraduate load[1] in the same fields. Apart from the apparent anomaly of the first four years in the case of postgraduate numbers, which appears to be due to a change in the definition of a part-time medical postgraduate, the trend is upwards throughout. It is important to note from Figure 3.9 that in one year only, 1977/78, did the total number of scientific staff fail to increase above that for the previous year; indeed, apart from this slight hesitation (- 0.5%), there is no correspondence in the graph of staff numbers to the cessation of growth in research expenditure which took place after 1973/74.[2]

The similar shape of the staff and student curves indicates that the student load per number of staff did not change a great deal. This can be seen from the student/staff ratios in Figure 3.10. Again, disregarding the first few postgraduate points, the postgraduate/staff ratio has remained within ±0.04 (± 3%) of its 1978/79 value of 1.39. The undergraduate ratio has, however, increased from its lowest figure of 5.7 in 1974/75 to the 1978/79 values of 6.5, ie an increase of 14 per cent. This evidence in itself does not suggest that the teaching load has increased significantly over the period, but a somewhat different picture emerges when individual subjects are examined (see below).

The other important statistic to examine is the research expenditure per member of staff, and how it has changed over the period, since this is perhaps the most sensitive measure of research support. Figure 3.11 shows total direct and departmental research expenditure per staff. Both graphs increase to a peak in 1973/74 and then decline until the rise in the last two years.

Analysis by Individual Subjects

As has been mentioned earlier, neither scientific equipment nor computing services can be allocated to subjects, so this more detailed analysis has to be limited to departmental research expenditure. Both in-house (UGC) and external funding (grants and contracts) are, however, tabulated by subject in the DES statistics, as are staff and student numbers.

Figure 3.12 shows departmental research expenditure (D_r) for each of the six science groups listed in Table 3.1. Apart from the sharp upturn in 1978/79 and 1979/80, which is common to all groups except applied biology, the most significant feature is the steady and substantial increase in

---

[1] Postgraduate numbers have been calculated by adding half the number of part-time postgraduates to the number of full-time postgraduates.
[2] The CVCP Office informs us that the staff record maintained in the University Staff Record (USR) was restructured in 1976/77, and the apparent fall in staff numbers in 1977/78 may be an artefact.

FUNDING AND POLICY IN THE NATURAL SCIENCES 107

FIGURE 3.9
Staff and student load 1965-80

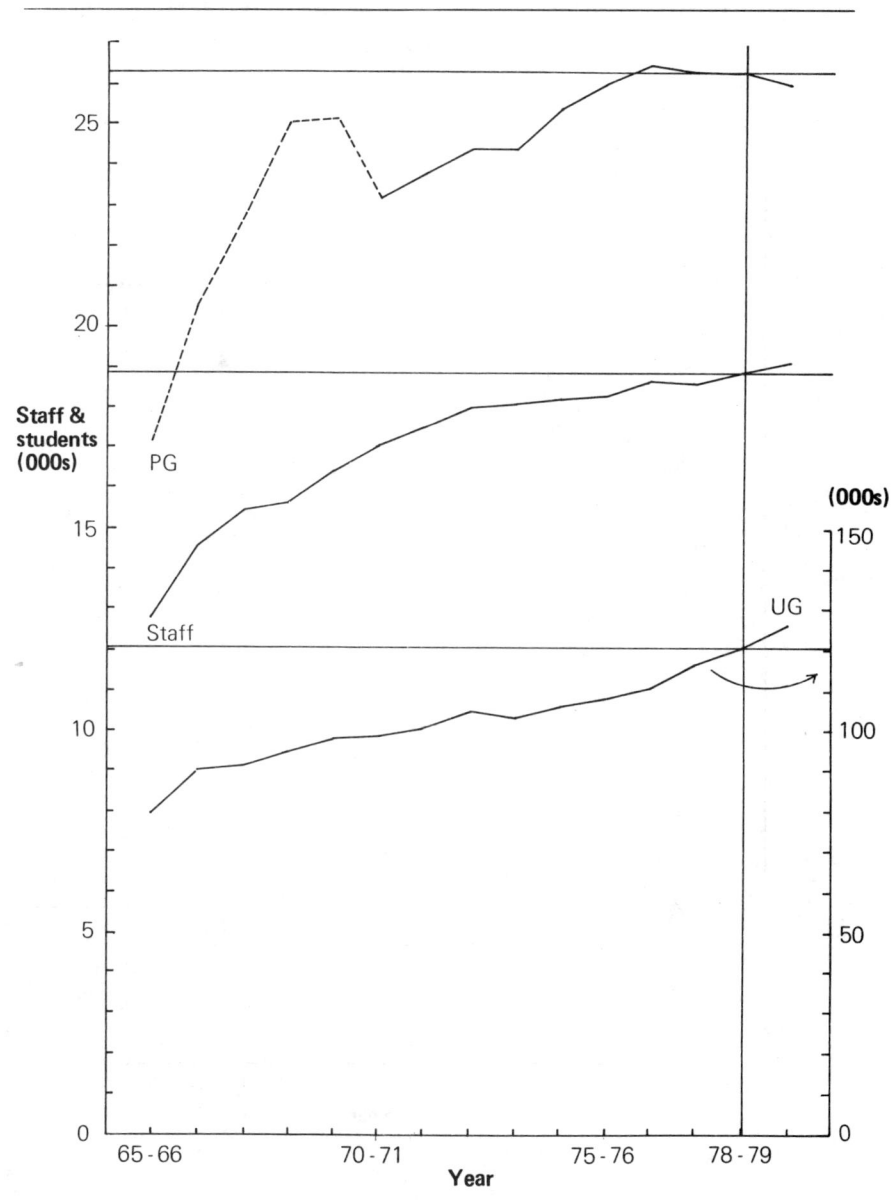

FIGURE 3.10
Student load/staff 1965-80

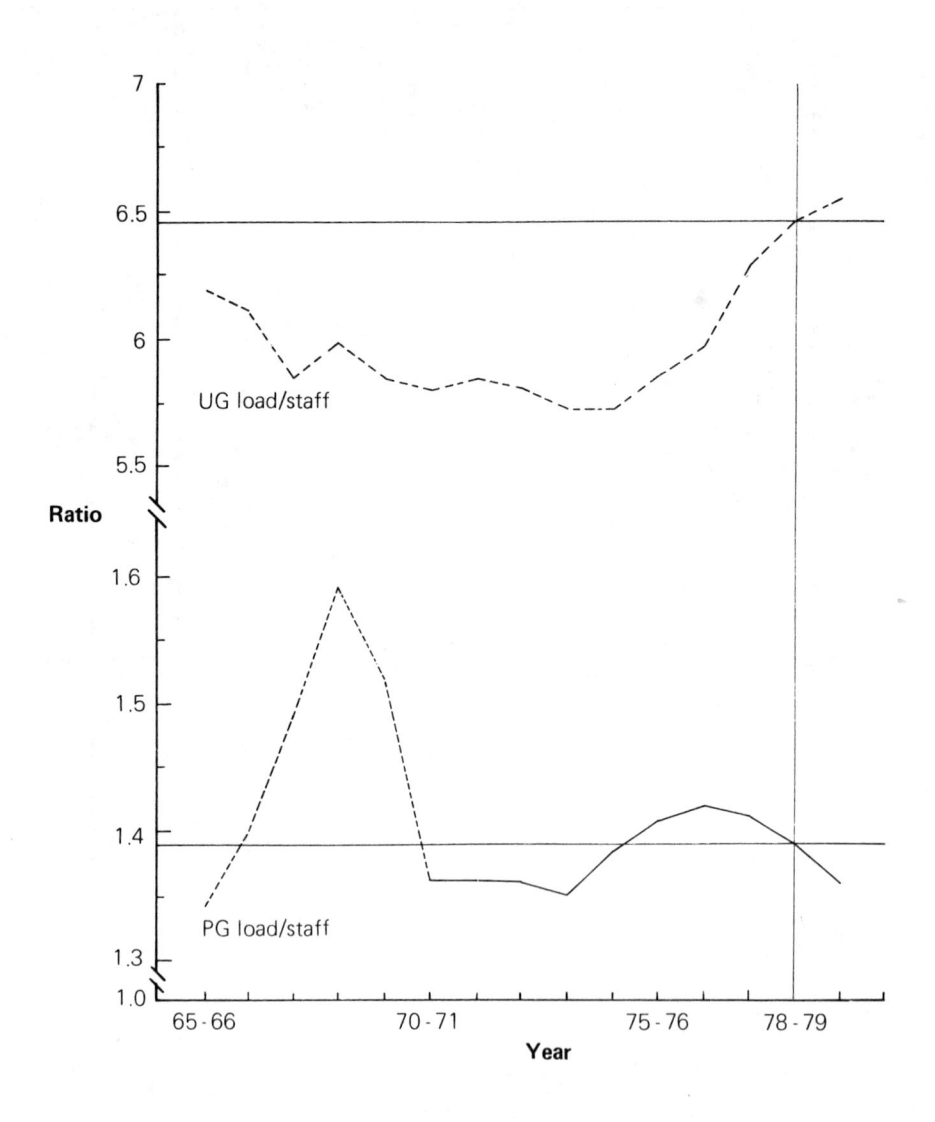

expenditure in the medical and biological sciences, particularly the former.[1] It must, however, be remembered that these figures do not include expenditure on either computing services or equipment, which is likely to have gone more to the physical than the biological sciences. With this central expenditure ranging from £30m to £80m over the period, its allocation by subjects could significantly alter the pattern of Figure 3.12 in favour of the physical sciences though not to the extent of changing the dominance of the growth in medical and biological sciences.

Trends in staff numbers are shown in Figure 3.13. Again, the outstanding feature is the sustained rise in medical sciences staff, whose numbers increased by over 60 per cent during the period. Staff numbers have remained static after 1973/74 or declined in all other subjects except biological sciences, in which some growth is present throughout.

Trends in student load for individual subject groups are shown in Figures 3.14 and 3.15. Although subjects reflected the rise in science undergraduates (Figure 3.14) from the mid-seventies onwards, only medicine and biological sciences showed a sustained growth throughout (by more than 60 per cent over the period shown). In contrast, the undergraduate load in the physical sciences, although it picked up towards the end of the decade, was smaller by 1980 than it was in 1967. The trends in postgraduate load (Figure 3.15) are less pronounced but follow the same general pattern, except that engineering and mathematics join medicine and biology in showing sustained growth, while the decline in postgraduate load in the physical sciences is more consistent.

Undergraduate load/staff ratios for individual subject groups are shown in Figure 3.16. The ratios have increased significantly since 1974/75 in all except medical sciences, but because most groups showed a fall in the earlier years the overall trends are less clear. Applied biology is, however, exceptional in increasing throughout, by nearly two-fold, while the biological sciences ratio has increased since 1971/72 (by 30%). In contrast, the undergraduate/staff ratio in the physical sciences is about 10 per cent lower than it was in 1965/66, due to the significant decline in undergraduates in this category of sciences. The trends in postgraduate/staff ratios shown in Figure 3.17 are less pronounced except in applied biology, where they were some 40 per cent higher in the later years compared with 1965/66. Significantly, the overall trend in physical sciences has been downward, the 1979/80 ratio being some 17 per cent below that in 1965/66.

Finally, Figure 3.18 shows departmental research expenditure per staff by subject group. There are no marked trends, but the upturn in 1978/79 and 1979/80 evident from the combined data in Figure 3.10 is seen to apply to all subject groups except applied biology.

---

[1] It will be recalled from p.87 that our category 'biological sciences' combines both the DES category (x) Biological Sciences and the DES category (ii) Pre-clinical Medicine and Dentistry.

FIGURE 3.11
Research expenditure (£m 1978/79) per staff 1965-80

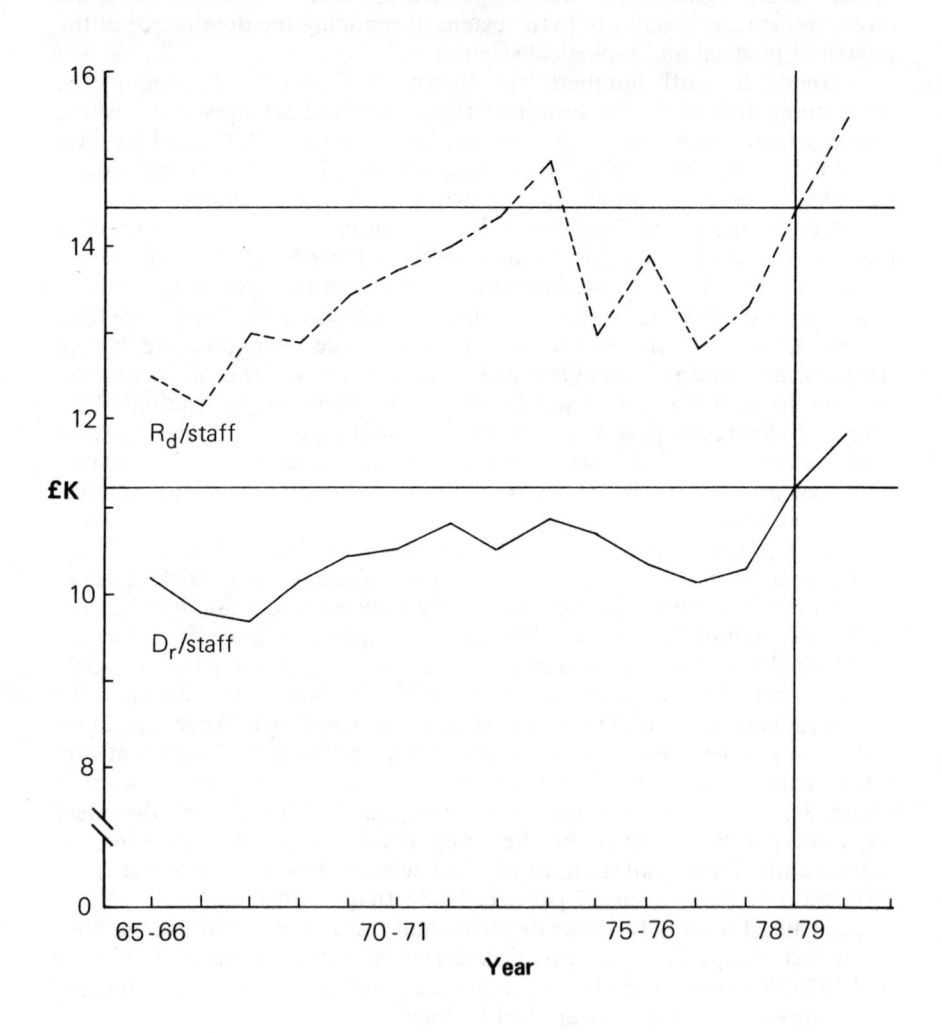

FIGURE 3.12
Departmental research expenditure (D_r) by subject groups 1965-80

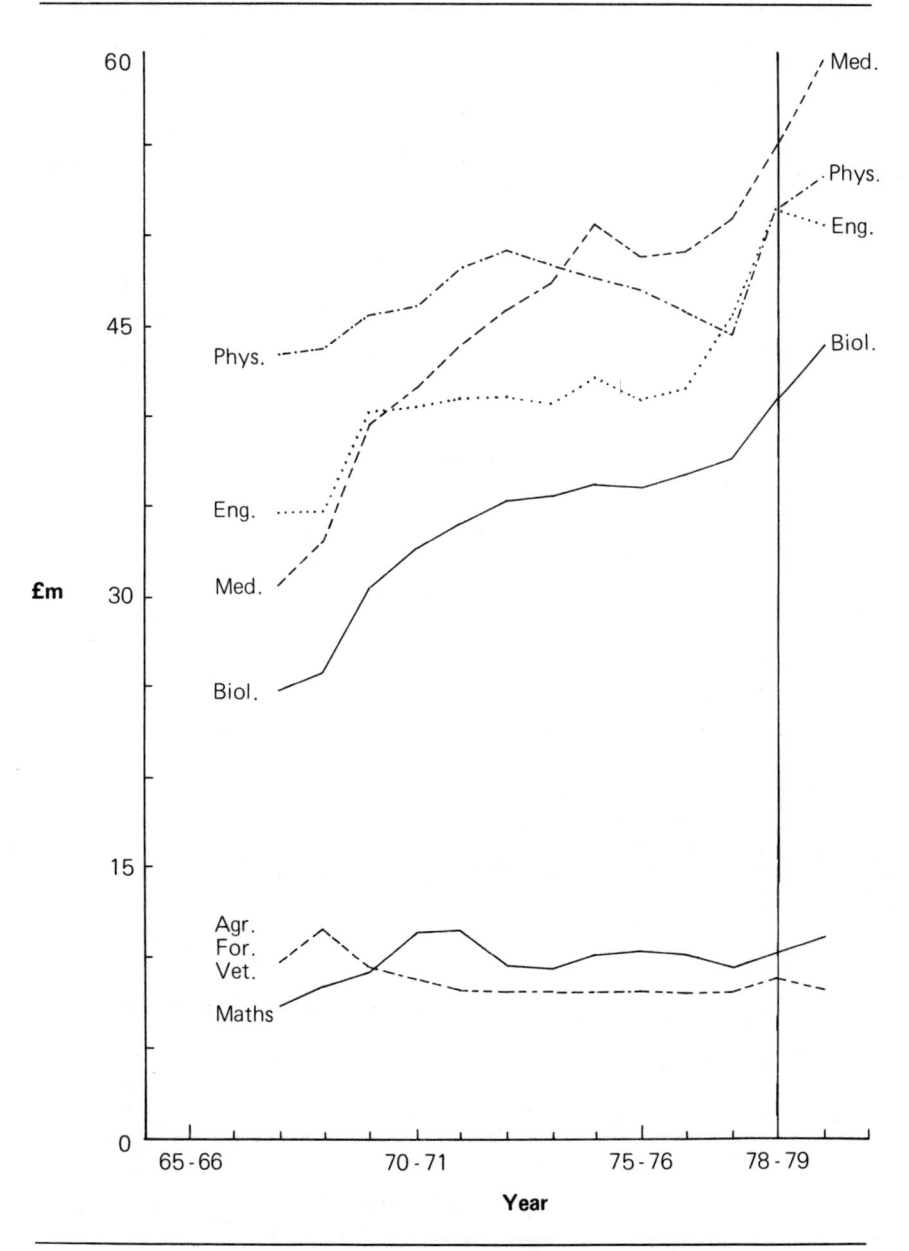

112 THE FUTURE OF RESEARCH

FIGURE 3.13
Staff by subject groups 1965-80

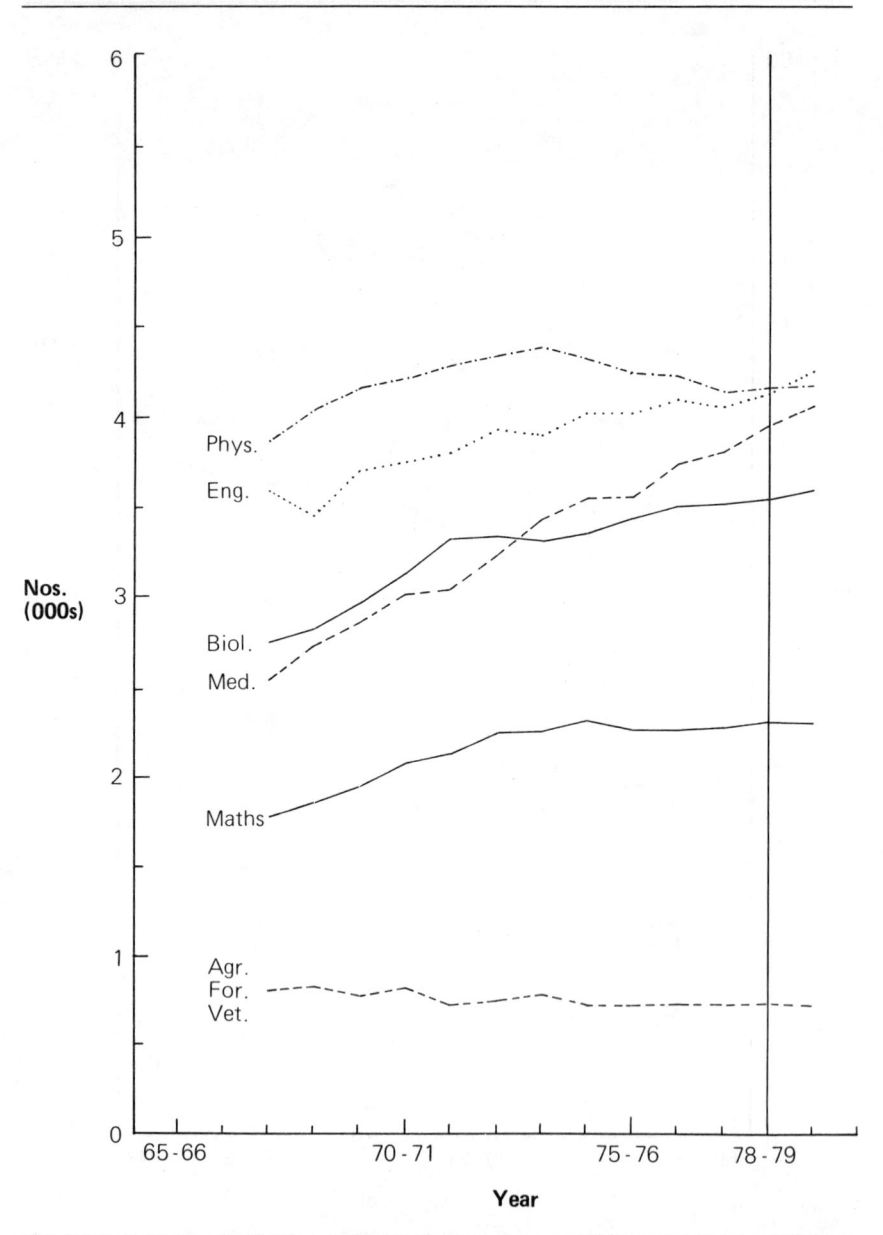

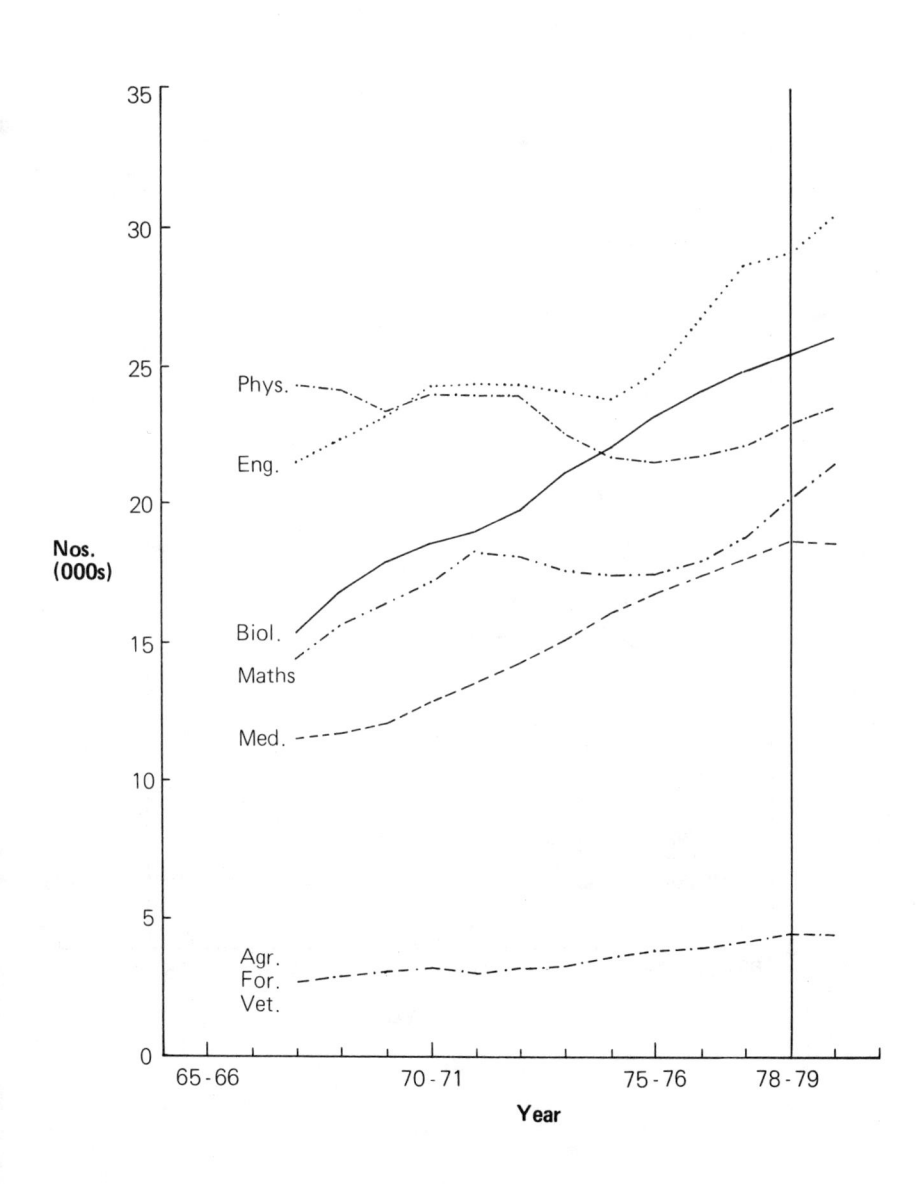

FIGURE 3.14
Undergraduate student load by subject 1965-80

FIGURE 3.15
Postgraduate student load by subject 1965-80

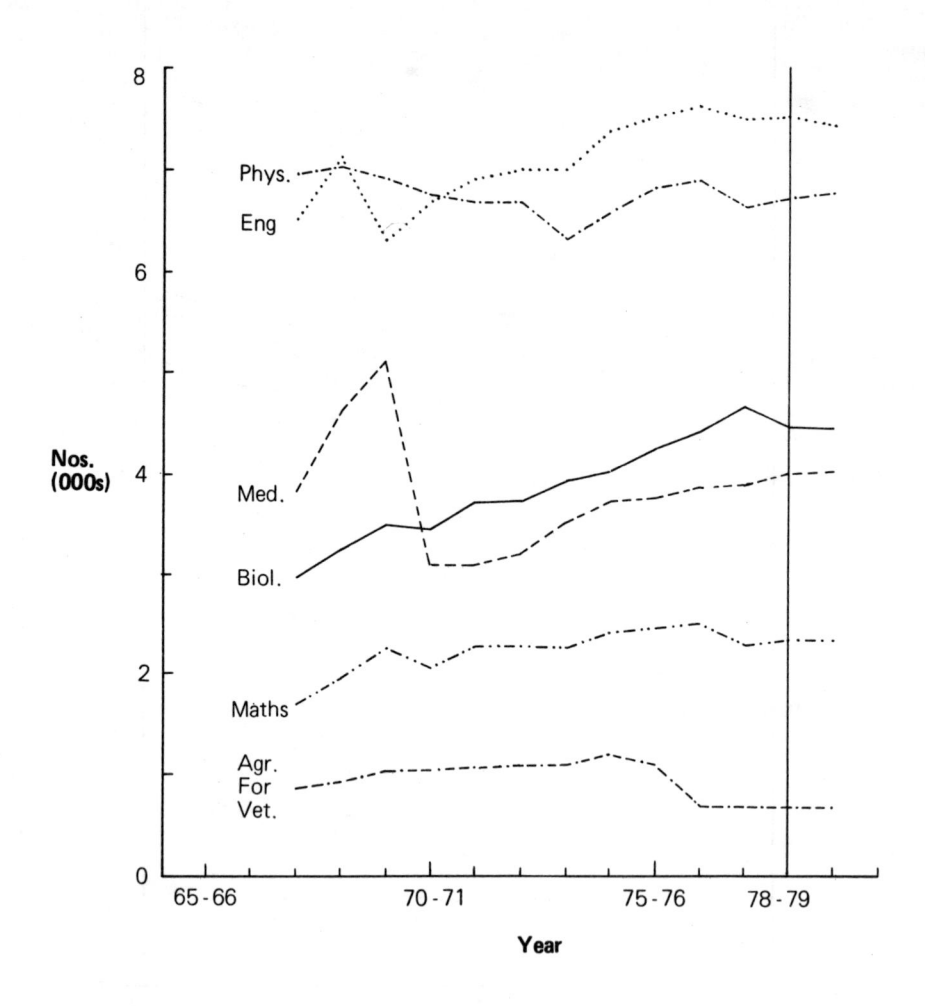

FUNDING AND POLICY IN THE NATURAL SCIENCES 115

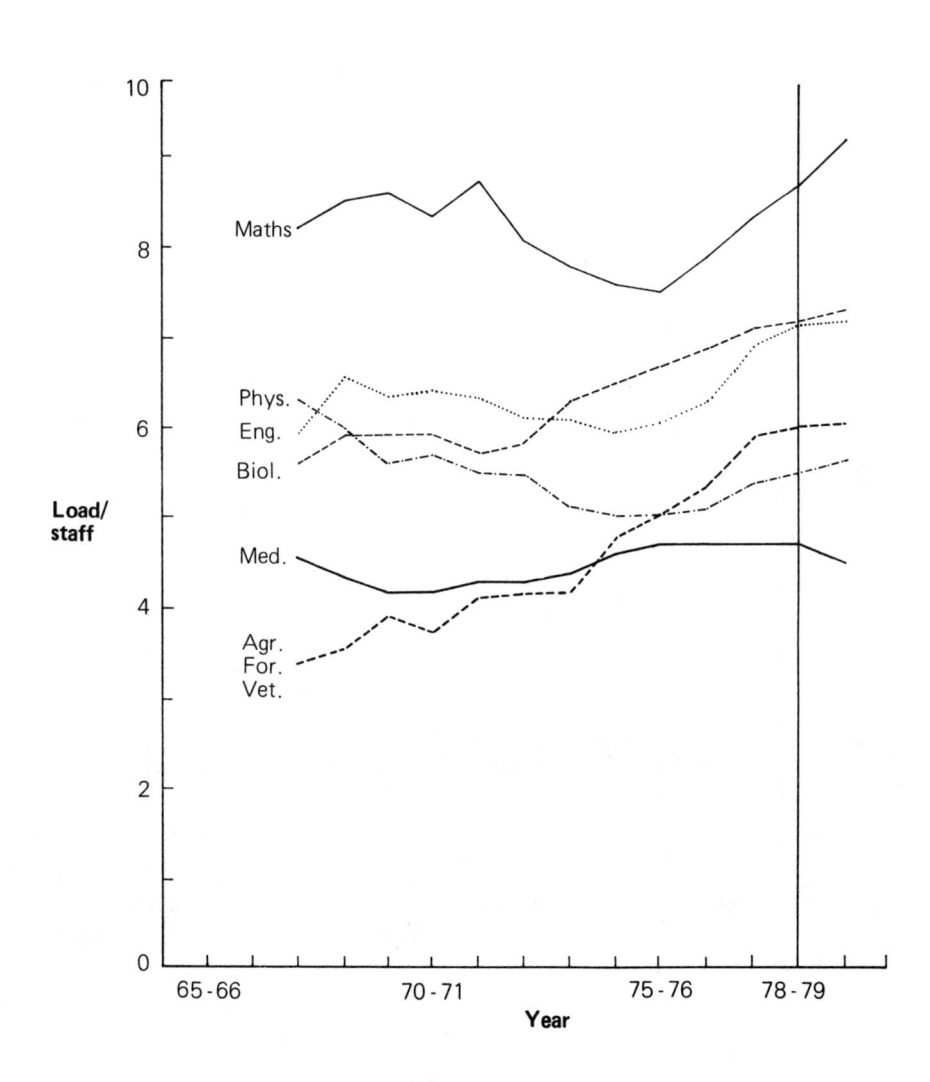

FIGURE 3.16
Undergraduate load/staff by subject 1965-80

FIGURE 3.17
Postgraduate load/staff by subject 1965-80

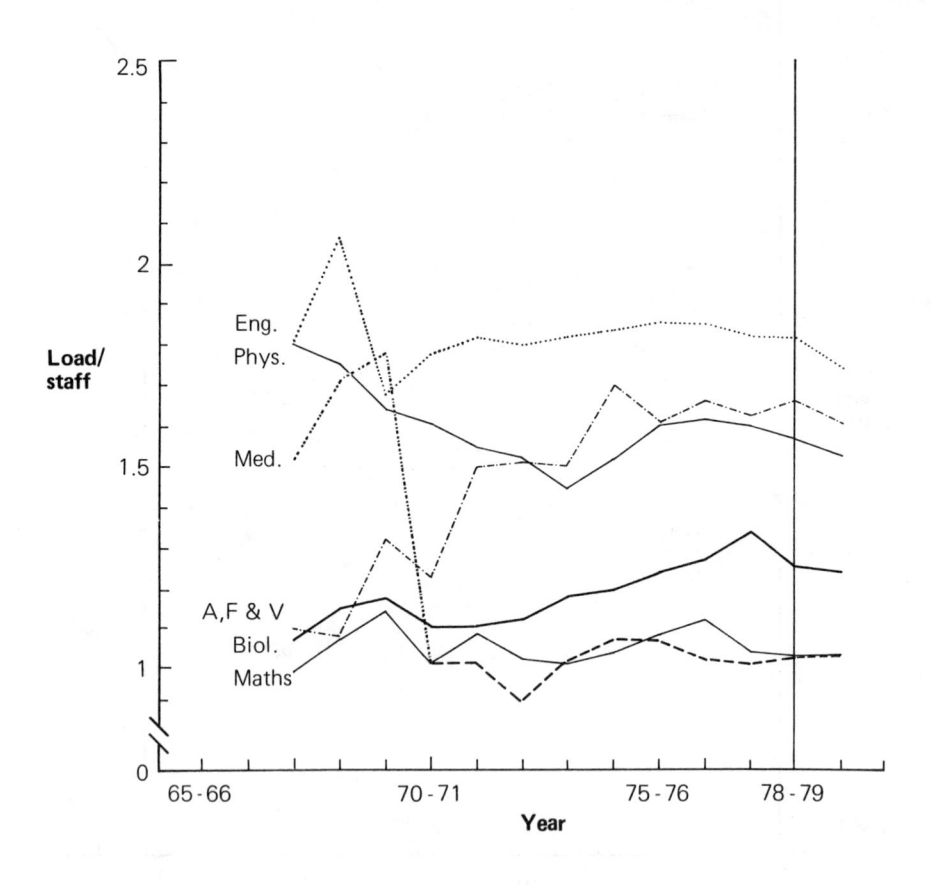

FIGURE 3.18
Departmental research expenditure (£K 1978/79 prices) per staff by subject group 1965-80

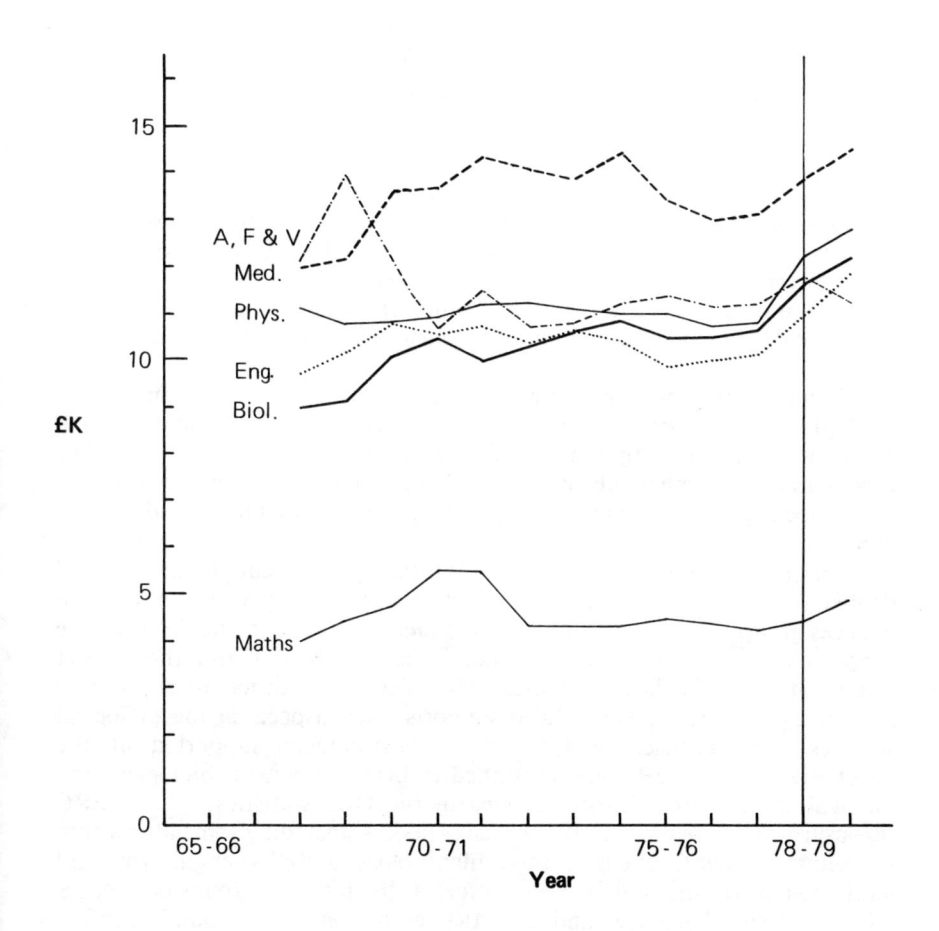

External Sources of Funding of Research

Figure 3.19a shows the trends in the total grants and contracts over the period and in the research grants from the research councils concerned with the natural sciences.

The latter, with their total grants in 1978/79 which make up about half the total grants and contracts expenditure by the universities, are:

		£m 1978/79	%
Agricultural Research Council	(ARC)	1	2
Medical Research Council	(MRC)	17	33
Natural Environment Research Council	(NERC)	3	6
Science and Engineering Research Council	(SERC)	31	59
		52	100

Both sets of data have remained effectively constant since 1970, showing little of the perturbations which have characterized the 1970/80 decade of funding from internal (UGC) sources. Figure 3.19b shows, however, that the proportion of total external support coming from the research councils has tended to decline, despite fluctuations from around 60 to 50 per cent over the period.

Figure 3.20 shows how the percentages of the six science groups in the total grants and contracts have changed. Again, medical and biological sciences stand apart; they alone having increased their percentage. The proportions of the other subjects have either remained effectively constant (as in engineering) or declined (as in physical sciences, mathematics and applied biology).

Except for the ambiguity concerning pre-clinical medicine and dentistry, the MRC grant aid corresponds fairly closely with our medical sciences group. There is no such correspondence between the fields of science supported by the other three science research councils and the subject classification in the DES statistics. The ARC, in addition to supporting specific agricultural research, also supports other aspects of the biological sciences. The sciences of the natural environment supported at the unversities by the NERC are subsumed in both the general biological and physical sciences and forestry groups in the DES statistics, while SERC research grants cover nearly all the basic sciences (including some also within the remits of other Councils, eg molecular biology) as well as engineering and mathematics. In what follows we therefore distinguish two groups of sciences only: the medical sciences and the MRC grants on the one hand; and the non-medical sciences (including engineering and mathematics) with the aggregate grants from the other three councils (ARC, NERC and SERC) on the other.

FUNDING AND POLICY IN THE NATURAL SCIENCES   119

FIGURE 3.19a
Grants and contracts 1965-80 (£m 1978/79): total and research councils

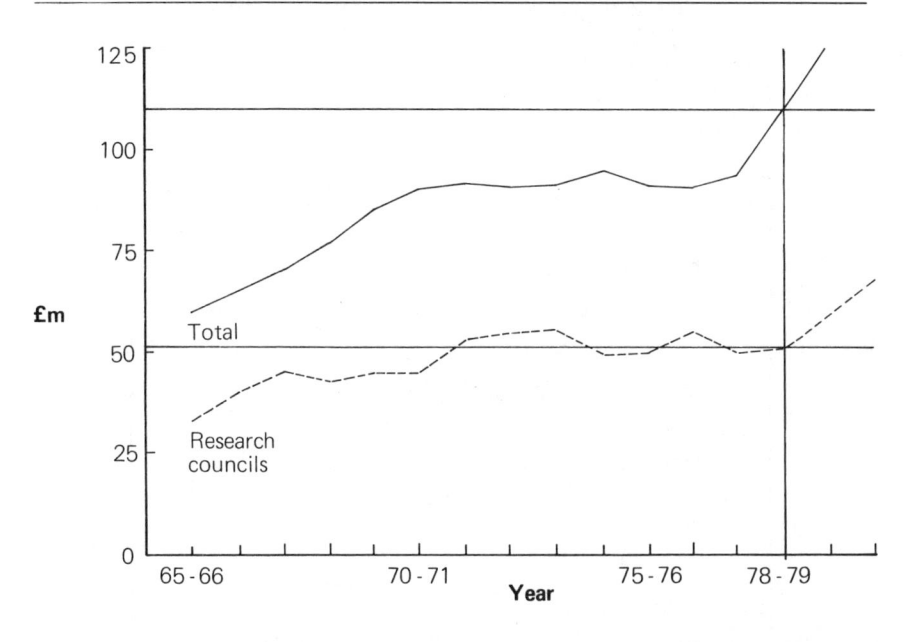

Figure 3.19b
Grants and contracts 1965-80: research council grants as percentage of total

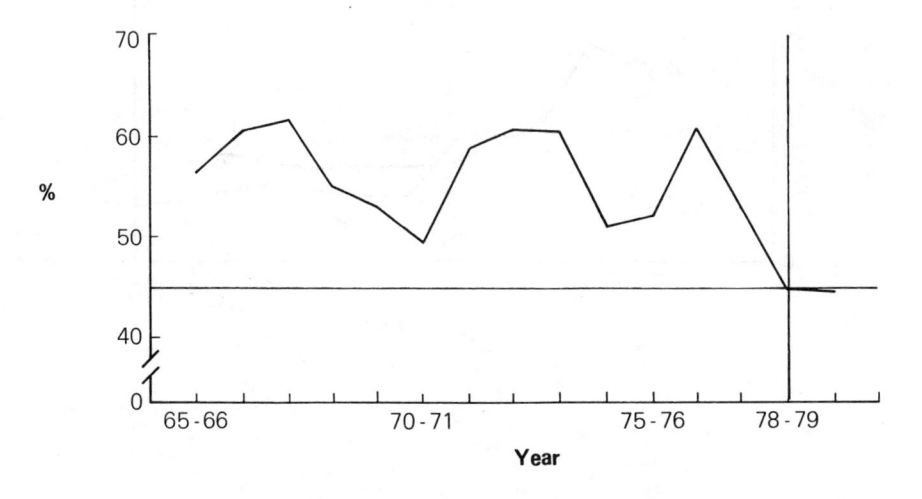

FIGURE 3.20
Percentage composition of grants and contracts by subject 1965-80

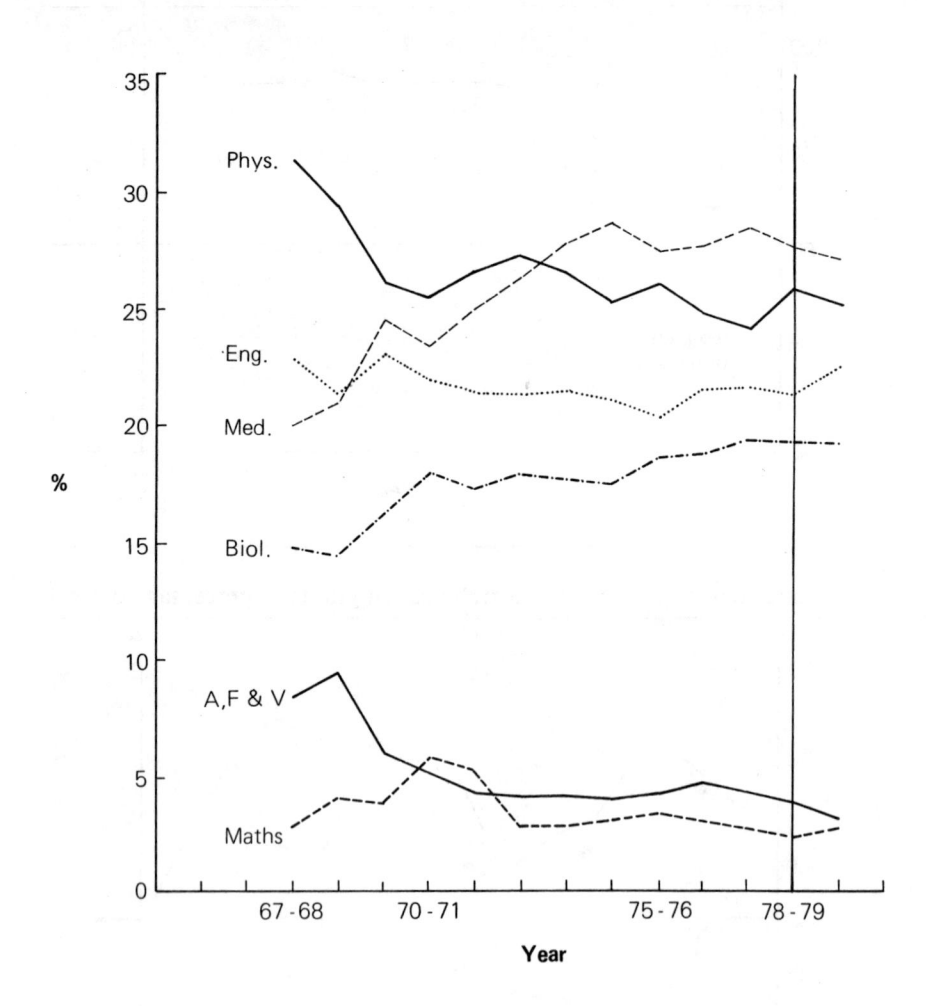

Figure 3.21a shows the trends in expenditure of total medical grants and contracts, and MRC grants. Both show growth during the period, although the MRC grants stayed level through much of the seventies. Total medical grants, however, increased steadily by nearly three-fold over this period. This differential movement is seen in Figure 3.21b which shows how the percentage of MRC grants in the total has declined from nearly 70 to 40 per cent, albeit with fluctuations. It follows, of course, that other sources of funding for medical research, partly from the Department of Health and Social Security (DHSS) but also from private trusts, foundations and industry, have increased greatly over the period and especially in recent years.

A rather different picture emerges from the statistics of the research grants for non-medical sciences, shown in Figure 3.22 a and b. After rising at first, the total remained effectively constant from 1970/71 to 1977/78. The combined ARC, NERC and SERC grants continued to increase until 1973/74 when they too ceased growing. As a result, the proportion (%) of research council grants in the total external grant-aid for the general sciences has fluctuated about a roughly constant mean of about 55 per cent throughout the period. The increase, in real terms, in both research council and other external funding in 1978/79 and 1979/80 is noteworthy.

External funding for non-medical scientific research, other than research grants from the three research councils (which totalled £35m in 1978/79), comes from many sources. Funds from government departments, mainly as contracts, probably accounted for about one-fifth of the total, although no one of them contributed more than £1m-£2m. Private and nationalized industries together made up the majority of the rest, but details of the large number of research contracts, many of them very small, placed at universities and polytechnics are not published, mainly for reasons of confidentiality.

Research by Postgraduate Students

The last of the financial contributions to university research which we must consider is support for postgraduate students. We shall confine this analysis to those taking a three-year PhD course, of which there were about 20,000 in the total science sector in 1978/79. Roughly half of these were paid for by the research councils at a cost per student per year of about £3,000. In total, therefore, about £60m was spent as grants in support of PhD science students in 1978/79. A further £300 per student per year (ie £3m) was awarded to the departments as Research Training Support Grants, although this usually still left a significant dependence on the general departmental funds.

It is not easy to weigh this expenditure in terms that can be compared with the rest of university research expenditure. It has to be remembered that the prime purpose of the PhD course is for training in research. The projects are, or should be, chosen with this in mind and must also be capable of being

122   THE FUTURE OF RESEARCH

FIGURE 3.21a
Medical sciences: grants and contracts 1965-80: total and MRC

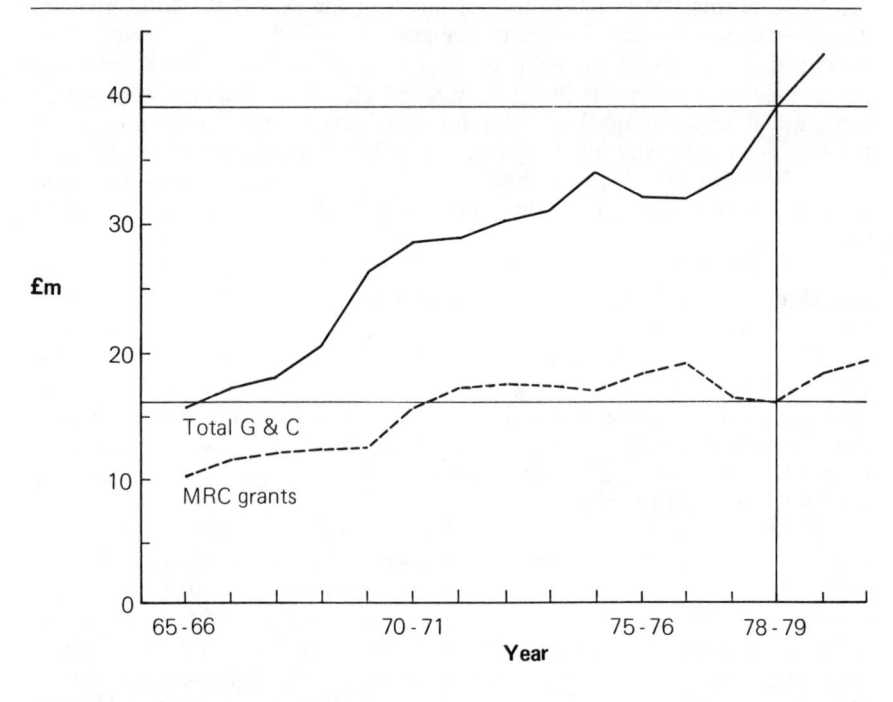

FIGURE 3.21b
Medical sciences: grants and contracts 1965-80: MRC grants as percentage of total medical grants and contracts

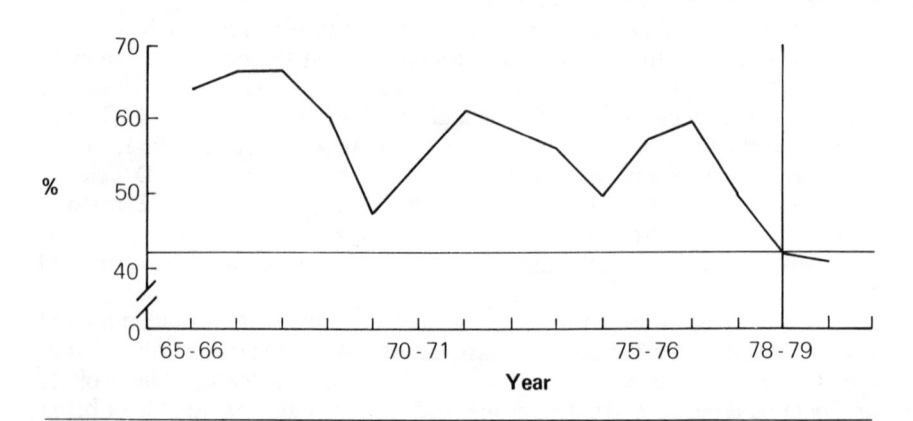

FUNDING AND POLICY IN THE NATURAL SCIENCES   123

FIGURE 3.22a
Non-medical sciences: grants and contracts 1965-80: total and research council

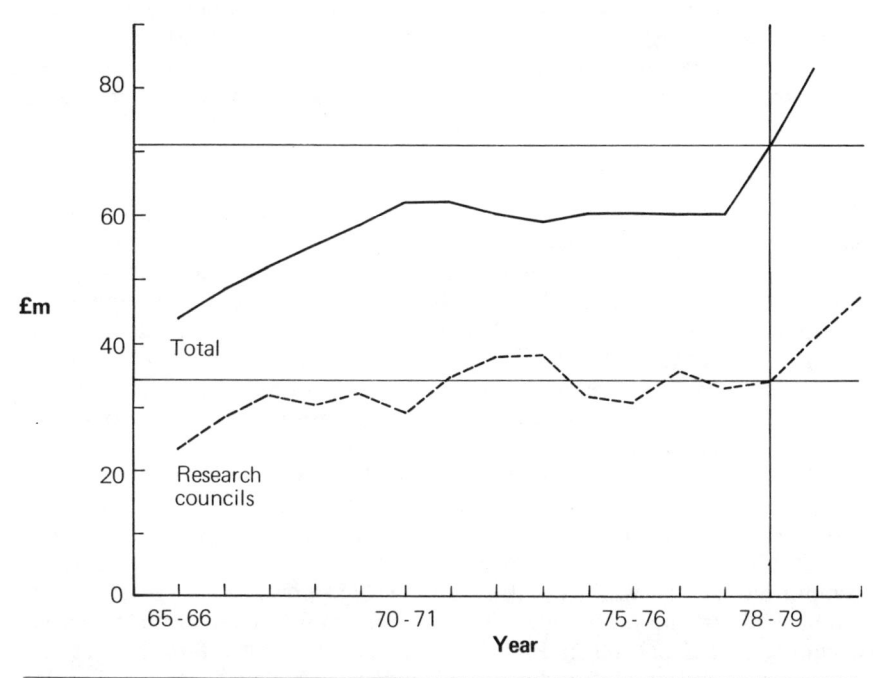

FIGURE 3.22b
Non-medical sciences: grants and contracts 1965-80: research council as percentage of total non-medical grants and contracts

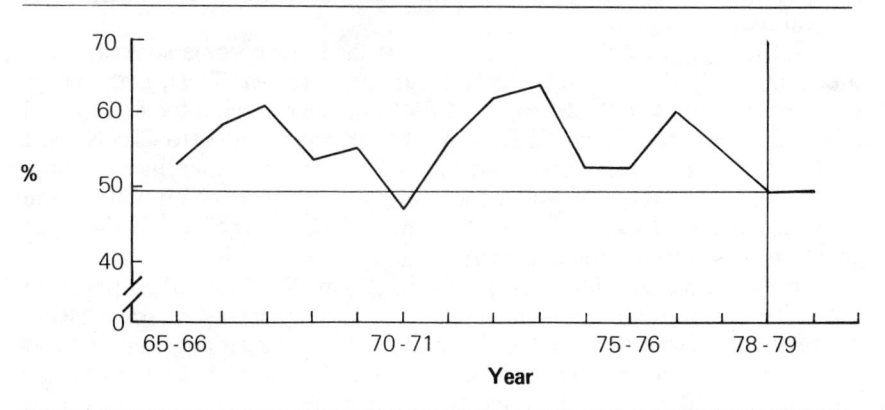

completed within the three-year period. As a result, many PhD theses are not suitable for publication in the scientific journals as they stand, even though they are fully up to the required PhD standard. However, they may well form an identifiable part of later publications, so that analysis of publications might provide a measure of research output which could be compared, per unit expenditure, with other research. In the absence of such information, we shall simply note that in our judgement something in the region of £20-£30m ought to be added to the overall research expenditure of the universities to take account of research undertaken by postgraduate students.

'In-kind' Support for University Research
The Science and Engineering Research Council is by far the largest provider of this kind of support, which is especially significant in the 'big science' area (eg high energy physics, astronomy, etc.) which falls mainly within the SERC remit. Since its formation in 1965 the SERC has made the support of university research by all means, financially via grants and studentships, and 'in-kind', the centrepiece of its policy, although the council also supports a substantial in-house research capability at its Rutherford Appleton (RAL) and Daresbury laboratories, and at the Royal Observatories. In 1965/66 the only central facility was the prototype Atlas computer. By the early seventies an ICL 1906 A and part of the time of an IBM 370/195 — the most advanced computer of its time — was available to the universities. By then, university scientists also had access to neutron scattering facilities and the NINA and NIMROD accelerators. Towards the end of the decade an interactive computing facility was available, and a high-powered laser laboratory established. In the most recent years, with emphasis on particle physics declining, the Synchrotron Radiation Source has been established at the Daresbury Laboratory for the use of chemists, biologists and molecular physicists, and an electron beam lithography unit has been set up at the RAL for use by universities and polytechnics. The SERC Annual Reports give detailed accounts of the evolution of these and other advanced facilities for general use.

In the biggest of the big-science fields facilities become so costly that they can be afforded only by international collaboration. Thus, high energy physicists now turn to the European CERN for their accelerator facility and other advanced techniques. SERC pays the UK subscription to CERN, part of that to the European Space Agency (ESA) and to other international research organizations, of which the university scientific community is the main beneficiary. In 1978/79, 30 per cent (£47m) of the SERC budget was spent on these international subscriptions.

In contrast, the Medical Research Council's 'in-kind' support to unversity research is mainly via research units they set up at universities. There are at present sixty such units, and in 1978/79 their aggregate budget was £23m, or 27 per cent of the total MRC budget. Only about half of these units are located in a strictly university medical department, and these vary greatly in the extent to which they are integrated into the day-to-day activities of their 'host' department. In some, such as Cytogenetics at the University of Edinburgh, the staff of the MRC unit work alongside their university colleagues on a day-to-day basis; in others, such as the MRC Laboratory of Molecular Biology on the New Addenbrookes site outside Cambridge, there is only a small amount of contact with the university departments.

In earlier years the Agricultural Research Council also supported a number of research units in university departments, some of which (eg insect physiology at Cambridge) became 'centres of excellence' in their field. Only four such units now remain, however, supported by the ARC.

The Natural Environment Research Council's main 'in-kind' support is, like that of the SERC, in the form of the use of expensive facilities, in this case research vessels and advanced geophysical equipment, without charge. Again like SERC, these facilities scarcely existed in 1965, when the council was set up. At the present time about £3m per annum is spent by the NERC in maintaining facilities (mainly research ships) for use by the university scientific community as well as their own staff. This 'in-kind' support is mainly in the fields of oceanography, and marine geology and geophysics, where it is a vital element of the research capability of the universities.

No more than a very rough indication can be gained of the financial significance of these various forms of 'in-kind' support for university research, in units which are additive with direct expenditure. In the case of the SERC it is conventional to regard the whole of the council's activities as basically in support of universities, all the intra-mural research and international subscription costs (£100m in 1978/79) therefore being regarded as supporting university research. Correspondingly, the MRC regard about two-thirds of the total budget of their research units as supporting university research.

Both these assessments would appear to be on the generous side if treated as equivalent, so far as the universities themselves are concerned, to their own resources for research. It would be better to conclude that the total 'in-kind' support for university research in 1978/79, expressed in terms of equivalent university expenditure, would be in the range of £50m to £80m, and probably nearer the lower figure than the upper. This obscures, however, the many other ways in which the research councils assist university research, for example by encouraging joint research between universities and their own institutes, by establishing senior fellowships in key fields, and so forth.[1] The financial implications of these are small taken individually, but their real significance in creating a broader community of interest and awareness in many fields of research is enormously greater.

---

[1] In addition to the Annual Reports of the Research Councils, the NERC has published a separate account of its relationships with the universities: *Universities and NERC Institutes* NERC, March 1976.

Overall Assessment of University Research Expenditure, 1978/79

It is now possible to assess the limits within which total expenditure on research at the universities, from all sources, in the reference year 1978/79, will have fallen. The four elements we have considered are:

(a) Total direct expenditure R_d. This is estimated at £273m, but it is probably an upper limit because we have assumed that all expenditure on grants, contracts, equipment and computer services was strictly on research. A lower limit for R_d would be £220m.

(b) General overheads. With R_d at £273m these are £130m; but with the lower estimate of £220m for R_d, overheads would be correspondingly reduced to £110m.

(c) Postgraduate research, which we have put at £20-£30m for comparative purposes.

(d) 'In-kind' support, which we have estimated to be in the range £50-£80m.

These assessments are combined in Table 3.5 below.

TABLE 3.5
Overall expenditure on university research (£m 1978/79)

Category of expenditure	Lower estimate	Upper estimate
Total direct, R_d	220	270
General overheads	110	130
PG students	20	30
'In-kind'	50	80
TOTAL	400	510

We therefore conclude that overall university research expenditure in 1978/79 was in the range of £400m - £500m and it is interesting to see how this figure compares with the national expenditure on research. The 1981 issue of the CSO Annual Abstract of Statistics does not give comprehensive statistics for research and development beyond 1975, but it is possible to construct an estimate which is sufficient for present purposes. Thus, 'net central government expenditure' on research and development in 1978/79 was £1,891m, and in previous years this source of funding was about 93 per cent of gross expenditure which, in turn, comprised about half the total national research and development expenditure, most of the rest being by private industry. Assuming that these relativities applied in 1978/79 gives a total of £1,891 x 1.08 x 2 = £4,085m. Calling this £4,000m in round numbers, means that university research represented in the region of 10 to 12 per cent of the total UK expenditure on research and development in 1978/79. Like all such broad statistical comparisons, this assessment must be interpreted with care. It should not be overlooked, for example, that in fundamental research generally the universities play a major role and, in some fields, they represent nearly the whole of the nation's research capability.

SUPPORT FOR UNIVERSITY SCIENTIFIC RESEARCH 1965-80

Summary for years 1965-1980
The general picture shown in Figures 3.2-3.4 is of steady growth, albeit at a decreasing rate, in both overall and research expenditure, up to the year 1973/74. Research expenditure then fell in real terms by 12 per cent in 1974/75 and although most of this fall was attributable to a drop in capital expenditure, there was a slow decline in recurrent expenditure for the next four years. Not until 1978/79 did the overall research expenditure exceed the 1973/74 level; by 1979/80 it was in the region of 10 per cent above the 1973/74 level.

For a complex system of fifty largely autonomous units dependent on a single central source for most of its funds, the transition after 1973/74 from a regime of steady growth to an appreciably lower level was quite sharp. The fact that both staff and student numbers continued to increase put further pressure on the system. Manoeuvrable reserves, in this case mainly capital for equipment and day-to-day running expenditure and maintenance, were mobilized to sustain the commitments of staff and fixed assets, thus causing greater year-to-year fluctuations and weakening the resilience of the system in the longer term. These changes would have been sharper still if it were not for the fact that external support (grants and contracts) remained steady (Figure 3.5).

Alone among all the specialized services, resources for computing continued to increase strongly throughout. Had this not been so, there is no doubt that the effectiveness of the research effort at the universities would have been seriously weakened. It is significant that policy and resources for computing are the responsibilty of the Computer Board, accountable directly to the DES but independent of the UGC and able to publish its own annual report on progress, needs and policy. In contrast, scientific equipment is the responsibility of the equipment sub-committee of the UGC. It is difficult to avoid the conclusion that this is a much less effective way of formulating a clear policy for a specialized requirement and making a convincing case for the necessary resources.

Among the subject groups, a striking feature is the sustained growth of the medical and biological[1] sciences, in money (Figure 3.12), staff and students (figures 3.13, 14 and 15). Although grants from the Medical

---

[1] It will be recalled that it has been necessary to include pre-clinical medicine and dentistry in both of these cases; the latter on their own do not show as marked an increase in expenditure.

Research Council barely maintained their effective level throughout the decade, other sources of funding for medical research rose throughout the period, as did the priority given to sustaining the growth of intra-mural support for medicine by the UGC itself, even when financial stringency was most acute (Figure 3.21). No less significant is the decline in support for the physical sciences, though how much of this is attributable to chemistry as distinct from the pure physical sciences is impossible to say.

The student of population dynamics would recognize the general picture as symptomatic of a population whose growth rate is not subject to the negative feedback processes which normally control its size, and yet whose resources of food and space are strictly limited. The onset of greater fluctuations in size and the mobilization of reserves, which happened in the university system in the second half of the decade, are characteristic of a population under stress for this reason.

The analogy goes further when it is remembered that most universities were striving to enhance their claims to a larger share of the UGC grant by sustaining growth in student numbers. This produced the effect of a positive feedback between growth and size, which leads to inherent instability in any system unless resources are unlimited.

The Official UGC Commentary
The scene for most of the seventies was set by the publication in 1972 of the government White Paper *Education: A Framework for Expansion* (Cmnd 5174). Most of this paper concerned schools. It said practically nothing about research, but it endorsed the Robbins principle for the universities and planned for student numbers to increase from 236,000 in 1971/72 to 375,000 by 1981, ie an increase of nearly 60 per cent. It envisaged the recurrent grant increasing by 23 per cent in real terms, over the period from 1972 to 1976. What actually happened is, of course, quite different. Student numbers increased but to nothing like the planned extent; published figures (1979/80) show a total of 292,738, while overall university expenditure in real terms remained static from 1972 to 1976 (Figure 3.2). The country's economic position changed radically for the worse during this time, triggered by the oil crisis, and it is hardly surprising that the optimism of 1972 was not sustained. The question we now wish to examine is whether the conclusions we draw from our analysis of one statistical record are consistent with the official commentaries at the time.

The two main sources of information are the Annual Surveys (AS) of the University Grants Committee[1] and the Annual Reports of the Research Councils.[2] The first significant comment is in the UGC's Annual Survey for 1972/73. This was the first year after the termination of the quinquennial grant system and the committee was concerned that the money to be made

---

[1] Published by HMSO as Command papers.
[2] Published by the councils individually.

available by the government was based on the assumption of a much slower growth in the number of postgraduates than had been the case hitherto. To make ends meet (in an expanding system, nevertheless) it was decided that reductions in the growth proposed by the universities should be

'. . . smallest in medicine, social sciences and business studies, and greatest in physical and biological sciences and in technology'

and for medicine and the physical sciences this is accurately reflected in the statistical record. No facts or arguments are advanced in support of this fundamental decision about strategy for science. It makes somewhat bizarre reading compared with present-day thinking, less than a decade later.

The Annual Survey for 1973/74 paints a gloomier picture, stressing the failure of the government's allocation adequately to meet the inflationary increase in recurrent costs. It speaks of the universities intensifying their already severe programme of economies in maintenance and departmental expenses, and refers to

'. . . restrictions, in some cases an absolute prohibition, on the filling of posts falling vacant among teaching and non-teaching staff.'

Our analysis reveals that some financial economies had indeed been in progress before this year; yet total university staff numbers increased in 1973/74 by 2.3 per cent on the previous year. Figure 3.13 shows, however, that growth of staff in the science sector after 1971 occurred primarily in medicine and to a lesser extent in engineering and the biological sciences. Staff in the physical and biological sciences decreased in number after 1973/74.

The year 1973/74, it will be recalled, was the last year of growth, in real terms. It might be thought from the Annual Survey for that year, as perhaps did the government, that the UGC was crying before it was hurt. The following year 1974/75, however, was the period of high inflation, and this caused real problems for the universities as it did for most sectors of the economy. The Annual Survey for 1974/75 refers to the

'. . . prospect of insolvency for some institutions and great financial uncertainty for the system as a whole.'

There is reference to 500 academic vacancies having been frozen (although the record still shows a continued net growth in total staff) and concern is expressed lest funds should be diverted to balancing the catering and residence accounts at the cost of teaching and research. In the event, additional money was made available to restore solvency and the 1975/76 grant was settled at a figure which, according to the UGC, allowed for inflation. Our analysis shows that this optimism was unfounded.

It is also recorded that

'. . . a very large part of the capital finance available has been devoted to the claims of expanding medical education and the target intake set for 1979 was given the highest priority.'

References to achieving the target set by government for the intake of medical students by the end of the decade occur in several Annual Surveys, but this is one of the few instances of the pressure thereby placed on the system being acknowledged. Perhaps this was at least a contributory reason for the scientific equipment grant in 1974/75 falling to half its previous level.

A significant event spanning 1974 and 1975 was the inquiry by the former House of Commons Select Committee on Science and Technology into Scientific Research in British Universities. The minutes of evidence and conclusion, which began to be published in the second half of 1975, are as pertinent to present-day problems as they were then, a fact which is itself illuminating and disturbing. Among their recommended short-term measures are several that reveal the committee's concern about the implications of growth in student numbers; thus in para 88(i):

'The UGC and the universities should seek to ensure that if activities have to be reduced, research should not be arbitrarily sacrificed in order to maintain a pre-ordained level of student numbers.'

And again, in para 88(vi):

'The Department of Education and Science should not expect, and the universities should not accept, growth targets for student numbers which, unless there is a sudden improvement in the economic situation, could only be achieved at the expense of the universities' research activities.'

The UGC itself was not unaware of the implications of the relentless growth in student numbers, as the Annual Surveys for the latter part of the decade reveal. Yet perception by the universities of the advantage of maintaining linkage between growth in student numbers and hence an increasing share of the UGC funds was not dispelled. Nor, apparently, did the UGC do anything to restrain the universities from using some of those additional resources to increase their tenured academic staff so as to maintain their staff/student ratios. It is as though the Robbins principle of a decade before, with the added momentum of the 1972 White Paper, had become so deeply enshrined in national thinking that no one — neither government, the UGC, nor, least of all, the universities — had the will to question it, even although it was becoming apparent to more critical observers that resources were falling far short of what was needed to carry through that principle.

In the last three years, 1975/78, the UGC continued to emphasize the financial stringencies under which the universities were operating, which is in conformity with the statistical evidence. Because 75 per cent of university expenditure is attributable to salaries and wages, economies fell heavily on libraries,[1] laboratory consumables and maintenance of buildings. The extra cost of implementing the requirements of the Health and Safety at Work Act of 1974, for example, constituted a serious problem in the straitened

---

[1] The percentage of total recurrent expenditure going on library services stayed, however, nearly constant, at between 4 and 4½ per cent throughout the period.

circumstances of the end of the decade. Concern is expressed in the 1975/76 Annual Survey, possibly a little belatedly, about the low and seriously inadequate capital provision, eg for improvements to facilities. For the first time, anxiety is expressed about the strain on the Dual Support System arising from the fact that by this time many of the science departments were no longer in a 'well-found state.' This concern is increasingly stressed in the final years of the decade leading, in 1980, to the announcement of the setting up, jointly with the ABRC, of the joint 'Merrison' Working Party to review the arrangements for the support of university research. The decade ends with the announcement by government that from October 1980 the grant would relate only to home and EC students, other overseas students being required to pay the full economic charge for their tuition and residence. This proved to be the first significant step by the present government in a direction which culminated in the Spring of 1981 with the announcement of the major reductions in the grant to universities.

The Contribution from the Research Councils
The annual reports of the research councils reflect, indeed anticipate, the concern expressed by the UGC about the efficacy of the Dual Support System. They voice also their own anxieties which, for the SERC, centred on a decrease, in real terms, of their total grant of 2 to 4 per cent over the years 1974-1978. The MRC was especially anxious about the growing inability of the universities to offer tenure to the many hundreds of postgraduate and post-doctoral staff supported on limited-term contracts by the council.

The MRC, along with the NERC and ARC, had another problem to contend with in the seventies, namely (as noted on pages 84-85) the transfer of portions of their budgets to 'customer' departments as part of the 'Rothschild' arrangements brought in by Cmnd 5046. Although all three councils were able to protect the universities from the direct effect of these transfers, their own science budget funds from which came their support for university research, were obviously smaller. The combined effect of these pressures on the research councils is reflected in the cessation of growth in research council grants after 1973/74 (Figure 3.19a).

With the science budget holding firm at the close of the decade, the SERC gained a small growth in real terms after several lean years and tried to help the universities rectify what was by then seen as a very serious problem of obsolescence in equipment. An invitation to universities to put in bids resulted in requests totalling some £50m, which is some indication of the consequences of several years of seriously deficient funding from UGC sources. The SERC was, of course, in no position to increase its equipment grants by more than a few million pounds; and even this caused the council to overspend its cash limit in 1980/81 and incur the displeasure of the Public Accounts Committee.

Although the science budget component of the incomes of the other councils maintained its value in real terms, all were in difficulties through decreases in their commissioned research funds from customer departments. They nevertheless increased their support to the universities as far as they were able — mainly by providing not only specialized equipment but also other more general departmental requirements which hitherto would have been regarded as the responsibility of the UGC. The SERC did the same. Thus, the balance of responsibility for funding on the Dual Support principle shifted by a perceptible amount towards the research councils. Whether this shift can or should be increased in the future is discussed later.

EXPENDITURE ON RESEARCH AT THE POLYTECHNICS

The status of research at the polytechnics has never been clearly defined, and collated statistics of its financial support comparable with those for the universities do not exist. This is true for polytechnic finance generally.

The first official reference to the research function of polytechnics is contained in Appendix B of Administrative Memorandum No. 8/67 issued in 1967 by the Secretary of State for Education and Science to local education authorities and major establishments of further education. In that document it is stated that the main responsibilities of the polytechnics will be as teaching institutions

'. . . but it will be necessary to make the provision for research which is essential to the proper fulfilment of their teaching functions and the maintenance and development of close links with industry. . . .'

The document goes on to say that the Secretary of State hopes that

'. . . provision will be made for suitably qualified members of the teaching staff to pursue research where it will contribute to the better performance of their teaching duties. . . . He does not, however, envisage that in the ordinary way it will be necessary for members of the academic staff to devote the whole or most of their time to research.'

The first quantitative data on how this principle was operating in practice are contained in the 1974 report of the working party set up by the Council for National Academic Awards[1] under the chairmanship of Professor G.D. Rochester, FRS. Information supplied to the working party for the period 1969-1971 showed that research funds received by polytechnics from external sources ranged from £50K. to £80K. per annum (ie about £200K. per annum in 1978/79 terms). The full expenditure on research, including that derived from 'general college income' (equivalent to the UGC grant to the universities) was acknowledged to be difficult to estimate; figures quoted ranged from 0.7 to 15 per cent. The Rochester Working Party did not attempt to define what should be the optimum figure, but expressed the view:

'. . . an institution teaching to degree level, whether a university or a polytechnic, must sustain an adequate level of research activity, as part

---

[1] *Report of the Working Party on Resources for Research in Polytechnics and other Colleges* CNAA, 1974.

of its teaching function. Universities and Polytechnics cannot therefore be distinguished on any ground of principle in their concern for research although there may be differences of content and balance.'

And it goes on, in its conclusions, to say
'There is value in avoiding a rigid division between those who "do research" and those who "carry the teaching load".'

The question of expenditure on research by polytechnics was taken up again by the Committee of Directors of Polytechnics (CDP) in 1979, a survey based on questionnaires being conducted by Sir Norman Lindop, Director of Hatfield Polytechnic. Estimates of the external sources of funds for research in 1979/80 ranged from £7K. in the case of Wales to £466K. for Hatfield. The CDP estimates that a total of £6.6m was received by the polytechnics for research from external sources, which in 1979/80 was 2 per cent of the total polytechnic expenditure (£360m). Again, no figures are available for internal expenditure on research, but if the ratio of internal to external funding for research were the same for the polytechnics as for the universities (Figure 3.4b), then the total research expenditure by the polytechnics would be in the region of 5 per cent of their total budget, ie £15m. This is a little lower than the estimate provided to us by the Secretary of the CDP, which is that research expenditure is in the range of 6 to 10 per cent of the total polytechnic budgets, but the difference is not significant.

The nature of scientific research undertaken by the polytechnics differs from that at the universities, being much more applied and being mainly in the fields of physical sciences, technology and engineering. Their remit does, of course, expect them to give particular emphasis to applied and industrial research and development. Other sciences such as medical, agricultural and environmental are well represented only in a few polytechnics, and as a result most research council grants to polytechnics come from the SERC. Even so, it is interesting to find that research grants to the polytechnics from the combined research councils in 1979/80 (£2.7m) made up a similar proportion of total external funds (41 per cent of £6.6m) as they did in the case of the universities (£70m out of £151m, or 46 per cent).

To sum up, it seems that the best estimate that can be made of expenditure on research at the polytechnics is that it is in the range 5 to 10 per cent of the total polytechnic expenditure, ie between £18m and £36m in 1979/80. In that year the total direct expenditure on research at the universities was about £350m (at 1979/80 prices), so that polytechnic research expenditure was also between 5 and 10 per cent of that undertaken at the universities. It should be noted, however, that other forms of research support, ie postgraduate studentships and the 'in-kind' support from the research councils, goes largely to the universities. Taking this into account means that the lower figure of 5 per cent is probably the better measure of polytechnic research activity compared with that of the universities.

THE IMMEDIATE FUTURE

The Starting Point for the 1980s
The year 1980/81 has turned out to be the base from which the present cuts are of necessity being measured. It is unfortunate, therefore, that no comprehensive statistics are available for that year, nor are likely to be for some time to come if past publication times persist. Such clues as there are indicate that the overall position for the universities was certainly no better than in 1979/80 and probably marginally worse.

As we have shown, the up-turn in research expenditure from 1978 to 1980 came largely from external sources. Full data on grants and contracts in 1980/81 are unavailable, but at least the grants from the research councils continued to increase (see Figure 3.19a). Expenditure on scientific equipment also increased significantly in 1980/81 in real terms (Figure 3.7a), although much more will be needed to rectify the accumulated obsolescence of the preceding seven years. Computing also remained buoyant, especially when the substantial 'in-kind' support from the SERC through the further development of the interactive computing network is taken into account.

Encouraging though these signs are, it is probable that the pressure increased at the domestic level in the universities. The UGC Annual Survey for 1979/80 forecast a loss of £35m in 1980/81 on income from some categories of overseas students. On the other hand, the numbers of both students and staff continued to rise in 1979/80 (by 1.3 per cent and 1.7 per cent respectively). The margin of uncommitted money probably declined further and economies must have continued to be made where manoeuvrable resources still remained, eg in staff-dependent costs other than salaries and wages, and in departmental and laboratory maintenance.

In these circumstances a key question is whether the proportion of time devoted to research by the academic staff has decreased. Only circumstantial evidence is available. The ratio of undergraduates to staff in most science subjects has tended to increase (Figure 3.16), although the trends in the postgraduate/staff ratios are less marked (Figure 3.17). The relative decline in departmental running expenses has probably meant that academic staff now have to spend more of their time on various domestic duties than formerly, a trend which will be enhanced if the proportion of technician and other assistant staff is reduced to achieve economies.

The actual situation of course varies greatly both from one university to another and between departments, and could thus be revealed only by intensive inquiries. Our impression, nevertheless, is that research time has decreased appreciably for two other reasons than the above. One is that standards of teaching have risen, partly in response to student expectations. The other is that because a greater proportion of research funds now come from outside sources, correspondingly more time has to be spent by scientists in preparing and negotiating their bids for those funds. Both developments could be held to be desirable — in the interests of better teaching and greater accountability, respectively, but a price has to be paid.

Our conclusion is therefore that even if no cuts had been made, the university system generally, and university research in particular, was already in difficulties. Firm action would have been necessary to redress the imbalance between staff and students on the one hand and resources for research on the other, so that proper levels of maintenance and services could be restored. Judging by the record of the seventies, such changes would not have happened easily. They would have raised fundamental questions about the way research at the universities was to be organized and promoted under conditions of a static budget, with much reduced scope for introducing new blood and with a Dual Support System already under strain.

The 1981 cuts

The first announcement of a significant change in government policy for the universities since the 1972 White Paper came in March 1980 with the publication of that year's Forward Expenditure Plans.[1] This forecast 'a small reduction' in funding for the universities from central sources, in real terms for the next four years. The reality was, however, more ominous, in view of the anticipated fall in income for those universities who normally had substantial numbers of overseas students.

It was against this background that the government announced in March 1981 that the institutional expenditure (net of tuition fee income) for distribution among the universities would be reduced progressively over the next three years, so that by 1983/84 it would be 'rather more than 8% below the level planned in Cmnd 7841'.[2] This is generally held to mean a cut of over 8 per cent on the 1980/81 level. In addition, the UGC estimated that this would require student numbers to decline over the same period by 3 to 5 per cent. Taking this loss of revenue into account, and also the loss of income from overseas students, the chairman of the UGC estimated the effective cut by 1983/84 as 11 per cent '. . . at the absolute minimum'.[3] The CVCP put the figure at 15 per cent. None of those estimates made any allowance for the cost of redundancies, which were now realized to be inescapable.

Some idea of the implications of those changes for the university system as a whole can be gauged by reference to Figure 3.2. Assuming that total expenditure in 1980/81 was about £1,150m (at 1978/79 prices), a reduction of 15 per cent results in a figure of £980m, which is about the level of expenditure in 1968/69. The total full-time student population in 1980/81 was about 295,000, which a fall of 5 per cent would reduce to 280,000; but

---

[1] *The Government's Expenditure Plans 1980/81 to 1983/84* (Cmnd 7841) HMSO, March 1980.
[2] *The Government's Expenditure Plans 1981/82 to 1983/84* (Cmnd 8175) HMSO, March 1981.
[3] *Minutes of Evidence to the H. of C. Education, Science and Arts Committee, Session 1980/81* HMSO, July 1981.

this is to be compared with a student population in 1968/69 of only 212,000.

There was no reference to staff numbers in the 1981 Public Expenditure White Paper (Cmnd 8175) but the pressure that will be created by these differential changes in funds and student numbers is clear. Even if staff numbers were to be reduced in proportion to expenditure, there would still be the problem of adjusting general overheads (eg maintenance of buildings and common services) if the already inadequate level of maintenance expenditure were not to become even more imbalanced.

The time-scale over which the cuts are to be achieved — three years — becomes critical when considering practicalities. The 'natural wastage' of academic staff has been recorded for the past few years in the UGC Annual Surveys; the figures for the three most recent years are given in Table 3.6.

TABLE 3.6
Natural wastage of academic staff

	% natural wastage of academic staff
1977/78	4.4
1978/79	3.8
1979/80	3.6

The decreasing percentage may well be symptomatic of declining job opportunities elsewhere, in which case the actual figure for the immediate future is likely to be lower still, possibly not more than 3 per cent. Remembering also that in an organization like a university it is not possible to allow all posts becoming vacant through natural wastage to remain unfilled if efficiency is not to be seriously impaired, the rate of net 'usable' natural wastage over the next three years may well not exceed 2 per cent. In other words, it would take between seven and ten years to achieve a staff reduction of 15 per cent by natural processes, allowing some scope for new recruitment of the most essential kind, academic and administrative. Although the staff question is by far the most serious and distressing, some other adjustments, for example economies on accommodation and mergers within and between universities, also require time-scales of five to ten years.[1]

[1] The Chairman of the UGC, in his evidence to the Select Committee on Education, Science and Arts (July 1981) said that the present rate of change is '. . . about twice the minimum rate at which you can do the job in an economic fashion.' We would put it at nearer three times the economic speed.

It is not possible to go further on the 'macro-economic' scale, treating the university system as an entity, because in practice the cuts were distributed far from uniformly and individual universities of course differ widely in their financial resilience. Nevertheless, this analysis is enough to show the magnitude of the problem when changes which at first sight may not seem very severe in scale or timing are imposed on a system with a long intrinsic time-scale for significant change. The reaction of government when the implications of its timetable for the cuts were brought into the public scrutiny, mainly by the press and the universities themselves, gave the impression that their full significane may not have been appreciated.

Distribution of Cuts by the UGC

The first letter from the Chairman of the UGC to all vice-chancellors was published in *The Times Higher Education Supplement* of 22 May 1981. It gave general indications as to the basis on which the cuts would be administered but no details for individual universities. Of particular significance was the announcement that target student numbers for 1983/84 would be allocated to each institution, and that while 'grants' would be related, among other factors, to the target student numbers, 'levels of activity' in research would also be taken into account. It was stated that

'... particular attention must be paid to retaining capacity for research, and there have been consultations with the Research Councils to this end.'

The letter went on to say that adequate provision had not been made for redundancies and that it would be for each institution to inform the committee about the redundancy implications when it knew how it would be affected by the cuts.

The allocation to each university was announced by the UGC on 2 July 1981 and reproduced in full in the *THES* of 3 July. Figure 3.23 shows the frequency distribution of the cuts to individual universities (to 1983/84). While the majority lie in the 10 to 20 per cent bracket, the allocations produced markedly differential reductions between universities.

In the case of student numbers the UGC recommended that the overall reductions are to be achieved by a reduction of 8 per cent in arts subjects and 2 per cent in science subjects, but a growth of 5 per cent in medicine. Within sciences and medicine the strategy is for:

(a) Some growth in student numbers in the physical and mathematical sciences, in engineering and technology, and in certain aspects of biology (eg bio-technology).

(b) Decline in other aspects of biology and in agriculture, and a reduction of one-quarter in the number of places available for subjects allied to medicine, notably pharmacy.

Although the individual letters to vice-chancellors were not released by the UGC, it was not long before the diligence of the reporters enabled much of the substance of the UGC's advice to be brought to light.[1] It was clear that this advice, in some cases relating to the phasing out of some departments altogether and the merging of others, was far more detailed and explicit than had ever before been issued by the UGC. This naturally raised the question of the criteria used by the UGC in making their individual allocations — especially as some of the heaviest cuts fell on institutions active in the favoured subjects.

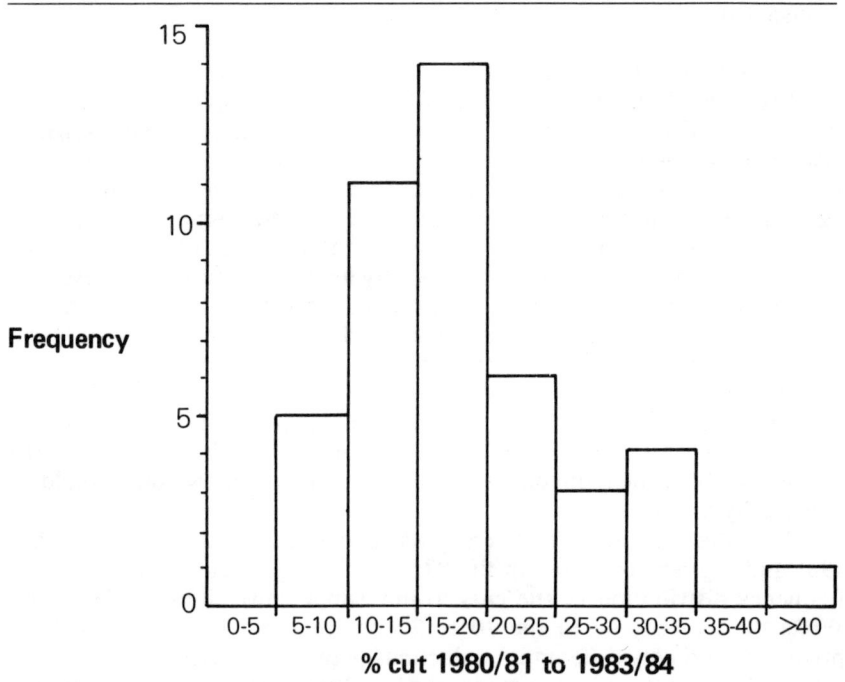

FIGURE 3.23
Frequency distribution of 1981 cuts

% cut **1980/81 to 1983/84**

The replies given by the Chairman of the UGC to a question on that point by the House of Commons Committee on Education, Science and the Arts in July 1981 were not as informative as might have been hoped. He emphasized that decisions had been made primarily about the subjects that should be strengthened or run down at the national level. He explained, for example, that while medicine had hitherto been a protected area with

[1] The *THES* was at the centre of those journalistic activities, but *Nature*, *New Scientist* and some other specialized publications (eg the journal of the Institute of Biology) carried accurate and informative reports.

'Government-prescribed targets' for it,[1] this would no longer be so. The extent to which objective criteria on individual institutions or departments (staff numbers, student demand and quality, external income, etc.) were overlaid with subjective value judgements is unclear. Whatever the process, however, it is clear that even within a given subject, institutions were treated very differently. In addition, therefore, to formulating a policy for the future support of university science, the UGC also made an assessment of what distinguishes a 'good' from a 'less good' department or university in which to encourage both teaching and research in the favoured subjects.

The fact that the UGC did not adopt the simpler solution of pro-rata reductions all round, at least within particular subject areas, is generally regarded as to its credit. It would have been impossible for the committee to have escaped criticism from some quarters, no matter how it had acted, but it is interesting that the *THES*, not normally noted for its benevolence towards authority, commented later in July 1981 that the UGC's overall strategy probably corresponded fairly well with the 'general will' of the universities.

Response of the Universities
Since their receipt of the July 1981 round of letters from the UGC, the universities have been in varying degrees of ferment in trying to decide how to react. Those facing the more severe cuts were understandably distressed, and the *THES* has almost weekly carried reports of the heart-searching that has been going on. Measures that have been considered involve plans to avoid redundancies by still further economies elsewhere or by fund-raising schemes, by foregoing or covenanting salary increases, by premature retirements and by employing staff for only nine months out of twelve. The more heavily hit institutions are facing the need to close whole departments or merge smaller ones to achieve economies of scale.

In so far as a pattern is discernible, the tendency seems to have been for universities to start with a sharply selective policy — which may or may not have coincided with UGC guidance. As plans have gone through the institutional hierarchy, support for the threatened areas has mobilized, and the difficulty and hardship involved in the exercise of sharply selective cuts in a tightly-knit community have become apparent. It is still too early to draw any firm conclusions, but the outcome seems likely, in most cases, to be more egalitarian, with hardship widely shared, than it was at the start and perhaps than the UGC intended.

So far as the future is concerned, one message is however clear. It is that

---

[1] This accounts for the evident priority afforded to medicine throughout the seventies, despite the progressively worsening financial situation. Yet, even now, the UGC is recommending an increase of 5 per cent in medical students; how this is to be reconciled with the statement by the Chairman of the UGC is not clear.

if universities are left to make adjustments individually on the scale now required, there is no guarantee that the outcome, at least so far as research is concerned, will conform either to the UGC's or to any other plan at the national level. For example, concern is already being expressed lest in the search for economies in what is now a less favoured area of biology, every university will close its marine station — clearly an undesirable result. To be any part of a rational plan, universities need to know what others are doing and how outside funding agencies (particularly the research councils) view the options available.

Financially, the position is further complicated by the efforts universities are making, understandably enough, to supplement their UGC funds from outside sources, but everything depends on how many redundancies will result and how much of the cost will be met by a supplementary grant by government. Until that question is clearer, how the UGC's stated intention to 'retain the capacity for research' will be implemented by the universities is impossible to foresee.

EMERGENCE OF A POLICY FOR THE LONGER TERM

A Fresh Approach
All the evidence and ideas from many sources that we have attempted to summarize points to the conclusion that the future of university scientific research depends on the explicit recognition which government and the UGC are prepared to give to it. We showed how a policy for the expansion of higher education, deriving from Robbins in the sixties and reinforced by the 1972 White Paper, led the UGC to give primacy to the teaching function when resources became significantly limited. Even without the 1981 cuts, we noted, a continuation of this de facto policy could have led only to a further weakening of the universities research base.

The UGC's approach to the administration of the 1981 cuts thus marks a turning point. We have noted above that the UGC not only announced firm targets for student numbers, but also conveyed more explicit advice to individual universities than it had ever done before on the emphasis to be given to different subject areas. It acknowledged the need to retain 'the capacity for research', and referred to consultations with the research councils in this connection. These are three of the essentials for the emergence of a policy for university research. We must now examine their implications and consider whether they are sufficient to satisfy other essential criteria — among these being the need to foster the zest for enquiry in an atmosphere of true scholarship, and to be able to generate excellence (at individual, group and national level) through selective and concentrated support. No less important is it that university research should be widely seen and appreciated as a vital element in the nation's overall scientific capability.

Teaching and Research
The first point we would stress is that the setting of firm target numbers for students should be more than a temporary expedient to cope with the present crisis. It should become a lasting and well-publicized feature of UGC policy. This will require the UGC to develop a long-term policy for undergraduate support which takes account not only of the subjects that happen to be popular at the time with students but also of future manpower requirements, difficult though the latter may be.

This alone would mean that the needs of teaching and of research would have to be to some extent differentiated. Such a step has long been foreseen by some; yet it is still a controversial subject, with the arguments for and against both confused and often subjective. We have referred to the views of the select committee of 1974, but this was not the first open challenge to the principle that university teaching should never be separated from research. In 1971, a working group set up by the then Council for Scientific Policy and chaired by Sir Harrie Massey,[1] although advancing strong reasons for associating scientific research with university teaching in the interests of scholarship, also recognized that

'... if there is to be any further large-scale expansion of undergraduate teaching in the universities, that association — or at least the degree to which it is maintained and the form it should take — may be called into question.'

It should be noted that the main deliberations of this working group were held in the late nineteen sixties, before any of the later pressures on the university system had been experienced. In 1973 another study group on higher education and research, this time set up by the British Association and chaired by Lord Ashby,[2] concluded in much more forceful terms:

'(b) We believe, however, that the expansion of research cannot and should not run *pari passu* with the expansion of undergraduate teaching as we move toward mass higher education. To do this would result only in a grave dilution of the quality of research and an inefficient deployment of funds for research.'

It is clearly nothing new to conclude that UGC policy should address separately the needs of undergraduate teaching and of research. Only thus could a perceived national need for more (or less) trained manpower in a particular subject be met without at the same time necessarily committing resources for expanding (or contracting) research in that subject. The converse is also true: for example, while there is no doubt that there is currently a national need for more research in biotechnology, it does not follow that biotechnology is an appropriate subject for a first degree.

---

[1] *Report of a Study on the Support of Scientific Research in the Universities* (Cmnd 4798) HMSO, 1971.
[2] *Higher Education and Research* (Report of a Study Group) British Association for the Advancement of Science, Publication 73/1, 1973.

The position of the postgraduate student, particularly if studying for a PhD, needs, however, to be clarified in this connection. Because a PhD is essentially a training in research, the criteria for allocation of PhD studentships are much influenced by the quality of the research undertaken by the department in question and the calibre of the supervisor or the individual research project. Thus, support of students at the PhD level may need to be linked more explicitly with support of research at a particular university than it has been hitherto, as has been the policy of one of the research councils for some years. The requirements for the more vocational one-year MSc training are likely to be intermediate in this connection.

External Support of Research

That the UGC 'consulted' with the research councils before making the 1981 allocations implies that it had taken into account the distribution of the councils' *selective* support in arriving at its allocations to particular universities.[1] Effectively this amounts to a loose application of the principle of 'resonance', whereby the level of central (ie UGC) funds to a university or department is positively related to the amount of research income which that university or department can generate from outside sources. The scale of the latter, comprising, as noted, over 40 per cent of the total direct expenditure on research (R_d, Figure 3.5b) — over 50 per cent if allowance is made for the 'in-kind' support from the research councils — means that it will necessarily be a major determinant in central resource distribution.

We have already noted that in the last two years there has been a shift — small but significant — in the balance of the Dual Support System towards the research councils. The view has been advanced that this trend could with advantage go much further; but in practice to do so would have profound administrative and constitutional implications. At present the respective spheres of responsibility of the universities and the councils are reasonably clear. If, however, the research councils were to provide the kind of physical resources normally coming from UGC funds it would involve them in the managerial affairs of the universities and in decisions on which they would have insufficient information and no real accountability. These problems would be even more acute if the councils were to take responsibility for the salaries of tenured staff. The extent to which it would be feasible for the universities to look to the research councils for additional funding without calling into question the whole principle of the Dual Support System is therefore marginal.

Of the other external sources of research funds, government departments are unlikely to provide more than a small additional income.

---

[1] This was a point taken up by *THES* and explicitly criticized by some (more hard hit) universities who felt that in so doing UGC had taken insufficient account of their ability to earn external income from other, non-research council sources — mainly industry.

Their existing contribution in overall terms is not substantial and there is little evidence to suggest that there is much which the universities could do to increase it. In the medical field, outside support from charities and trusts is substantial, and still growing. In the non-medical fields, the private sector is the most likely source of enhanced research income.

For certain of the more technologically orientated universities closer links with industry would no doubt be of mutual benefit, and greater dependence on industrial funding no disadvantage. Whether the same would be true for universities generally is another matter. Industry has hitherto been interested in supporting only the more basic research at universities which it could not undertake itself. Although the extent of university/industry co-operation in research has been enhanced in recent years, for example through schemes promoted by the SERC, to increase significantly their income from this source would probably require the universities to move appreciably away from their traditional role of fundamental inquiry in which the free flow of scientific ideas is not always compatible with the requirements of commercial confidentiality. Again, the amount of senior scientists' time that needs to be devoted to talking to commercial firms, preparing proposals for contracts and generally establishing mutual awareness and confidence, should not be underestimated.[1]

To try to mobilize more of the nation's best scientific thinking in furthering our industrial capability is an attractive aim. But if it is to be at the price of a corresponding reduction in our capacity for fundamental inquiry, then care is needed. There is no magic formula for the optimum ratio of basic to applied research, but when the ratio shifts appreciably the implications deserve close scrutiny. Just such a shift, towards applied research, has occurred in the last decade in nearly all government research laboratories and in two of the research councils through the introduction of the Rothschild customer-contractor system. If the trend were now to extend more widely to university research, it might be found that the search for short-term relevance has gone too far.

However matters develop along these lines, there is a principle which we believe to be important. It is that when a university or a polytechnic negotiates a contract to undertake a specific piece of research for a customer (whether in the public or private sector) who requires the results of that research, it should be charged at the full academic cost, with overheads. In this way the institution will derive a legitimate contribution from that contract at least to maintain its research base. This would avoid putting further strain on the Dual Support System.

---

[1] The experience of an institution such as the Cranfield Institute of Technology, that derives the greater part of its income from the private sector but which also maintains an advanced teaching and research function, is relevant in this connection.

Support of University Research by the UGC

External sources of support, though important, are necessarily diverse in their origins and objectives and thus could never fall into a coherent pattern. The need for the UGC to continue to give orientation and emphasis in allocating its resources, as it started to do in outline for the first time last year, therefore seems to us inescapable. This calls for a broad 'strategy' for research in the sense used in the 1971 Report of the Dainton Working Party,[1] a concept familiar enough to the research councils[2] but unfortunately excluded in the 'Rothschild' philosophy which has dominated much of British scientific policy in the last decade. In its essentials, the concept of strategic planning for research acknowledges that to make the best use of limited resources it is advisable to try to identify and encourage those fields of science, and the facilities needed to prosecute them, which are likely to be most rewarding, in cultural or practical terms, in the years to come.

To evolve such a strategy, providing the rational basis for selection and concentration of research effort yet still preserving the essential freedom for research initiative, is a formidable task, involving complex issues of fundamental importance to the country's future. In our view it should be worked out in open and continuing debate with the universities themselves, the research councils, government and polytechnics and other bodies who can contribute. The aim would be, in this way, not only for a broad consensus to emerge but also for the reasoning behind it to be understood (if not always accepted) by all.

To call for wide debate presupposes a forum for the purpose, and we recognize that no existing organization is ideally suited. Of the official bodies, the UGC as presently constituted is too closely associated with the executive function of administering a budget for the universities, given to it by government. The ABRC's responsibility, on the other hand, is limited to the research councils. The CVCP for the universities and the CDP for the polytechnics, however, are able to represent the corporate views of their respective institutions, and clearly could play an important role. Yet again, the Royal Society as an entirely independent and authoritative voice of science is able to take a broad view across the whole of research including government and industry as well as the universities.

How one, or a combination, of these four bodies might best provide a forum for the debate, we must leave unresolved. It could, indeed, be advantageous to devolve responsibility for the preparatory stage of the

---

[1] *The Future of the Research Council System* Report of a CSP Working Group under the chairmanship of Sir Frederick Dainton (Cmnd 4814) HMSO, 1971.

[2] Eg the response of the Natural Environment Research Council to the Rothschild proposal in NERC Annual Report for 1971-72, Appendix X, HMSO, 1972.

planning debate to the various existing bodies most competent in their respective fields, provided all work to a common aim in a co-ordinated way and publish their findings. What matters is that the outcome should be a coherent strategy which carries the confidence of the scientific community and of government, and changes the image of the UGC's support from that of a passive 'floor' to a positive 'framework', with a structure and purpose. (To achieve this, better information and statistics of the university research function will be needed; some observations on the requirements are given in the appendix to this chapter (pp.146-148).)

Implementation — Control and Accountability
Given linked but distinguishable strategies for teaching and for research, it would still, under the present system, fall to the UGC to make the executive decisions on grants to individual universities and how they are to be used. While clearly these executive procedures are properly matters conducted with due confidentiality, it is worth commenting on the point raised on pages 137-138 that the *criteria* used in making those decisions could with advantage be made public. To do so would not only be justified on grounds of 'accountability' but should provide institutions with the guidance and incentives on which to base their future claims for resources. Recent reports that government may lift some of the UGC's traditional requirements of secrecy are thus to be warmly welcomed.

The question that now must be faced is whether the traditional unspecific 'block-grant' procedure used by the UGC for allocating recurrent funds to the universities would be a sufficient means of implementing a more deliberate strategy for research. Even on the assumption of a static budget (in real terms) after the present upheaval is over, money will still be tight and significant new developments will require compensating economies elsewhere. If the overall funds available to the universities are to be used to best advantage, such adjustments should be optimized across the system as a whole. The need to facilitate mobility of staff between universities is also likely to be a significant factor in determining the future level of recurrent funds.

It is therefore probable that to make its intentions clear and to ensure that scarce funds are used for the purposes intended, the UGC will be obliged to 'earmark' portions of its recurrent grants to universities. If this prospect causes misgivings, it should be remembered that some of the research institutes in the research council system are, like the universities, private bodies, employing their own staff. They are grant-aided by their parent council on a more detailed basis than would probably be needed in the case of the universities, yet can claim to be true centres of excellence for basic research in their respective fields.

Such an arrangement does, of course, imply a different kind of relationship between the universities and the UGC in the future. The universities will have to be prepared to accept a greater degree of involvement by the UGC in their affairs; while the UGC, and particularly its permanent staff, will need to be strengthened. These developments should be made easier if there is a generally agreed strategy for support of research, to the formulation of which the universities have themselves contributed, and if allocations are made with reference to known criteria. In that way, and with understanding on both sides, the true freedom of the universities should not be at risk.

APPENDIX: INFORMATION REQUIREMENTS

Existing statistical information, though it reveals the broad trends in university research support on a macro scale, is inadequate as a base for the kind of strategic planning advocated in this chapter. Since it is rumoured that even the present DES publications may be severely pruned in the interests of economy, it may be helpful to suggest how they could be improved.

Subject Classification

The first requirement is that information should be collected and made available down to at least the level of the scientific discipline or perhaps, in some cases, the sub-discipline. Sufficient data about associated manpower, equipment, facilities and special services will also be needed if limited resources are to be deployed to best effect.

A category such as 'physical sciences' embraces the whole of chemistry and such diverse subjects as solid state physics, high energy physics, astronomy, geology, oceanography and meteorology. Few universities promote a substantial research activity in all these disciplines, some of which are confined to a few 'centres of excellence'. Each needs different equipment and services, looks to different outside bodies for support both financially and 'in kind' and has differing significance in terms of national interest.

Similar difficulties arise in other categories in which the statistics of university science are at present divided. The confusion between 'pre-clinical medicine' and 'biological sciences' is brought out on page 87 and in Figure 3.1. Diversity within the general 'biological sciences' category itself is as wide as in the physical sciences; criteria for support of the newer fields of molecular engineering and biotechnology, for example, are not the same as those for environmental biology or taxonomy. Similar diversity is to be found within the 'engineering and related technologies' categories, while there are important fields of research on the boundaries between mathematics and the applied sciences which could, with advantage, be separately identified.

Departmental Statistics

These examples lead to the conclusion that the basic 'unit of information' for strategic planning concerns the department or sub-department, rather than the institution as a whole. Information at the departmental level would also be valuable for the support of multi-disciplinary fields and, as seems likely in the future, associations of departments from different universities. These considerations apply also to staff and students; postgraduate student numbers are of particular importance because of their close links with the research function of a department. The research councils already work at the departmental level in carrying through their part of the Dual Support System: this needs to be paralleled in the statistics of research activity funded by the UGC.

Operational Indicators
The value of simple and sensitive indicators of the marginal economics of the research function, such as expenditure on departmental and laboratory maintenance, has been demonstrated in this paper. Other indicators of the strength or otherwise of the support for research include the amount and quality of general scientific equipment and its maintenance, the number and calibre of technical support staff, and the quality of specialized services (eg computers and libraries). Statistics on some of these are already given in the DES publication, but only at the level of the institution. To be of help in carrying through the kind of policy for support of research that we envisage, these indices would be needed at the departmental level and related to the finer subject divisions outlined above.

Research Time
The proportion of academic staff time spent on research is a key statistic, but the question whether it is worth attempting to collect data on it regularly needs consideration. To obtain reliable results requires some form of time recording, however simple, and the resulting data must be processed.[1] Without such information, however, anxiety about erosion of research time cannot be properly documented; while if the teaching and research functions become more differentiated in the future, the need for separate statistics for each may be more important than it has been in the past.

Adjustments for Inflation
It is unfortunate that a certain degree of sensitivity surrounds contemporary inflation indices of university and research council expenditure because they are involved in the negotiations for cash-limited budget allocations. This should not apply to historical data, however recent, in view of the almost real-time publication of Retail Price Indices by the CSO. A prerequisite for the fuller use of selected indices of the economics of research activity is that the inflationary trends in each (eg laboratory maintenance, libraries,

---

[1] Experience has shown that to guess the amount of time spent on research over a period gives unreliable results. Recording to a precision of 5 per cent (ie to one day a month) is ample and need take only a few tens of minutes per month of an individual's time. Modern computerized techniques can make the processing of the resululting data largely routine.

computer services, etc.) should be available.

Timeliness of Publication
It was noted at the beginning of this paper that the latest published edition of Volume 6 of the DES Estimates is for the year 1977/78 (ie up to August 1978, or nearly four years ago). It was only through the good offices of the staff of the UGC that we had access to manuscript versions of data for 1978/79 and 1979/80. It is thus hardly surprising if what has been happening to the resources for university research in the last few years is not well known, or that the true economic base from which the present cuts operate is somewhat obscure. Information in typescript or computer print-out would often be sufficient, provided it was fully accessible, and certainly better than a quality publication several years late.

Concluding Remarks
It would be inappropriate to go into further detail here about the information system needed to assist the development of a more rational policy for support of research at the universities and polytechnics. We would, however, urge that a thorough study of requirements and their implementation be put in hand. Considerable experience and skills now exist on the costing of research activities generally. Lessons have been learnt about what to do and what not to do, and modern techniques of data processing have greatly reduced the time and money required.

ACKNOWLEDGEMENTS
The authors wish to express their gratitude to the many people who have provided information and advice in the preparation of this paper. Among those we would wish specially to mention are members of staff of the University Grants Committee, the Committee of Vice-Chancellors and Principals, the Committee of Directors of Polytechnics, and of individual Research Councils and Polytechnics. Needless to say, none of these or others who have been kind enough to help us with this study are responsible for any errors or omissions which the paper may contain. We would also like to thank Mrs Diana Swann for undertaking the final typing against a very tight schedule.

SEMINAR DISCUSSION
Discussion on the Beverton and Findlay paper focused around four main issues.

Statistics
There was a consensus among the discussants that better statistics on research expenditures were required. Without them it will be difficult to formulate policy. There are, however, a number of difficulties. In the first place, most universities and polytechnics do not collect information about research expenditures at the level of detail that is required. Without this basic information central authorities such as the UGC or the DES cannot compile aggregate information.

A second difficulty with existing statistics is that they mostly ignore expenditures on the development end of the research and development spectrum, which means that the technological universities spend considerably more on research and development than shows in the statistical record. Research done by students also fails to appear as 'research' in many statistical returns, especially when the students are financed by industry. A part of the problem is due to inadequate statistical data-gathering systems but a part is due to accounting technique. Sometimes it may be to the institutions' advantage to show the income as for research, at other times and in other circumstances it may be more advantageous to show it under a teaching heading.

It was noted that statistics only showed the inputs to research, but what is really needed for policy purposes is a better measure of research outputs. Failing the availability of indicators of research performance, then input statistics are better than no statistics at all.

Management
Several speakers referred to what was called the 'catastrophic system of management' which prevails in the universities. This affects the accounting systems and hence determines to some extent the type of statistics that might be collected. But once this issue had been raised, there was general agreement that management reforms as a whole were urgently needed.

Selectivity and Concentration of Research Activity
The paper showed the sensitivity of the research system to relatively small changes in funding. Several speakers supported this point, and it was widely acknowledged that unless there was a large increase in research funding there would have to be more selectivity and concentration of research effort in fewer institutions. There were few suggestions, however, about how selectivity could be achieved in practice. It was badly needed, but it would be difficult to implement. Most participants would have liked to see the universities take the lead but many thought that in the end the decisions would have to be imposed from outside about which universities should continue to do research in specific scientific disciplines.

Selectivity would also have to take place within some sort of overall framework. That framework and the size of the total research budget would depend on the justification for research. Research is not an 'unqualified good'. It has to be justified.

The Relation between Teaching and Research
The Beverton and Findlay paper sparked off a lively discussion on the relationship between teaching and research. This was a topic which recurred time and again throughout the seminar. With only one or two exceptions the speakers were united in their opposition to the view that teaching and research were inseparably linked and that a good teacher had simultaneously to be a good researcher. The few studies which have been made on this subject are either inconclusive or suggest that the reverse is the case. Certainly the case for the inseparable link is not proven. It is an important issue because the present method whereby research is funded through the Dual Support System assumes the two are inextricably linked and provides money for research on the basis of undergraduate numbers. The implications of these discussions was that it would be in the interests of both teaching and research if the criteria for funding the two were clearly split. However, since it is difficult to evaluate a teacher's performance there will continue to be a lot of pressure within the higher education system to continue to use research performance as *the* criterion for promotion. This will make the separation of teaching and research difficult to achieve in practice.

4

THE RESEARCH FUNCTION IN THE SOCIAL SCIENCES

by Cyril S. Smith

The first wave of development of social science research which this country has ever known is now receding.* It gathered momentum very slowly until the 1960s but then for a spell of fifteen years it was in full spate. There were only 212 university teachers in social science in 1938 but by the mid-70s the total was over 7,000.[1] They became a very significant element in the universities, accounting for one in five of all academic staff, and in the polytechnics they were even more dominant.[2] Alongside this increase in the teaching staff of higher education there grew up a substantial commitment to research funding by government which reached its peak in real terms in 1975/76; and more than half of these funds found their way into institutions of higher education. The total research funding from all sources for 1977/78 of £55m can be compared with only £5m for 1962/63 (but allowance would need to be made for inflation).

The wave has now broken and the waters are receding fast. The weakening of university finances throughout the 70s has meant that the unit of resource for students has worsened by ten per cent overall — but the social sciences have suffered more. The current cutbacks in university allocations are falling disproportionately on the social sciences despite the UGC's intention that staff/student ratios should be improved.[3] Since 1979 government departments have reduced their research commissions by more than a third, and the budget of the SSRC has been cut by a quarter. However, if the experience of other countries is any guide this recession will only be temporary; the *third* wave in the USA is only just receding, and in France the second wave is beginning to swell.[4] This is a good time to reflect on our experience and ask whether we could arrange things differently next time.

An assessment was made for the SSRC in 1978 of the size and shape of the national research effort in the social sciences, and despite the omission of several important elements for which information was not available, the total was estimated as over £55m.[5] Over half this sum came from direct funding of government departments, especially from the DHSS, the DoE, the DE, the Home Office, the ODA and the DES. About one-tenth of the total came from the research councils, and in particular the SSRC. Using the assumptions derived from the CVCP study (that university teachers spent

---

*The views expressed in this paper are those of the author and not necessarily those of the Social Science Research Council.

thirty per cent of their time on research) this accounted for another one quarter of the total.[6] One-tenth came from business sources and only four per cent came from the charitable foundations.

It will become clear in this chapter that there is no convincing way in which this can be described as a *system* for funding the national research effort in the social sciences. The major sources of funding have acted independently of each other in making their decisions and often without informing other sponsors of their plans. This is perhaps understandable in the relations between government departments and the UGC, but less so in the relations between the UGC and the research councils (which are partners in the Dual Support System) or between government departments and the SSRC. It raises the fundamental issue addressed here — Should there be a system of research funding, especially for applied research, and if so what role should higher education institutions have within it? Our own tentative answer to this question will come after an examination of the way in which the major sponsors of research effort have reached their present positions.

THE UNIVERSITY GRANTS COMMITTEE

A substantial part of the present research capacity in the social sciences has been created through the decisions of the UGC to make funds available for teaching posts in the social sciences, for embedded in the notion of the university teacher's role was the expectation that he should spend a substantial amount of time on advanced studies and scholarship. Most universities still also have sabbatical arrangements for extended periods of study.

The UGC's role in providing funds which are used for teaching posts in social science depends of course on the willingness of universities to use them for that purpose, and on the supply of students wishing to read social science. It is not generally appreciated how the range of proportions of undergraduate reading the social sciences has varied. At one extreme two universities in 1977 had over half their undergraduate populations registered for social science degrees, and at the other extreme eight had less than one in five. As might be expected the proportions are high in the new universities, but not in those which had been colleges of advanced technology.

Student demand has been the important pre-condition of expansion for university teaching of the social sciences, and is now to some extent a protection against pressure for contraction. It is important therefore to try to understand what determines the level of student demand, although unfortunately there is surprisingly little relevant research available. The level is conceivably related to the availability of teaching at 'A' level, and there are one or two studies which relate job choices to subjects studied at university. Student demand for social sciences in the schools and in higher education itself helped create some of the jobs which students were looking for, in teaching and research, but that expansion is unlikely to be repeated on the same scale as in the 1960s.

Two of the subjects most affected by the growth of social science in the school curriculum were economics and sociology. Economics became available at 'A' level in 1951 and already by 1966 there were 15,000 entries, but by 1971 this had reached over 26,000.[10] A study by PEP in 1968 showed that two-thirds of the university economics students interviewed had studied the subject at school, and most saw it as a route into accountancy.[11] A fact relevant to this vocational orientation is that over 80 per cent of economics students are male, and the choice of economics at degree level may be related to the availability of teaching of economics in girls' schools.[12]

Sociology was not introduced at 'A' level until 1964; it too expanded very rapidly (17,569 entries in 1979), but compared with economics was much more popular with girls. It is known that many girls choose sociology courses at university with some thought of becoming social workers, and indeed one study has shown this is the most frequent choice of employment on graduation, and for postgraduate training.[13] Opportunities in social work expanded greatly in the 1970s after the publication of the Seebohm Report, but have now almost closed off. The expansion of sociology teaching in schools also increased the demand for sociology graduates: there were over 43,000 'O' level entries in 1979.

Applications for any particular subject seem to reach a peak and then fall away, and economics reached its peak first (1966), sociology followed in 1974, but psychology seems not yet to have reached its ceiling.[14] Acceptances for courses (which have to be related to resources for teaching and to internal targets for admissions) do not vary so greatly from year to year as applications. The number of acceptances for economics (first-year courses) showed a steady increase from 1,425 in 1966 to 2,126 in 1978, and likewise sociology rose from 863 to 1,359 over the same period (although with a slight dip in 1974). Psychology has shown the greatest growth from only 250 in 1966 to 1,313 in 1978. Government and public administration lagged some way behind with only 689 acceptances in 1978.

The growth of the undergraduate population over the last two decades has predictably created a demand for full-time study at postgraduate level, but this has been to some degree constrained by the availability of financial support. This has not had the same effect on part-time students, where there has been a very substantial increase. According to USE figures about a third of the total number of full-time social science students depend upon research council support and another forty per cent are supported by central or local government (many of this latter group will be in vocational training such as for social work). Most of the remainder are self-supporting. Postgraduate students not only provide universities with direct financial support through the fees they bring with them, but they are also counted as part of the teaching load supported by the UGC (not of course overseas students) and this is particularly important to the social sciences.

According to the USE figures for 1979 21.3 per cent of all full-time postgraduates (including management but not education) were reading social sciences: some 6,237. These figures are however inflated by the numbers taking social work and other vocational training, which fact particularly affects the numbers shown for sociology — over 2,000 (which is shown to be grossly inflated when it is compared with the undergraduate entry for 1978/79 of only 1,359). As these are figures for 1978/79 they do not show the effects of the cuts in the SSRC's budget in 1979 and since, which led to a reduction of one half in the number of new awards. Nevertheless, even with these reservations the contribution which graduate education still makes to the viability and reputation of university departments in the social sciences is crucial. Moreover, SSRS provides a Research Training Support Grant for departments which have SSRC-supported students. Apart from being a source of funds and staff, postgraduates do make their own significant contribution to their subjects, as recent studies of published output from theses have demonstrated.[16] They also have a key role in scientific change by migrating to promising areas of development.

It should have become clear from the discussion this far that the UGC has a central role to play in determining the level of research capacity in the social sciences, but there are other aspects of its role which need to be discussed: its commitment to the Dual Support System, and its support for essential university facilities such as libraries. The principles of the Dual Support System are a set of understandings which have been reached over the years between the UGC and the research councils and which have evolved with the needs of the natural sciences particularly in mind. Under this system the universities have responsibility for providing the floor of research funding, including laboratories, libraries, accommodation, and the salaries of permanent academic staff under whose direction research projects funded by the research councils are conducted.[17] The UGC makes grants from its equipment fund mainly to the natural sciences to help universities provide their contribution to the Dual Support System, but the natural sciences often also benefit from industrial support.

In the social sciences most research is conducted on a small scale, and typically a grant from the SSRC will cover the cost of one or two research workers at a junior level.[18] Supervision of such a small team is well within the realm of possibility for a university teacher, and there is no charge for his supervision. There is, however, little equipment provided by the university and certainly not on the scale allowed for in the natural sciences by the UGC. Until now the UGC has apparently taken little notice of a university's ability to attract research funds in determining the level of its block grant. This last year, in applying the cuts in allocation and deciding which universities should reduce student numbers it has directly consulted the research councils.

In considering the role of the UGC a number of questions have to be raised. Has the UGC given sufficient priority to research in its decisions? Should universities be encouraged by the UGC to develop research policies which form part of a national pattern? If they did, what would be the effect on the research effort of individual university teachers? I consider such questions after looking at the role of other funding agencies.

THE POLYTECHNICS AND THE LOCAL AUTHORITIES
The expansion of the social sciences in the universities has been matched by the same in the polytechnics; in 1976 nearly 40 per cent (37.9 per cent) of the advanced course enrolments were in social, administrative and business studies — over 60,000 students served by approximately 7,500 staff.[19] Relatively few of these students are reading for higher degrees — between five and six hundred.

It would be useful to know more about the current level of research activity in polytechnics, and there is a working party of the CNAA which is now considering the matter. Staff contracts vary from institution to institution, and sometimes from department to department, in the time set aside for research. Research appears to have expanded in recent years and there no longer seems to be any force in the doctrine that polytechnics should be teaching institutions, but in the recent survey carried out by Halsey the polytechnic lecturers sampled claimed to spend only 18 per cent of their time on research.[20] Very few government contracts are placed with polytechnics and very few SSRC grants are held by them: only 37 of 576 in January 1982. There is no equivalent of the Dual Support System between the local authorities and the research councils.

THE RESEARCH COUNCILS
Until the mid 1960s there was no apparent role for a social science research council in intervening between government and the universities. The Clapham Committee set up by the wartime coalition government to examine provision for social and economic research considered the idea, but when they reported in 1945 they rejected it on a number of grounds. They saw the chief need to be the strengthening of staff and provision for routine research (ie economic and social statistics) and secondly, they saw a 'danger of a premature crystallization of spurious orthodoxies'. As for the universities, they wanted the UGC to increase the number of teaching and research posts in economics and statistics. The Labour government accepted their recommendations.

It was another twenty years before the Heyworth Committee was to revive the issue and recommend the setting up of the SSRC, but the period in between was not without initiatives on the part of government to fund research in the social sciences. Conditional Aid funds from the USA were used to examine the human factors in industrial productivity and support for this work was continued by the DSIR and MRC. The Colonial Office set up the Colonial Social Science Research Council. One or two departments of state such as the Treasury and the Home Office sponsored or supported work of direct interest to them in the 1950s.

The Heyworth Committee was appointed by R.A. Butler in 1963 but reported to a Labour government in 1965.[21] Their chief recommendation, which was to set up an SSRC, was accepted by C.A.R. Crosland, the Secretary of State for DES, and the SSRC began its work, under a royal charter, in the same year. One of its first tasks was to increase the number and quality of research workers, and the instrument of this policy was to increase the number of studentships for postgraduate study. However, much of the early investment in training was siphoned off into the expansion of tenured teaching posts in higher education. For the rest, the experience of full-time research was a relatively brief affair — often a few years as a research assistant, and the absence of any dependable career in research has meant that experience of research has rarely been cumulative. Even the experience of holding an SSRC research grant has as yet tended not to be repeated.

Unlike other research councils the SSRC did not invest heavily in its own research centres.[22] Only five units were started (one closed in 1976) and six Designated Research Centres were set up in 1978. Programme grants, some of which were renewed, offered a five-year life, but again they formed a small part of the total research expenditure. The study already referred to, of grants awarded by the SSRC, showed that the typical grant was a small-scale project lasting two to three years, and employing one or two research assistants.[23] It represents not only the aspiration of the typical academic applicant, but also the norm of the subject committee which assessed the applications.

Until 1974 the SSRC operated largely in a responsive mode but then in the backwash of the Rothschild Report it began to make its case for a larger share of the Science Budget (the source of its funds since 1972) in terms of relevance to national needs.[24] In 1974 Council appointed a Research Initiatives Board to identify areas of national interest, which by 1978 was spending 8.6 per cent of the total budget, and 26.9 per cent of the research budget.

1979 saw an important change in the fortunes of the SSRC, and this was brought about by two events — the Review of the Rothschild Report, and the election of a new government. The first event was important because it made explicit something which had been appreciated at the SSRC for some time. Despite the very considerable growth in government funding of social science research almost no commissions had been placed through the SSRC. As the Review Report put it: 'Departments did not find it necessary or useful to look to the SSRC as an intermediary.'[25] It recommended that government departments should examine the SSRC arrangements for commissioning social science research with a view to operating a satisfactory 'modus operandi'. The Heyworth Committee had seen the SSRC as the source of advice to government on its needs for social science research but that advice had not been sought.

The second event was the election of a Conservative government committed to cutting public expenditure. Within two months the budget for the SSRC was cut by 20 per cent, most of the impact of which cut was felt by those university departments holding an allocation of SSRC postgraduate awards. Over the next three years awards were cut by over 50 per cent. In the coming financial year 1982/83 the budget of the SSRC will be cut again — by 4 per cent — although the Science Budget as a whole is to enjoy level funding, and Lord Rothschild has been asked to conduct an urgent inquiry into the scope and efficiency of its work.[26]

It may be asked what special role the SSRC has managed to establish for itself in the funding 'system'. It has neither developed its own research capacity as far as other research councils nor has it been asked to act as an agent for government departments. On the positive side it has established through the peer review some common standards for social science research which are generally accepted as high, and it has sought in recent years to offer a different kind of policy relevant research — with a longer and wider view than any single government department might take. It has also sought to encourage independent views, and to enhance the value of ideas as well as facts. It has supported a regular supply of research workers from postgraduate training even if they lack the experience (and some employers would add 'the skills') of research.

DIRECT DEPARTMENT FUNDING

Direct funding by government departments accounted for one half of the funding in the social sciences in 1977/78, and although it has since been cut by over a third it remains a central element in the funding 'system'. Direct funding was almost unknown in the 1950s, and indeed steps were taken by government to find ways of funding which ensured independence of outlook and a long-term perspective. This may be illustrated by two examples.

In 1957 R.A. Butler, then the new Home Secretary, decided that 'The slow pace of change in the prisons combined with agitation, and even alarm at the continuing rise in crime, particularly by the young, had led to a call from all sides for more effective action.'[27] He was 'determined that there should be a long term plan; a course of action that would lay a path for an enlightened penal policy'. He pledged as his 'first priority the expansion of the research programme. But how was it to be achieved? How was the work to be organized? What would be the respective roles of the government and independent organizations?' Although in May 1957 he announced the formation of an in-house research unit (at that time consisting of only two research workers and four civil servants), he 'was convinced that (he) should do everything possible to promote an Institute which would be independent of the Home Office'. To do this he approached London and Cambridge Universities but it was clear they could only respond if the funds were provided for the institute. Butler insisted that the independence of the unit could only be safeguarded if the funds came from the UGC or from an independent foundation, and through his good offices these funds were secured.

The second significant example in the 1950s concerns a civil servant, Sir Robert Hall, then at the Treasury, who asked the NIESR to begin a programme of economic forecasting — the first such programme in the country.[28] He was convinced that the research resources at the Treasury were not equal to the demands being made upon them in the management of the economy. Since it was important to the Treasury that such work should be seen to be independent of government, and that government should not be associated with its forecasts, a campaign was launched to raise funds from foundations and from business. The Ford Foundation made a substantial contribution from 1957 to 1962 but from 1962 onwards the Treasury began to make grants for specific projects and a contribution to overheads. When the SSRC was established it also made a substantial contribution to the work of NIESR.

Irrespective of the success or otherwise of these endeavours in achieving their objectives there was some long-term objective in view and there was a serious attempt to ensure independence from government. Developments in direct funded research during the 1960s were much less scrupulous about the need for independence and much more geared to the short-term needs of government. Two of the more radical and innovating of the ministers in the Wilson government of the 1960s were at the centre of much of the growth in social and economic research. R.H.S. Crossman, first at the Ministry of Housing and Local Government (during which time he helped to create the Centre for Environmental Studies — now disbanded), and then later at the DHSS, encouraged a very rapid growth in research programmes. Barbara Castle when she was Minister of Transport and later at the DEP gathered around her groups of young economists and encouraged a substantial number of research commissions in the universities and elsewhere.

The expansion of government support for social science research in the late 1960s was, however, more broadly based than the particular interests of individual ministers. It found wide support among civil servants, especially those committed to the reform of the machinery and processes of government. The establishment of specialist classes in the civil service for certain social sciences such as economics and psychology opened up the doors of government to research from within. Even though many of its particular recommendations were not welcomed, the Fulton Committee had many supporters in the civil service in its concern for a more professional and expert administration.[29] One recommendation, the expansion of training for administrators in the late 1960s, was a ready way to open up the minds of civil servants to social science, and another, the setting up of Planning Units, provided an obvious home for the analytic approaches of social scientists in the civil service.

The Green Paper based on the Rothschild Report (Cmnd 4814) and the White Paper which followed it in 1972 (Cmnd 5046) had no immediate impact on the scale and direction of social science work commissioned by government departments since its main concern was the use of the natural sciences.[30] However, the new machinery set up by departments to relate the needs of the customer more closely to research contracts did have its effects, especially since departments often had needs in both natural and social sciences. The appointment of Chief Scientists and the establishment of research requirements machinery began to constrain the freedom previously enjoyed by that part of the academic community which had been closest to government. While money was plentiful this constraint was not unduly irksome but with the public expenditure cuts of the mid-1970s it was beginning to lead to serious differences of view between the civil servants and the academics. Not only were there differences about the choice and formulation of problems to be studied but the underlying difference of interest between government's need for flexibility and the research worker's need for stability of employment and programme became a serious issue. And one outcome was, as Kogan puts it in his study of DHSS, 'In the view of some, the science was not good enough,'[31] but it must also be added that it gave social scientists a much better appreciation of the realities of policy making.

The tightening of public expenditure in the mid-1970s placed the system under strain but it was the coincidence in 1979 of the review of the Rothschild Report and the election of a new government which forced re-appraisal of direct department funding of the social sciences, and which accelerated changes that were already in train. Budgets to social science were severely reduced. There was an increasing tendency to place contracts with commercial agencies and independent institutes, and a loss of confidence in the universities. The elaborate machinery for identifying customer needs was dismantled, or left incomplete. There were considerable cuts in the staff of in-house units, and in the staff supporting the Chief Scientists. Many of these changes were of course a consequence of general public expenditure cuts and were not aimed specifically at social science.

Throughout the period of rapid expansion through 1965-75, and now the period of contraction, there has been a minimum level of co-ordination inside government. A small unit set up in the Cabinet Office in the late 60s was disbanded in 1975, and in any case its role had been limited to increasing the flow of information. A Cabinet committee of officials met infrequently with little result and was eventually stood down. Through these decisions the SSRC lost two of the small windows through which it could officially see the social science activity of Whitehall. Interestingly, the Committee on Economic Research (then in the Treasury) continued to monitor and co-ordinate economic research but separately from other social science research.

For a period of ten years, from 1965 to 1975, certain government departments, both their ministers and civil servants, invested heavily in social science research. In their decisions on research they acted increasingly in the short-term interest; politically they became preoccupied with the needs of a particular government, and administratively they were constrained by the Rothschild principle of customer needs. They also acted without much regard for the role of the SSRC, and for the long- or medium-term impact of their initiatives on the university system. In this period of affluence a whole range of research institutions was created in universities but on a shallow foundation.[32] Since government departments paid the full costs of overheads their contracts were much more attractive than those of the SSRC grants which were governed by the principles of the Dual Support System. The decline in direct funding has not only seriously reduced the level of research in teaching departments, it has made university research centres extremely vulnerable over the medium term, and it is unlikely that the UGC and the SSRC can, or will be able to do much to help.

THE RESPONSE OF THE SCIENTIFIC COMMUNITY TO FUNDING OPPORTUNITIES

Governments naturally act on the assumption that they can control events, but scientific events have a way of eluding government intentions. Any simple expectations which governments may have entertained in the past that rapid bursts in scientific investment will lead to equally rapid results have been as liable to disappointment in the social sciences as in the natural sciences. There have been years when budgets in government departments and the SSRC have been seriously underspent, yet about a half of the university social science departments contained no funded research. It has taken much longer than planned to encourage the best minds to turn themselves to problems defined by government officials and committees, and sometimes the pressures to produce results quickly have meant settling for less than the best. It is important to understand what it is about the internal dynamics of the scientific communities which renders them so resistant to change, and so unpredictable in the face of government-inspired action.

The first thing to understand is that as with other scientists the most important people in the professional life of a typical social scientist are other social scientists.[33] They are the source of his reputation, they give direction to his ambitions, and motivate his efforts. When he carries out research it is intended for publication in academic journals or at conferences of his learned society. He started work in a university and will probably finish it there (often the same university).[34] Of course this picture does not fit so closely to the small number who work in independent research institutes or in government departments; nor does it apply so well to economists as it does to other social scientists. Those social scientists engaged in the vocational training of managers, teachers and social workers are also more sensitive to the currents of opinion of the outside world, and less bound to the professional reference group of their discipline.

Another fact about the scientific community is that the questions which motivate them to carry out research are usually the questions which interest other people in their discipline, and indeed these questions become the increasingly specialized preoccupations of groups within the discipline.[35]

Government departments, which are also specialized, but in a different sense, find it much easier to encourage work in their field when it converges on an existing academic specialism. If such a specialism does not exist it may be a long and expensive business to create one. Applied specialisms may also be developed for professional practice outside the universities, such as in economics and psychology — and these practitioners may then seek to influence the direction of research in the universities. Specialization, whether pure or applied, may be particularly advantageous to staff in provincial universities which have to compete with the dominance of the metropolitan centres, particularly since their departments may be smaller in size. It cannot go very far in undergraduate teaching, but at postgraduate level, and in research, it offers the possibility of exploiting a useful but limited market. When the two needs for specialization, pure and applied, coincide, this is very propitious for the possible collaboration of academics with government funding.

It is commonly supposed that specialization and disciplinary-based work are somehow fatally flawed from the standpoint of government, for political problems, it is argued, are neither economic problems nor sociological problems but just problems, which require a multi-faceted attack from different disciplinary perspectives. In this way the case is sometimes made out for multi-disciplinary team work. Now it is certainly the case that most of the major centres which receive government contracts employ a range of social scientists but characteristically such scientists work outside their disciplines, and the information they collect is often not informed by theoretical or conceptual considerations. When a multi-disciplinary approach has been most creative is when it has also been institutionalized in university teaching, and particularly in the vocational training of managers, teachers and social workers.

Another important fact about the scientific community which has implications for government research funding is that its most distinguished members operate on an international network, and especially on the transatlantic net. The international nature of social science is not new, as it had its origins in Europe and was transplanted to the USA, but since the Second World War the traffic in ideas has been mostly the other way and a stream of the most able young social scientists have spent formative periods in the USA. Some of the leading North American intellectuals have also taught here, and many of the basic textbooks in social science are still imported from the USA. The impact of the American experience has been not only to increase the intellectual and technical sophistication of British social science, but also to shape the debates about the relationships between research and policy in Britain — for example influencing strategies for social reform, and more latterly the management of the economy through monetarist ideas.

This last point has much wider implications for British politics than the possible influence of American thinking as it raises the whole question of the 'scientific' nature of the social sciences, and of their ideological underpinning. The social sciences, and in particular sociology, are widely believed to be left wing in inspiration and inclination and the prominence of sociology students in the university troubles of the late 1960s may have reinforced this notion. It may be that there is an underlying unity of interest between intellectuals and reforming governments, or to put it differently an opposition between the business community and intellectuals,[36] but some of these presuppositions are ill-founded, and others may be of a temporary significance. The dominance of Keynesian thinking in British economics has now been challenged, and there are indications that Fabian views of social administration are also under attack. It may be a sign of the maturing of British social science that it is becoming more heterodox in outlook. In any case there is a sufficient number of social scientists of a non-political outlook in the universities who have been willing to serve governments whatever their political complexions.

A number of factors have been identified which get in the way of successful collaboration between government and the universities, but it has to be remembered that irrespective of what governments choose to do, university teachers will expect to continue to do research in their own time and of their own choosing. (It is interesting in this context to note the way in which the word 'research' has replaced 'scholarship'.) Some of this research at least will be directly relevant to the business of government and here the concern which government might legitimately express is whether the output is adequate — in quality or quantity. On the face of it there should be no worry about the scale of the output other than a fear of being overwhelmed by it. It has been estimated that the production of monographs in the social sciences in the UK rose from 2,774 in 1950 to 5,444 in 1960, and 9,394 in 1970.[37] In sociology alone the increase was 858 per cent over the period from 1950 to 1970. In all subjects the number of academic journals increased sharply and they found room for more and longer articles. Such journals are especially central to communications in the better established disciplines like economics and psychology, but in those disciplines it was a growing practice to circulate unpublished papers privately, partly to establish priority, partly to get results circulating faster, and partly because of the difficulties in getting papers published. The rapid inflation of costs in the 1970s has slowed the growth of publications down considerably and commercial publishers have become less enthusiastic about the market. The learned societies, and the universities with their house journals, who still dominate the control of serial publications in the social sciences, have also had difficulty in coping with the rising costs.[38]

But the impressive story set out above is not the whole story. For one thing it is clear that a small number of academics account for a high proportion of the publications and a substantial minority publish nothing at all for long periods.[39] Furthermore it is clear that postgraduate theses have been the source of a substantial fraction of articles in journals of learned societies, and of books.[40] It would be interesting to make a comparison of the output of one full-time research worker with the notionally equivalent research effort of three university teachers but there is no data available. It is difficult anyway to compare the value of the different kinds of channels they use for publication. It might be argued that an esoteric article in an academic journal is much less useful to a government department than a research report which has been specially prepared following a research commission, but two points would have to be made in reply to that argument. Would the research report have been as perspicacious if the authors had not themselves been fed on an academic diet? And secondly, the esoteric paper may provide the foundation for a popular article or programme in the media which may reach an audience of millions, especially if the topic is controversial. This seldom happens to technical research reports published by government.

The matter of judging quality is inclined to be subjective but one way of looking at it is to examine the international reputation of British social science and social scientists. Measured by publications in the leading international journals, by citations, and by international honours it must be said that there are only a few who measure up to the highest standards.[41] Most of the leaders in the social sciences now live in America. British economics, history and anthropology are still widely respected but with notable exceptions British sociology, psychology and political science have not yet really established themselves in the international league.

The review of the roles of the main agencies of research funding underlines the point made at the beginning of this paper: it is difficult to talk of a funding *system*. The UGC and the polytechnics have been preoccupied with the problems of creating the capacity in higher education to absorb more students. They have not given a great deal of thought to the research capacity they were creating. The government departments, under pressure of fast moving political events, have acted quickly to satisfy their short-term needs and with very little thought for the consequences. The SSRC might have acted as the broker to these changes, or at least the central source of information and advice, but has not been able to establish its right or power to do so. It is after all a very small organization when set alongside the UGC and government departments, and one which has to rely on moral persuasion rather than on implementing a clear scientific policy coming from the government. It has nevertheless had an important role in the development of postgraduate work in the social sciences. We have not discussed the role of the foundations, although it was very important in the formative years of social science, nor the role of business support, as both are minor elements in the overall picture of funding. As government support for the social sciences contracts their role may become important once again.

COULD WE DO BETTER NEXT TIME?
There is very little likelihood of a major revival of interest in social science

research in the foreseeable future, but a breathing space may be helpful in thinking through a strategy for future development. It must be said that any attempt to develop a system of funding with roles assigned to the major sponsors presupposes an agreement about the objectives of such a system, and a shared assumption that the social sciences have contributed something to politics, culture and society.

Any manifesto for the social sciences for the future must seek to be more realistic than the Heyworth Committee about what social science can achieve, for very little progress has been made with the list of problems set out in Chapter IV of their Report.[42] In any case it is time to abandon the simplistic notions of social engineering which guided that committee, for research can not only legitimate political solutions to social problems, it may also establish valid criticism. It may of course be possible to find solutions to some social and economic problems but it is rare for these to be directly derived from research. More often than not it is the analysis, the interpretation, or the tentative explanation which is valuable to those who have to make decisions. Such enlightenment is an important element in the popular culture of a modern democratic society for politicians now have to come up with satisfactory explanations of what they are (or are not) doing, and those explanations have to satisfy an increasingly educated and sceptical public.

The ways in which this kind of thinking gets absorbed into conventional wisdom has been well put in an editorial in the American journal *Science*:

> 'Ironically, the social sciences seldom get full credit for their theoretical accomplishments, because the discoveries, once labelled, are quickly absorbed into conventional wisdom. This is easily demonstrated; note the number of social science concepts common in our vocabulary: human capital, gross national product, identity crisis, span of control, the unconscious, price elasticity, acculturation, political party identification, reference group, externalities. Obviously, the phenomena revealed through such concepts existed prior to the relevant research, just as DNA, quarks, and the source of the Nile existed prior to their discovery. Yet concepts generated through research are discoveries that make phenomena intelligible and accessible that previously were inaccurately or incompletely understood.'[43]

Certain knowledge-based professions such as education, management and social work, which are a key element in the ordering of a modern social structure, are particularly dependent upon such ideas and concepts. The élite of each of these professions are increasingly recruited from university training where they have become directly acquainted with the fruits of research and sensitized to the potential of research methods.

When social science is looked at in this way — when it becomes difficult to distinguish the pure from the applied, scholarship from research, the instrinsic from the instrumental, it is difficult to conceive of any tightly articulated system of research funding geared to useful ends. The focus of intellectual activity must continue to be located in the universities and polytechnics if it is to comprehend all these possibilities. Nevertheless, some better way has to be found of increasing the research output of universities and of linking the applied research activity in higher education to national needs. Such needs have to find expression in some national forum, and the price of the ticket of admission to this forum is that the university subscribers should have something special to offer.

Universities will have to be prepared to choose the ground on which their staff will compete, and the reward from the UGC, the research councils and government departments should be to give preferential treatment to the successful. This will mean concentration of effort and specialization of function. The SSRC could encourage this by concentrating its postgraduate awards on such centres, and concentrating its grants and contracts on centres which can offer scale and continuity. Government departments are already attracted by the possibilities of using SSRC centres for project funding. It is a policy which could enable the smaller department of a provincial university to compete fairly with the larger metropolitan centre.

Kogan has made the very useful point that 'Legitimation of research choice is as important as intellectual quality', but it is not easy to see the best form and location for a national forum to consider applied research needs. In France the CNRS and the DGRST have had an important role in defining research needs in the context of the national social and economic plans, but such centralized planning is not part of the British tradition of government. It is difficult to see any existing organization having this role. It cannot be the UGC since that body is not close enough to government, except for its DES connection. It cannot be government itself as it is defined too narrowly in a party sense. It cannot be the ABRC as that is concerned in the main with basic research in the sciences. The SSRC might be one possibility but it would have to be moved nearer to the centre of the governmental stage if it were to be taken seriously. The answer may lie in setting up or using differently a number of bodies such as NEDO or the Schools Council but in other fields of policy. One problem which would have to be overcome is how the recommendations of such bodies could be converted into resource commitments by the bodies which control the funds. Another problem is that the further the discussions about policy research are removed from the operational level the less informed the discussions are likely to be, and the less likely that research findings will be heeded.

The other strategy for a better use of the national research effort must lie in more flexible combinations of research, scholarship and teaching in higher education.[44] It is time that the convention of 30 per cent of a university teacher's time for research should be openly questioned. How could it be thought to apply equally to all subjects in a university? And to all individuals — the energetic and the lazy? And at all levels of student numbers? Staff will naturally want to resist any further worsening of staff-student ratios but these may improve (as long as participation rates do not change) because of demographic factors in the late 80s. This may give the UGC an opportunity to encourage more variations in the basic university contracts with some posts seen as research lectureships with very little or no teaching, and research grant holders might be rewarded with a smaller teaching load. There are already local variations of an informal kind but these need to be made more explicit and generally applied. Universities might also be willing to favour departments which have had a successful record in attracting research funds. A great many variations could be conceived if there were a real incentive to reward research.

We have tried to describe and analyse the roles of different agencies sponsoring research in the social sciences, and how these developed independently of each other in the 60s and 70s. It would be unwise now to go to the opposite extreme and look for a highly articulated system for the future. There are good reasons for retaining a degree of redundancy of action and vagueness about role definition. Some progress might be made if a national forum could be established for discussing applied research needs as seen by all sponsors of research, and for those who are in command of public resources to find better ways of relating their individual research programmes. In any case something must be done to create real incentives in higher education to increase the level and quality of research activity, especially during a period when promotion opportunities will be extremely limited.

NOTES

1 Social sciences in this chapter are taken to include the subjects covered by the three UGC committees on social studies, education, and business and management studies. Social studies includes administration, American social studies, anthropology, applied economics, banking, Commonwealth studies, conveyancing, criminology, demography, economic history, economics, econometrics, environmental studies, town and country planning, geography, government, history of science, human relations, international studies, jurisprudence, law, occupational psychology, philosophy of science, politics, psychology, social administration, social psychology, social science, sociology, social statistics, work studies, youth work. The figure for 1938 is from the Heyworth Report and is less widely defined.

2 Two of the basic sources for this paper are:
   i   Williams, G., Blackstone, T. and Metcalf, D. (1974) *The Academic Labour Market* Amsterdam: Elsevier.
   ii Westoby, A., Webster, D. and Williams, G. (1976) *Social Scientists at Work* London: SRHE.

An up-to-date analysis of the situation in the polytechnics is contained in Balmer, D.W. (1980) *A Preliminary Investigation of the Demand for Recruits to Polytechnic Teaching in the Social Sciences* Unpublished SSRC Report July 1980.

3   Advice to the universities in the letter from the UGC dated 1 July 1981. It is expected that the number of full-time social studies students (UK/EEC) will fall by 12 per cent by 1983/84.
4   The current position in the USA is well analysed in Prewitt, K. and Sills, D.L. (1981) Federal funding for the social sciences: threats and responses *ITEMS* 35 (3) September.
5   Jackson, A. (1979) *The Flow of Funds to Social Research in the UK in Recent Years* SSRC, unpublished. Local authorities were not included but it is estimated that there were over 1,000 research workers employed in 1978.
6   The Committee of Vice-Chancellors and Principals asked university teachers in eleven universities to keep diaries for three separate weeks in 1969/70. The findings were published by the CVCP in 1972. The replies probably over-estimate the actual amount of time spent on scholarship and research.
7   Clapham Committee (1946) *Provision for Social and Economic Research* (Cmnd 6868) London: HMSO.
    Specific governmental decisions have also caused the UGC and the universities to create a limited number of full-time tenured research posts since then.
8   Robbins (1963) *Higher Education* Report of the Committee on Higher Education under the Chairmanship of Lord Robbins 1961-63 (Cmnd 2154) London: HMSO.
9   DES and SED (1978) *Higher Education into the 1990s* A discussion document. London: HMSO.
10 Lumsden, K., Atiyah, R. and Scott, A. (1980) *Economics Education in the UK* Heinemann.
11 Draft Report of the PEP Survey of 1968 Economics and Statistics Graduates (not published) Report to SSRC HG 25/35/1.
12 Booth, A.E. and Coats, A.W. (1978) The market for economists in Britain 1945-75 *The Economic Journal* 88, September.
    Also see Institute of Manpower Studies, University of Sussex (1981) *The Employment of Postgraduate Social Scientists* and the various associated reports, especially MIP/5a.
13 Webb, D. (1973) *The Employment of 1970 Sociology Graduates* Privately published.
14 Statistics from the Annual Reports of the Universities Council for Central Admissions.
15 DES *Statistics of Education 1978 Vol 6 Universities.*
16 Hay, A. and Maddock, S. (1980) *The Contribution of Postgraduate Thesis Research to the Published Literature of Human Geography in the UK* London: SSRC.
    Benewick, R., and Solomos, I. (1980) *Report on the Contribution of SSRC Supported Research Students to the Published Literature of Political Science and International Relations* London: SSRC

Atkinson, A.B. (with Isaacs, C. and Richmond, D.) (1980) *Report on SSRC Supported Economics Research Students 1970-75* London: SSRC.
17 Merrison, Sir A. *The Support of University Scientific Research* Joint Working Party of the ABRC and UGC. It is not yet clear whether this report, which examines the Dual Support System, will be published.
18 In an SSRC study by Shaw, S. (1980) (unpublished) over three-quarters of a sample of completed grants had employed only one or two staff.
19 Balmer — op. cit.
20 Halsey, A.H. *Higher Education in Britain 1980* Final Report to SSRC on Research Grant HR 3441, Lodged with the British Lending Library.
21 Heyworth, Lord (1965) *Report of the Committee on Social Studies* (Cmnd 2660) London: HMSO.
22 *Annual Reports of the SSRC* (1976) 10th Anniversary Newsletter.
23 Shaw — op. cit.
24 Rothschild, Lord (1971) *The Organisation and Management of Government Research and Development* (Cmnd 4814). *A Framework for Government Research and Development* (1972) (Cmnd 5046) London: HMSO.
25 *Review of the Framework for Government Research and Development* (1979) (Cmnd 7499) London: HMSO.
26 The terms of reference for this Enquiry were given in answer to a Parliamentary Question on 23 December 1981.
27 Butler, R.A. (1974). In Hood, R. (Editor) *Crime, Criminology and Public Policy* London: Heinemann.
28 Hall, Sir, R. (now Lord Roberthall) writing in the 50th issue of NIESR's *Economic Review* November 1969.
29 Fulton, Lord (1968) *Report of the Committee on the Civil Service* (Cmnd 3638) London: HMSO.
30 Blume, S.S. (forthcoming) *The Commissioning of Social Research by Central Government* London: SSRC.
Social Research Association: Terms and Conditions of Social Research Funding in Britain (1980) London.
Departments are required to publish annual reports on their expenditure on research and development.
31 Kogan, M., Korman, N. and Henkel, M. (1980) *Government's Commissioning of Research: a case study* (Ch. 7) Brunel University.
32 Perry, N. (1975) Table 3 p.24 in *The Organisation of Social Science Research in the UK* Occasional Paper No. 6 in Survey Research. Table 3, p.24. London: SSRC.
Crawford, E. and Perry, N. (Editors) (1976) *Demand for Social Knowledge* (in particular Ch. 2) London: Sage.
33 Haggstrom, W.O. (1965) *The Scientific Community* Basic Books.

34 Halsey — op. cit. Also Halsey, A. and Trow, M. (1971) *British Academics* London. Both studies show a mobility of less than 2 per cent between universities in the two years examined (1967/68 and 1975/76).
33 Haggstrom — op. cit. There is now a growing literature on specializations in the social sciences: for example Stehr, N. (1974) Paradigmatic crystallisation — patterns of interrelations in sociology *Social Science Information* 12 (1) 119.
36 See Orlans, H. (1973) *Contracting for Knowledge* (Ch. 1) San Francisco: Jossey-Bass.
37 Line, M. and Roberts, S. (1976) The size, growth and composition of social science literature *International Social Science Journal* XXVII (1).
38 Royal Society (1981) *A Study of the Scientific Information System in the UK* London.
39 See Williams — op. cit. Table 18.5, p.365; and Halsey — op. cit. Tables 12, 13 and 14, pp.32-33.
40 Hay and Maddock et al. — op. cit.
41 Nelson, D. (Editor) (1971) *Bibliography of British Psychological Research 1960-66* London: HMSO. This examined the state of British psychology for the SSRC but is now somewhat dated. A number of studies have looked at the British contribution to the American journals which dominate the international scene. For example: Lovell, M.C. (1973) The production of economic literature: an interpretation *Journal of Economic Literature* II (1) pp.27; Collison, P. Webber (1971) British Sociology 1950-70: A journal analysis *Sociological Review* 19.
42 Some examples from Heyworth Ch. IV are 'What are the physical, psychological, genetic and social factors affecting delinquency?' or 'What factors affect the relationship between police and public?'
43 ITEMS — op. cit.
44 *Research in Universities* (1980) London: CVCP: 'There is no doubt that for education at the level of a UK honours degree and for postgraduate work, the interplay between teaching and research is of immense value' (p.8 Introduction by Sir Rex Richards). There is unfortunately no research which has corroborated this view, and other countries seem to have managed a very successful research programme divorced from teaching.

SEMINAR DISCUSSION

The discussion on the social sciences covered many of the same issues as the sessions on the natural sciences. For example, what is the relationship between teaching and research in the social sciences? Can a national policy be formulated for social science research? Does the Dual Support System work for the social sciences? What special requirements are there to ensure a national capability in the social sciences? But the social science discussion came to somewhat different conclusions.

Training and Research
Except for certain individual preferences there seems to be no fundamental reason why research in the social sciences should be so inextricably linked to undergraduate teaching. There is much to be said for separating the two and permitting more interdisciplinary research groups to operate. This will be necessary if the appropriate research capacity is to be formed to solve both long- and short-term social problems.

Institutional Research Policy
Many speakers considered it inevitable that there would have to be greater selectivity and concentration of research in the social sciences, but doubted whether the present university management system would permit such choices to be made. Making priorities between groups and departments and areas of work is a divisive activity. But whereas the same arguments were made in the session on the natural sciences it was then felt by some that the imposition of priorities by outside bodies was possible to contemplate. In the social sciences, however, one of the main activities of academic groups must be the independent critique of society and government policy. It is therefore difficult to accept the legitimacy of priorities determined by government bodies. The only possible alternative would be for the SSRC to play a more active role in making the choices. This implies some loss of autonomy within the institutions of higher education.

National Priorities for Research
If it is wrong for government bodies to impose priorities, are there other more acceptable mechanisms which can formulate national priorities for social science research? There was little agreement on this. Some felt that a national forum which brought together users and researchers could help to determine priorities and growth areas, but this should not go under the title of a national social science research policy. Others were more sceptical about any mechanism which established these sorts of priorities and preferred instead all initiative for research to come from the researchers themselves. It was pointed out that other countries had managed to identify national needs in a way that seemed to be acceptable to the researchers in those countries. The debate was inconclusive on this point.

Funding
There was a lot of criticism of the way the Dual Support System has worked in the social sciences. There seems to have been very little consultation between the UGC and the research councils. The result is that there are too few incentives for good research. There was criticism too of the relationship between the SSRC and many government departments. It seemed to be rare for a government department to make substantial comments on research proposals sent to them by the SSRC. Some participants argued that it was not appropriate for government departments to be asked for such comments since the role of academics should be to criticize and not just be a tool of government.

One feature of the present cuts to university budgets is the arbitrary way in which some social sciences research units are being affected. Both government departments and the SSRC have helped finance several good policy research units in universities, but since they are university-based and are subject to cuts in their core budget they have been vulnerable to UGC initiatives.

All of the discussion on the balance between UGC and non-UGC funding for research must have seemed very academic to the representatives from the polytechnics. Whether research survives in these institutions depends entirely on staff enthusiasm and administrative support.

Special Difficulties in the Social Sciences
One of the principal difficulties in social science research in Britian seems to be the fragmented nature of the activity. What is required is research capacity for tackling long-term policy problems. When this capacity exists it can also be drawn upon to solve some of the short-term policy problems of government. A second difficulty is the need for interdisciplinary teams to

solve 'real world' problems. Too many academics are bound within the confines of their discipline. One solution to these difficulties would be for universities, the UGC, and the research councils to get together and between them decide in what areas it was important to have long-term social science research capacity created in this country. They should then help build up more designated research centres with both UGC and research council support.

5

THE FUNCTIONS OF RESEARCH IN THE HUMANITIES

by David Daiches

Organized research in the humanities — or what used to be called the arts, both liberal arts and fine arts — is a relatively modern activity. Until fairly recent times inquiry into literary or historical or philosophical problems was in the hands of cultivated gentlemen who worked as individuals in their own time on a subject that had captured their interest. There were indeed men of letters who made a living by the publication of their researches — Dr Johnson, with his *Dictionary of the English Language* (1755) and his edition of Shakespeare (1765) is one of the most notable examples — but they were individuals working on subjects of their own choice that they considered to be of interest to the general public. From the seventeenth century on, antiquaries, biographers, linguists, philosophers, historians (who succeeded antiquaries as ideas of historical development and causation emerged), literary and art critics (who became possible when a sufficiently varied body of creative works had become available and when scholars had access to them by means of libraries and similar institutions), musicologists (Charles Burney's Pioneering *General History of Music* appeared in 1776-89), textual scholars in the classical languages (the great name here is Richard Bentley, 1662-1742), orientalists, and other men of learning in a variety of humanistic fields, published the results of their researches for the most part without institutional sponsorship or academic formality. The picture remained in considerable degree the same throughout the nineteenth century, when the ideal of the man of letters contributing to the sum of knowledge and understanding as a private 'gentleman and scholar' burned brightly, in spite of the professionalizing of some areas of research, notably history, a field in which William Stubbs, who became Regius Professor of History at Oxford in 1866, and whose work on English constitutional history was intended to be and long remained aids to students of the subject, pioneered what might be called a professional academic approach. In this respect Stubbs differed from such other nineteenth-century historians as Lord Macaulay and J.R. Green. Many literary and historical scholars in the nineteenth century were in fact clergymen, as Green was and as the literary scholar, biographer and editor A.B. Grosart was; others like the historian J.A. Froude and the biographer and critic Sir Leslie Stephen gave up ecclesiastical and academic prospects on principle early in their careers to lead an independent life as men of letters.

The researcher as independent man of letters gave way in the present century to the researcher as professional academic. The development of the

PhD degee at universities was part cause and part effect of this. The notion of a research thesis leading to a doctoral degree had been established in Germany and had been adopted by the Americans under German influence. It was under the joint influence of German and American academic experience, and partly in order to attract American postgraduate students, that British universities developed a similar programme. Many older academics resisted the notion that a university should provide formal teaching in the humanities at the research level. If there was a topic that attracted a potential researcher, then the university would provide a library for him to work in and even scholars for him to consult, but it was up to the researcher to get on with the job in his own way. If I may be allowed a personal reminiscence, I might mention that when I went from Edinburgh to Oxford to work for a DPhil degree I wrote my Oxford doctoral dissertation without at any stage exchanging a word with my nominal supervisor on the subject I was investigating. He used to invite me to dine with him at his college once a term, on which occasions we would talk about anything except my thesis, but the actual planning and writing up of my research was left entirely to myself, working in the Bodleian Library. I also remember H.J.C. Grierson, the distinguished Professor of English at Edinburgh, once replying to a foreign student who asked him how long it took to write a doctoral dissertation: 'Two years; one for reading, one for writing.'

The generation of great scholars and teachers in the humanities who flourished in the earlier half of this century, of whom Grierson was one, rarely had research degrees. They may have had honorary doctorates conferred on them in later life, but for the most part they did their research and wrote their books in their own time and in their own way (as Grierson produced his great edition of Donne) during their tenure of a university Chair. The scholar had already become a professor rather than producing books in his spare time as a clergyman or simply as a private gentleman, and this was the first step to the emergence of the Doctors degree as a desirable if not a necessary qualification for the academic profession. In the United States the possession of a PhD degree as a password to the academic profession was well established quite early in the present century. In this country there was much resistance to any such requisite, and indeed there still is in some quarters, although the large majority of university teachers in the humanities have by now felt it necessary to obtain a Doctors degree.

The consequences of the establishment of the PhD as a passport to the academic profession have been far-reaching. The whole concept of research in the humanities has changed, as well as the circumstances and atmosphere under which research has been conducted. To have to produce a piece of research in order to get your foot on the academic ladder often means that instead of embarking on a scholarly investigation because the subject fascinates you, you embark on it as a necessary piece of drudgery, perhaps involving a subject suggested to you by a supervisor in which you have no special interest. It may be that in the sciences the slotting of an individual's research into a wider project in order to contribute to a well planned comprehensive investigation is a sound way of engaging in postgraduate work, but in the humanities the situation is generally different.[1] Educationally, it is much more important for someone pursuing an academic career in the humanities to widen his perspective by much reading, by learning new languages, by reflecting more on the significance of the knowledge he has already acquired than by endeavouring to extend the bounds of knowledge. It is true that most universities now define the object of a doctoral dissertation as contributing to the increase of knowledge *or understanding*, which relieves the research student from the necessity of actually making new discoveries, and 'understanding' can be defined in a great number of ways. Indeed, in literary research today a fairly high proportion of theses are essentially revaluations or re-thinkings of the significance of some literary work or works or of some concepts in literary criticism or critical theory. And this is true of most subjects in the humanities. Nevertheless, there remain ambiguities in the concept of research as applied to the humanities and confusions about the parallels between scientific and humanistic research.

At the beginning of this century John Burnet, a distinguished professor of Greek at St Andrews University and a passionate believer in the compatibility and mutual enrichment of humanistic and scientific study, expressed the view of what may be called the humanistic old guard on the matter of research:

'In our department, however it may be in others, no research worthy of the name has ever been done except by men who simply could not help doing it, and none has ever been done but for its own sake. A man is led by some feeling of kinship for what is greater than himself to devote his life to the interpretation of a poet, philosopher, or historian, to the elucidation of the language itself on its purely linguistic side, or to that of the art or institutions of antiquity. Such a man will freely give himself up to the most arid and laborious investigations. No erasure in a manuscript, no half-read scholium, no fragmentary inscription will seem unworthy of his attention; no grammatical nicety or stylistic peculiarity will be passed by as too trivial for his patient study. All these things will live in his hands; for they are all transformed by his faith in something to which he can hardly give a name, but which, to him, is more real than anything else. . . . it is this search for the something more that makes the real scholar, and I do not see how it is to be "promoted" or "encouraged" by regulations or endowments.'[2]

The notion that a researcher is a dedicated scholar passionately devoted to the investigation of a subject that has captured his imagination has little place in the modern university, however much we may be in sympathy with it. And the association of this view with the view that endowments are irrelevant to true scholarship — which is of course quite a different issue — quietly shelves the question of how the dedicated scholar is to live while he pursues his researches. At the back of Burnet's mind seems to have been the old concept of the gentleman scholar with his private resources. Nonetheless, Burnet laid his finger on an essential aspect of the kind of academic research that was beginning to emerge in his time: it was professional, it was undertaken in order to advance a man's career; 'learning has become a trade and the trail of "banausia" (the attitude of a vulgar mechanic) is over it all'. Such a distinction between the disinterested pursuit of a scholarly ideal and the undertaking of research for reasons of professional advancement can apply as much to scientific as to humanistic study, and Burton's account of his ideal researcher is as relevant to Galileo or Einstein as to any humanistic scholar.

It was nevertheless under the influence of scientific research and the prestige that science had acquired in the nineteenth century that the promotion of research in the humanities developed in the twentieth. The boundaries of knowledge needed to be widened, and if the astrophysicist could make new discoveries about the physical nature of the universe then the humanistic scholar could make new discoveries in the field of the arts. In some areas the parallel was justified. It has proved possible to learn more about, for example, Shakespeare's text by extending our knowledge of Elizabethan handwriting and printing practices; we can learn the date of manuscripts by applying new knowledge of early methods of paper-making and of water-marks; we can search records and discover new biographical facts; we can learn about the physical processes involved in early painting that will enable us to date a disputed Renaissance painting, for example, with some precision; we can learn more about the nature of early musical instruments and music-making that will enable us to reproduce more faithfully the sounds intended by earlier composers; we can even use computers to investigate stylistic peculiarities and so settle the authorship of disputed texts. But there is a limit to this kind of extension of knowledge in the humanities. It can be argued that the most significant work done in this field is less likely to be the discovery and application of new knowledge than revaluation and re-interpretation of what is already known, and even that research is less important than reflection.

It is perhaps a question of definition: one could define 'research' to include revaluation, re-interpretation and even reflection, and indeed some such definition is implied in the description of the object of a doctoral dissertation already mentioned. Nevertheless, the proliferation of the PhD degree as a professional requirement for academics in the humanities has led to innumerable attempts to achieve a dubious originality or to extend the bounds of knowledge in profitless or even merely nominal ways, as in investigating A's alleged influence on B (in literature and the arts) or creating false classifications or categories. (The late Professor Nichol Smith used to warn research students in English literature at Oxford against setting themselves meaningless objectives in research by creating false categories: an example he used to give was 'London in English literature', a topic which he insisted could yield no real insight of any kind, since the collocation of references to London in works of literature throughout the ages could not possibly add up to any significant new understanding.) It is not an exaggeration to state that in many humanities subjects the large majority of doctoral dissertations being turned out in unversities throughout the Western world are useless. Certainly, in my own field of English literature the bulk of theses churned out in vast quantities in the United States and elsewhere are at best exercises in methodology and at worst a total waste of time for everyone involved. It may be true that in the sciences, or in some of them, one must work on the frontiers of knowledge if one is to be an effective university teacher of the subject. This is not necessarily true of the humanities. It is possible to be learned, widely read in different languages and literatures, perceptive, critically astute, master of a lucid and elegant style in both lecturing and writing, capable of sustaining illuminating dialogue with others interested in the subject under discussion — it is possible to be in possession of all these qualities and in consequence to be a great university teacher in such a field as literature without ever having engaged in anything that could be called 'research'.

Another consequence of the emergence of the PhD degree as a requirement for entry into the academic teaching profession is the proliferation of specialization in areas where traditionally a broad background of knowledge and understanding was considered the most important qualification of all. Today the tendency is to define oneself from an early stage as 'a seventeenth century man' or as someone concerned with a single movement or even a single writer, and the traditional insistence on breadth for anyone working in the humanities has been replaced by an insistence on depth (of a sort). The days of the great university teacher in literature or philosophy who could fire his pupils with a genuine enthusiasm for the subject without himself having written anything that could be defined as a piece of research or even without having written anything at all — these days have now gone by, though memories of them persist in some Oxford and Cambridge colleges. The days when a graduate engaged in research out of pleasure in the subject rather than out of professional necessity are also gone. Where does that leave research in the humanities? If one takes the old-fashioned view that it should not be necessary to have produced a piece of research to qualify as a university teacher in the humanities (and such a view, though still tenable, is now very much a minority one) this does not mean that one does not want to encourage humanistic scholarship. What kind of humanistic scholarship do we want and what are the functions it should serve?

There is still the discovery of new information of the kinds already mentioned. This is perhaps not the most important kind of humanistic research but it can be used as a basic for important work. The whole modern science (and it is a science) of bibliography and textual criticism, for example, has brought a vast amount of new knowledge about early printed texts, knowledge that can be used by the critic and the interpreter in all sorts of ways. The subtlest critic of Shakespeare will be at a disadvantage if he cannot tell which readings in the text he is using are printer's errors, which revisions by a non-Shakespearean hand, which are Shakespeare's own. Similarly new biographical information, new facets of social history revealed by examination of sources hitherto neglected or unavailable, new facts revealed by archaeological excavations, can be taken as examples of useful research that may not in itself be of any great significance but which can in the hands of a scholar with the requisite range of knowledge and understanding yield important new kinds of understanding. This kind of research is a means to an end. What some historical and literary scholars call 'working at the coal face' — ie working with original manuscript documents in the Public Record Office or other archives — is itself often mechanical work that can be done by anyone endowed with tenacity and patience. The use of such material by scholars and critics of wide-ranging knowledge possessing the understanding that can come from such knowledge is the highly valuable end-product. Of course, many humanistic scholars themselves work at the coal face before proceeding to synthethize their newly acquired knowledge with other areas of knowledge and understanding to produce important new works of re-interpretation. To take only one of many examples, one can cite the work in Scottish history done by Professor Geoffrey Barrow, whose study of such documents as different from each other as Latin charters and Middle Scots poetry has helped him to re-write mediaeval Scottish history in a way that genuinely advances understanding, as showing how a scholar can possess both patience in the locating and studying of primary sources and a synthesizing historical imagination that enables him to make the fruitful use of those sources. There are other cases where the 'researcher' simply makes available primary sources which scholars of wider knowledge and imagination drew on in order to provide their revaluations and re-interpretations.

There can be little doubt that in the field of the humanities it is interpretation and evaluation that are most important. But it is not only interpretation and evaluation of works of art or historical movements or personalities and so on that we need; most of all we need new interpretations and evaluations of the function of humanistic study as a whole, its role in society, its meaning in terms of people's lives and the values we seek to encourage in living. This is what we must research into most of all — the human meaning and value of the subject itself. For the humanities, covering as they do all the arts and products of human imagination as well as intellect, constitute a culturally sensitive subject. In what sense are literature, music, fine art really teachable subjects? What part do they play and ought they to play in our culture? What is the ultimate objective (conscious or unconscious) of the professor of literature or history or philosophy or fine art? A major function of research in the humanities is thus the introspective one of seeking to define the nature and significance of its own subject.

This endeavour is bound up with the whole problem of the transmission of what is sometimes known as the 'high culture' of the past. Until fairly recently it has been taken for granted in our civilization that a major purpose of education, for that minority who are capable of acquiring it, is the development of an understanding and appreciation of the classics of literature, art and music and perhaps also of philosophy. What have become defined as classics in the course of the ages — Homer, Dante, Shakespeare, among men of literature; Bach, Mozart, Beethoven, among composers; Giotto, Titian, Rembrandt among painters; and so on — have as a consequence been accepted as especially worthy of what might be called educational and cultural attention. But the world is changing at an ever increasing pace. More and more works of art of all kinds are being produced. Is it still possible to transmit in our educational process an appreciation of the high culture of the past? Are the great names that punctuate the story of the development of the arts still 'relevant' — as the young people say — to the needs and interests of society? Even if this great tradition can still be transmitted, the question is now sometimes asked whether it *should* be transmitted.

There are those who say that what they call the 'élitist' high culture of the past is no longer of concern to society today, that it is only the vested interests of a minority of professional academics that keeps it alive, that it is more important that our young people should study say the social significance of the comic strip or the language of social protest than that they should devote time and thought to encountering the works of that tiny minority that produced what another minority have become accustomed to consider classical works. This is a real argument; it concerns the nature of cultural continuity, the significance of quality in works of art, the degree to which culture that is fully appreciated by only a minority can be properly called a culture, and many other questions. Above all, it concerns what might be called cultural memory. If everything that does not speak immediately and effortlessly to the surface feelings and prejudices of the majority is condemned as 'élitist' and removed from our educational programme, then cultural memory is lost, a whole heritage of human thought and imagination is abandoned, and our culture becomes what an individual would become with loss of memory, the helpless product of a series of discontinuous impressions. The nature of cultural memory, the relation between tradition and progress (in the arts as in other fields), the importance of awareness of how we come to be where we are in our social and cultural attitudes — all this constitutes not only an important but an urgent subject of investigation by the researcher in the humanities.

The matter is made all the more pressing by the increasing importance of leisure in our society. There can be no doubt that in the present and immediately foreseeable phases of technological development many areas of work that have hitherto been the sphere of people will become the sphere of increasingly sophisticated devices that will require only minimal human control. This means that employment will be permanently diminished, and the question of how people spend their leisure time will become increasingly important. Sociologists can study how people do in fact employ their leisure time, but it is the duty of the humanistic scholar to investigate ways in which the arts can enrich leisure, in which both understanding and appreciation of traditional arts and involvement in developing arts can make life fuller and more interesting for those who do not have to spend the greater part of their waking hours labouring in order to earn a living. If in the past the high culture of the western world has been available only to the privileged few, then the prospect that faces us today is that it can for the first time be made available for the leisured many. It must be added, however, that it is an oversimplification to say that the high culture of the past was always available only to a privileged few. Shakespeare appealed equally (and perhaps for different reasons) to groundlings and aristocrats and he is not unique in this respect. The conditions under which what came to be considered classics were available only to a small minority, together with such subjects as the relation of folk art and other forms of popular expression to 'high' art, are among the most significant topics requiring investigation by the humanistic researcher today. And they are all related to each other.

This question of relationship brings to the fore another important object of humanistic study as we should like to see it develop in the immediate future. This is in the field of interdisciplinary studies, where subjects that have developed as separate specialisms can be used to illuminate each other. It is hardly an exaggeration to say that in many fields of humanistic study, specialist work — by, for example, linguists, literary scholars, historians, psychologists — has gone as far as it can go without becoming involved in other fields. The fact that we have now such subjects as psycholinguists and sociolinguists, intellectual historians, social anthropologists, and so on, is an indication of how it has become necessary to move out of traditionally enclosed fields to seek illumination from other areas. As we have pointed out, the growth of the PhD system has meant the immense increase in specialization in humanistic higher education, but at the same time increasingly the areas of real growth have been those in which subjects intersect or interpenetrate each other. In the middle of the last century James Frederic Ferrier, Professor of Moral Philosophy in the University of St Andrews, invented the word 'Epistemology', theory of knowledge. The world has seen fit to take up this term and develop its implications, but it has not developed the parallel term he developed at the same time, 'Agnoiology', or theory of ignorance. But 'agnoiology' is in fact as relevant as 'epistemology', especially in a world of rapidly developing knowledge. There was a time in the history of the Western world when an educated man could be considered to have mastered virtually all the knowledge available in his culture. This was to an extent true in the Middle Ages. But with the explosion of knowledge in the Renaissance and after, it became increasingly difficult for any individual to be master of all available knowledge; as the sum of knowledge increased the proportion of it available to the individual became smaller, and we are faced with the paradox that increase of potential knowledge means increase of individual ignorance, if by increase of ignorance we mean knowledge of a progressively smaller proportion of what is known. Every new discovery in, say, astrophysics makes every one of us who is not an astrophysicist that much more ignorant. Ignorance therefore inevitably proliferates as knowledge advances. Boundaries close in as the material within each area becomes more abundant and complicated. 'That is not my field' becomes the cry of the scholar faced with something on the other side of the fence, as for example the classical scholar takes no responsibility for knowledge of what happened after the emergence of Alexander the Great.

At the same time something else has been happening: as we have pointed out, there comes a stage in the exploration of a limited subject when help has to be sought outside, and the solution to the problem posed by the theory of agnoiology as just defined has been in the exploration of inter-related areas, or rather in finding ways of seeing areas as inter-related that may not have been seen in that light before and then exploring the implications of that inter-relationship. Can we illuminate the tragic vision of Thomas Hardy by studying the text of his novels with care, perhaps showing how he was influenced by certain books he read as a young man, exploring something of the spirit of the age, and then perhaps raising the larger question of how that tragic vision was related to the tragic vision of, say, Aeschylus or Sophocles or Shakespeare? Or can we illuminate Hardy's pessimism by putting what the novels and poems say beside the fact of the great agricultural depression in England whose effects Hardy saw with profound concern as a young man? Should we study him by learning how to read his books with all the skills that literary criticism can provide, or by studying the influences that helped to form his mind, or by setting his work beside other great tragic writers, or by exploring the social and economic tragedy of his time that we know he was profoundly aware of? Or is it possible to combine these different insights into a comprehensive view of the nature of and meaning of Hardy's work? Some might say that the different disciplines involved are self-contained and cannot be synthesized. But in practice such syntheses are being produced in ever increasing numbers and nearly always illuminatingly. In studying the Victorian novel, is it helpful to employ the skills of the social historian and explore the impact of Moodie's library, with its insistence that novels should be in three volumes and its enormous influence on the sale of novels, or show how the practice of publishing novels in parts (with the socio-economic reasons for that practice) affected the actual form of novels? What were the socio-economic reasons for the drama becoming the most profound and exciting literary form in late Elizabethan and early Jacobean drama, whereas in the nineteenth century the novel performed the function that the drama performed in that earlier period? To discover the answers to these questions is to achieve new kinds of understanding of the way the literary imagination works in different situations. Psychology, sociology, history, biography, linguistics, are among the subjects that can be brought together with the analytic procedures of the formal literary critic to yield new insight into the meaning of literature. I take examples from literature because it is my own special field, but similar multi-disciplinary investigations have been developing in all humanistic subjects so as to increase our awareness of the human meaning involved in a great variety of products and activities.

There is one area of interdisciplinary research that is of common interest to both scientists and humanists, and that is the history of science. The exploration of how men came to give different answers to basic questions about the physical nature of the universe, of how and under what circumstances received answers came to be considered inadequate and new answers were sought, and the effect of all this on the way in which men reflected on the nature and meaning of their world (as revealed in, say, poetic images as well as in scientific works) is of profound interest and can bring together scholars of many different special concerns. To the humanistic student, the history of science is his best entry into science and to some scientists at least it has proved a way of fruitfully extending the bounds of their own interest. This is surely a growth subject, research into which may well help to bridge the great divide in our culture. If I may once more give a personal experience, I might mention that when I was professor at the University of Sussex, where we tried to explore all the possibilities of multidisciplinary studies, I once conducted a seminar together with the professor of physics, attended jointly by physicists and literary students, on the conditions under which old answers had to be rejected and new ones sought in both the sciences and the humanities, and it was a most intellectually exciting experience. What we need is research into the ways in which these kinds of subjects can be most effectively explored in our educational institutions.

Scientists and humanists can of course come together in other areas as well. It is one of the fallacies bequeathed to us by the Victorians that the ancient Greeks were an artistic rather than a scientific people, and that the language and thought of ancient Greece was therefore an appropriate study for someone on the arts side rather than on the science side. (It was the Victorians who first saw this as a real division between kinds of minds, a view that has been increasingly questioned in recent times.) But in fact the Greeks were primarily a scientific people: they did not even have a specific word for 'art' (their word 'techne' could refer equally to the art that designed the Parthenon and the craft of a cobbler making a pair of shoes) while they had many words for the sciences. As John Burnet once pointed out, the rediscovery of Greek in the Renaissance meant also the rediscovery of science, and it was through an exploration of the meaning of various Greek scientific terms that Renaissance science was able to begin where Greek science had left off. The career of Isaac Barrow (1630-1677), divine, sermon-writer, Greek scholar and mathematician, is most instructive for those interested in the relation between science and the humanities. Barrow gave up his professorship of Greek at Cambridge to become professor of geometry at Gresham College and then professor of mathematics at Cambridge (the newly founded Lucasian Chair). As professor of mathematics he lectured on Archimedes and Apollonius of Perga: one of his students was Isaac Newton, who learned from him the tradition of Greek higher mathematics and whose theory of fluxions owes much to the Greek mathematical term 'rhysis' of which it is a translation. An investigation of the conditions and ways in which 'art' and 'science' became opposing terms in Victorian education, to the extent that a pupil was considered to be suited for one *or* the other (a radically new development in the psychology of education) and the ways in which this view has affected the way both teachers and taught have subsequently behaved would be very rewarding.

Among individual subjects in the humanities we must single out philosophy as a special case since unlike other subjects it does not have a developing subject-matter. One of the problems in the study of literature is that as time advances there is more literature that ceases to be contemporary and is pushed back into the past to be studied as part of literary history. (There is also the quite separate fact that, pioneered in the United States, the study of the literature of one's own time is now regarded as academically desirable.) The subject therefore keeps growing and the problem of where to begin and what to leave out becomes ever more pressing. The same is true of the arts, and of all kinds of history. The Second World War is now as much a subject of historical research as the French Revolution was when I was a schoolboy. It is true that in literary and historical study scholars are often concerned with re-interpreting texts or events of the past. For the philosopher this is his major concern. He worries over what are substantially the same body of problems faced by his predecessors, although of course over a period of time once can observe definite shifts in perspective in the way in which a subject is approached (eg one generation may see as 'linguistic' questions which another generation sees as 'scientific'). But in general if one looks at what can be recognized as the traditional core of philosophy (metaphysics, theory of knowledge, philosophy of mind, ethics, political philosophy) and defines 'research' as what professional academic philosophers concern themselves with in books, articles and doctoral dissertations, then research in philosophy lies less in coming to terms with what is new than in working through some well-trodden field *for oneself*. Thus we may define research in philosophy as largely the re-thinking of old questions, not necessarily with a view to discovering new answers but in order to obtain the satisfaction of having come personally to grips with an established philosophical problem. This is not a barren study, but humanly rewarding and enriching.

Although what has just been described might be said to cover the bulk of 'research' in philosophy, there are also some areas of philosophy where genuinely new work seems to be going on. There is a new approach to the study of past philosophers, who have traditionally been read unhistorically as though their arguments can be understood as timeless abstractions and as though it were not necessary to understand fully the climate of ideas and opinion that prevailed when those philosophers wrote. The older tradition of history of philosophy paid little or no attention to whether the earlier philosophers would in fact have recognized themselves in the account of their ideas given by the historian and construed them as participating in a contemporary debate as such debates were conceived in the historian's own day. This has now given way increasingly to a revived interest in serious historical research in philosophy based on the recognition that shifts in concepts, background assumptions, the meaning of recurring key terms, and so on, really do occur and that much of the philosophical argument in any generation interacts with the scientific or political or theological or other concerns of its day, and that this happened to an even greater degree before philosophy became departmentalized in the modern university system. This kind of historical investigation is reflected in a number of recent publishing ventures. It is one of the most fruitful and promising of activities developing among academic philosophers and illustrates how philosophy in its own way is one of the many subjects in the humanities that is encouraging interdisciplinary work. It should be said that if this kind of philosophy is to be encouraged it requires the kind of resources (notably access to a great national or university library) that are only available in a few centres: it cannot be done at home, as the older kind of philosophy could be done.

Interdisciplinary studies are relevant to philosophical research in other ways than in writing the history of philosophy. The relation of logic to mathematics, of logic and philosophy of mind to computer science, of philosophy of social science to sociology, of theory of knowledge and philosophy of mind to psychology, the inter-relationship with other arts subjects through the study of aesthetics, and even the involvement of ethics with medicine, are some examples. There has also been a revival of interest in those aspects of philosophy that affect social, moral, legal and political life, and older questions about right and duty and obligation are beginning to be asked again (having been ousted for some generations by linguistic philosophy) and applied to actual contemporary problems. This is separate from, but no doubt has been influenced by, the impact of Marxist thought and the whole continental movement of Radical Philosophy which is having a belated influence in some areas of British philosophical study. The dropping in some quarters of the claims made in the recent past for the autonomy of philosophy as a subject, the recognition by some philosophers that they must master some other disciplines or body of facts in order to investigate issues involved in, say, euthanasia, minority rights or animal rights and not simply theorize in a vacuum, the mastery by some philosophers of the current literature on learning theory or artificial intelligence or sociobiology, to take only a few examples, in order to investigate the philosophical issues involved — all this reflects different ways in which philosophy and philosophical research is being involved with other subjects as well as with some practical issues of life.

In literary research the last two decades have seen a vast increase in the body of editorial commentary, in the form both of critical remarks and of all kinds of background information and explanation. This is in addition to the great modern advance in bibliograplhical studies and textual criticism already referred to. Editorial work, both on literary and on historical documents (and of course on works that are of interest equally to both literary scholars and historians, such as Pepys' *Diary*, where the nine-volume Latham-Matthews edition is a triumph of modern editorial scholarship) is a conspicuous feature of modern literary study. In English literature editorial attention has traditionally been devoted to poems and plays, but recently there has been a move towards the editing of prose, including novels, applying both modern textual scholarly methods and the beginnings of what appears to be a developing sophistication in the critical handling of works of prose fiction. There is much scope for expansion along these lines. What is involved is not armchair criticism but appropriate methodologies applied with knowledge, skill and perceptiveness. A major literary text edited in this way is one of the most important contributions a literary researcher can make and the publishing of such work a primary function of an academic press. Both the researcher and the publisher need material support to achieve editorial work of the required scope and scale, and it is sad to see some editorial projects abandoned by publishers on the grounds that they have not the economic resources to undertake publication.

Bibliographical aids of all kinds have been appearing in response to the demand of editors and researchers. The most significant new instrument here is the Arts and Humanities Citation Index, which will put the early stages of humanistic research on a quite new footing. There is also the prospect of computer applications, still in their infancy but rapidly growing. Already the compilation of reference books has been revolutionized, the first kind to profit being concordances. A concordance to the work of a major writer has long been recognized as a most valuable aid to acquiring insights into the way the writer's mind and imagination worked. Lane Cooper of Cornell University, humanist, classical and English scholar and literary critic, who flourished in the 1920s and 1930s, used to maintain that a proper concordance was one of the great peaks of literary research and he encouraged the production of concordances at Cornell. Each one — on a major poet such as Wordsworth for example — took many years of patient work to compile. Now, with computerization, the work is done in a tiny fraction of the time that used to be taken, and in consequence the number of concordances is increasing at an enormous rate. In this connection the older concept of the humanistic scholar working alone in his study or in a great library without the need of any of the apparatus required by the scientist has become outdated. A former dean of the faculty of arts, himself a professor of Italian, at one of our great universities recently wrote to me:

'I had an awful job as Dean to get *equipment* money out of the university for the modern tools of our job, partly because my older colleagues still think you only need a pen and a box of cards. But in the modern European languages the sheer financial problems of getting adequate access to the prime sources when they are in continental libraries is enough to deter any but the most determined researcher. We *do* need funding similar to that of the Science and Social Science Research Councils. . . .'

It is not only, therefore, in the preparation of computerized indexes that equipment is necessary. In modern languages especially, for reasons given in the remarks just quoted as well as for aid in the actual teaching of foreign languages, a variety of sophisticated equipment is now necessary if techniques of teaching are to be fully explored and exploited. The whole question of language teaching requires continuous research, and one of the problems of university modern linguists is that they are too busy with their day-to-day teaching to take time off and do research on the applied side of their work. There is much more to be done than sitting students down in a language laboratory, and it is surprising that with the expansion of theoretical inquiry into the nature of language, which flourishes now in a state of lively belligerence, there is nothing really commensurate on the applied side.

Here then is something that needs nurturing and funding, not only to improve teaching techniques in a subject that has proved, especially in Britain, so often unresponsive to teaching, or at least not as responsive as might have been expected, but also because in a world of progressively interlocking economies, of the EEC and of multi-national economic structures, the acquiring of modern languages becomes more and more the duty of a responsible citizen. The alternative of a world in which everybody speaks a kind of basic business English, which is a real possibility, would involve an intolerabe degree of cultural impoverishment, and institutions of higher education should do everything possible to rule it out.

On the literary rather than the linguistic side, one of the important developments in recent times is a second wave of comparative studies, after the lull of the 40s and 50s. Many universities now provide degree structures that allow for the study of English with a European or classical language and literature. But this in itself does not provide an adequate basis for true comparative research, which requires not only an inwardness with more than one language but also a familiarity with a vast body of critical and scholarly material in at least two literatures. This puts off many potential researchers, but those that do enter this field are producing really interesting work (Lary's *Dickens and Dostoievsky* is one example out of many) that points in an exciting direction.

While on the one hand literary studies have benefited enormously from an interdisciplinary approach, involving history, biography, psychology, aesthetics and other subjects, on the other there has been a recent development of interest in genre theory, which leads to the re-writing of literary history in terms of generic development rather than of influences, individual bodies of work, and so on. This is a minority movement in Britain, which has not been traditionally very hospitable to this kind of literary historiography, but it is presenting an interesting challenge to accepted methods of literary-historical research. (One must distinguish this approach from that of the American so-called 'New Criticism' that flourished in the 1940s and 1950s: this insisted on the timelessness and virtual anonymity of every individual work of literary art and regarded literary history as virtually a contradiction in terms. This approach bred no research that really deserved the name.) Another challenge has been presented by the theories of structuralists and attempts to apply them in practical criticism. This shows an openness to Continental influences that is not common in literary criticism in this country, and it has been vigorously challenged. However, the work of structuralists and their opponents, while contributing to a lively debate on the nature of literature and of literary criticism, can hardly be said to constitute research. Whether there is future for research in this area remains to be seen. But certainly there is scope for fruitful research into modern developments in literary theory.

More and more universities are now interested in the possibilities of providing graduate students with formal training in the methodology of research in the humanities. This used to be a matter that was left for the student himself to discover, with the help of advice from a supervisor. But the isolation of research students in arts subjects, most of whom are working alone on individual projects, has been noted as both socially and intellectually undesirable, and attempts have been made to provide social facilities that will bring them together as well as opportunities to exchange ideas and inform each other of the results of their research. This is a new dimension in postgraduate study of the humanities in our universities and one that requires encouragement and expansion. Formal training in the methodology of research is another matter, yet it is related to the question of the isolation of the humanities research student, for courses in research method bring research students together regularly in a way no other academic device can. But of course the main function of such courses is not social but educational. It is now generally accepted that, particularly in view of the sophistication of much modern research even in the humanities, formal courses in research method are most desirable. Oxford pioneered here as long ago as the 1930s, when research students in English literature were required to take courses in bibliography and textual criticism, the history of English studies and similar subjects before they could be registered as candidates for a higher degree. Cambridge followed with something similar in the 1950s, more as a result of efforts by individual dons than as a result of officially accepted theory: some dons lent their rooms for the discussion of papers by research students both with their fellow research students and with members of the university teaching staff. Almost all universities now provide some courses and some social facilities for postgraduate students in the humanities.

Whether a high degree should be granted entirely as a result of course work is a matter now much discussed by those involved in research in the humanities. There is much to be said for it. Enlarging one's perspective by involving oneself in a number of different special subjects, with a 'research paper' of limited scope done for each, may well provide a better training for a university teacher than long continued concentration on a single topic. Whether this would add up to 'research' as commonly defined is a matter of opinion. But certainly more and more universities, especially in the USA and Canda, are thinking of research in the humanities in this way and awarding the PhD degree entirely on the results of course work.

In this connection an interesting paradox might be mentioned. On the one hand the student of today vociferously asserts his independence; students run their own affairs through their unions and in many other ways insist on being treated like wholly responsible adults. Yet in the matter of research modern postgraduates are much less independent than their predecessors of of a few generations ago. I have already mentioned my own experience as a research student at Oxford, when I was left entirely to myself. But even if one was not left entirely alone and had a supervisor with whom one could consult about the progress of one's work, such consultations were infrequent and the bulk of the student's time was spent working alone. Today the research student is much more demanding; he wants continuous advice and help; and the role of a supervisor — quite apart from the function of courses in research method and so on — is to provide continuous guidance and be always available both to listen to what the student has to say and to provide his own views on how the student is doing. One result of this is that the universities today invest much more manpower in the guidance of research students than they used to, and the trend continues. An unexpected result of this closer relationship between research student and supervisor is that when the thesis is submitted the supervisor can appear to be as much on trial as the student. In some universities a supervisor is automatically disqualified from examining the finished work of a student he has supervised; in others he is automatically one of the examiners. There are problems and confusions here that require sorting out.

At the post-doctoral level the researcher is of course on his own and expected to be. Yet even here the provision of an environment where other researchers working on related subjects are part of the social and intellectual milieu is conducive to more effective research. There is little provision for this in British universities. The Institute for Advanced Studies in the Humanities at Edinburgh University is the sole example of its kind in the country. It has a very limited budget and operates on a small scale, in contrast, say, with the Institute of Advanced Studies at Princeton. Yet even on this limited scale the value of having a dozen or so senior researchers having study rooms in the same building, meeting daily over tea or coffee, giving talks and conducting seminars for anybody interested, is unquestionable. There are many ways of combating the loneliness of the research worker in the humanities, and the provision of such facilities for post-doctoral researchers in perhaps the most fruitful of all. The problem remains of how to fund such facilities, which are not a recognized part of a British university's budget.

The problem of funding research in the humanities in a period of prolonged economic recession when expenditure on all kinds of education is being cut and every educational activity that cannot be expected to lead directly to increase of material productivity is under suspicion, is clearly of enormous proportions. Although, as has been noted, high unemployment means that new opportunities for the use of leisure must be investigated, recognition of this necessity does not of itself bring government funds for such a purpose. It seems clear that in the foreseeable future, however urgent a case can be made out for the importance of research into what might be called the social function of the humanities (especially the arts), there will be no adequate government funding of it.

It has been suggested that in such circumstances it is important to investigate untapped resources in industry and commerce. Patronage of the arts used to be an important function of rich private individuals and of firms. Edinburgh University's McEwan Hall and the city's Usher Hall were both financed by brewers. Oxbridge colleges have in our own time been financed by wealthy industrialists. It is claimed that many of today's great multi-national companies are conscious of their image as philistine materialists and anxious to change it by public demonstration of their concern with the humanities, and that substantial endowments could be obtained from them if they were approached in the proper way — that is, by suggesting what universities and other institutions concerned with research in the humanities can do for them rather than the other way round. In other words, we can offer a vast public improvement of their image. A large endowment for significant research in the humanities, publicized as coming from a particular company and perhaps involving a building or a Chair bearing the name of the company, would be a striking way of demonstrating interest in things of the spirit. Only a few months ago an enterprising lecturer in history at Edinburgh University was able, in the course of a relatively brief conversation, to persuade a firm of whisky blenders to give £30,000 to fund an on-going seminar in mediaeval history. The seminar bears the name of the whisky — which is Antiquary, and therefore of some relevance to history! — and the firm thinks itself well served by the project. Distinguished mediaeval historians from all over Europe are brought to Edinburgh at regular intervals to give lecturers and conduct seminars under the Antiquary name. This is a small example of what might be done by way of involving industry and commerce in sponsorship of research in the humanities. Unlike the Americans, the British have little experience of fund-raising for universities among private industry. We already have some private sponsorship of theatre, ballet and sports. It is argued that this could be greatly extended to cover research in the humanities if the proper kind of approach were made and the appropriate kind of publicity for the donor guaranteed.

It is of course important to suggest subjects for research in the humanities that are relevant to society and promise to strengthen our culture. At the same time we must beware of trying to define too closely in advance exactly what any given research project sets out to achieve. Some of the most remarkable achievements in both science and the humanities have been brought about by people who started with something very different in mind from what eventually emerged. Flexibility of research is important, and while it is also important to define questions that require an answer one must not exclude the possibility of research devoted to one question turning up not only unexpected answers but also unexpected new questions. No endowment of research in the humanities should be so constricting that it discourages the researcher from following wherever his or her discoveries lead.

If one asks academics in the field of humanities what they most require in order to pursue their research, the answer most often given is 'time'. In the present economic climate, paid study leave for academics is becoming more and more unrealistic. Yet, with the increase of teaching load resulting from the cutting back of academic staff, it is more than ever necessary if academics are to produce the research they can do and want to do. Of course not all academic teachers are or wish to be researchers. It can be argued that researching and teaching are different activities not necessarily requiring the same kinds of skill. In the last century Sir David Brewster maintained that a research scientist should be freed from the drudgery of teaching, and there have been humanists who have taken a similar view. But certainly at least a proportion of academic teachers in the humanities as in other subjects should be working on the frontiers of knowledge in some area: that provides a kind of intellectual excitement that is important for the general atmosphere of a university. Whether one should have also research professorships with no teaching function at all is largely an economic question. Britain certainly cannot afford them in the humanities today. But if there were throughout the country a limited number of institutes for advanced study in the humanities financed perhaps from industrial and economic sources as already suggested this would be better than an occasional research professor working alone. There are certainly, as this chapter has tried to suggest, enough subjects crying out for exploration.

I should like to add a brief postscript after talking over some of the points raised here with other members of the SRHE Leverhulme seminar. I think I probably underestimated the amount of team work being carried out by researchers in the humanities. While it is true that most humanistic researchers work alone, there are some important team projects that are crying out for more adequate funding. They include projects in lexicography, editing, historical inquiry and archaeology. One such project I am personally concerned with, the Dictionary of the Older Scottish Tongue, which has been going on for about sixty years and is still far from complete is slowed down for lack of funds, and this is true of many others. I single this one out as it is a great national project, unique in Scotland, parallel to and not as well funded as national dictionaries in other European countries.

Another point that emerged in discussion is the relationship between research and teaching and the ambiguities involved in terms like 'research' and 'scholarship'. A closer investigation into the ways in which we use these terms and the different kinds of relationship between research and teaching that exist in different subjects and different situations would be well worth while.

NOTES

1 Not invariably, however. The 'Boswell factory' at Yale is an outstanding example of co-operative literary research in the field of editorial scholarship.
2 John Burnet (1929) *Essays and Addresses* London (p.34)

SEMINAR DISCUSSION

The discussion brought out a number of differences between 'research' in the humanities and the natural sciences. These differences included the following:
— Teaching and research seem to be more essentially interlocked in the humanities than in sciences.
— Scholarship with its emphasis on synthesis and reflective inquiry is a much more important activity in the humanities, although several participants argued for more scholarship in the sciences too.
— Scientific research is primarily creative and only secondarily critical of what has gone before. The creative people in the humanities are the novelist, the poet and the artist. Academics provide a critique of what the creative people do.
— Research in the humanities is done mainly by 'artisans', whereas in the natural sciences teamwork is often required.
— Research in the humanities is much less expensive than in the sciences.

It is important to recognize these differences since they have important policy implications. They mean, for example, that it is extremely difficult to formulate research policies which apply 'across the board' to all disciplines. It also means that it is unnecessary to advocate the establishment of a research council for the humanities. However, the polytechnics do not receive research funds from the local education authorities and they have to depend on local philanthropy for much of their humanities research funding.

Much research in the humanities tends to be what was called coal face research. This is where the researcher chips away at revealing small (and often trivial) bits of knowledge. These bits need to be synthesized, which is what is done by those who are engaged in scholarship. This point was further elaborated. The specialized approach seems to have been absorbed from the sciences where progress is usually achieved through increased specialization and fragmentation. Not only did this fragmentation affect how research was done but also the entire education system from school to the PhD. Some participants argued for a new approach to education which was based on synthesis and integration, which taught science in a social context, and which included the study of the evolution of scientific ideas.

A possible consequence of the emphasis of scholarship and critique in the humanities is that the PhD degree should only be awarded to those who could demonstrate maturity of judgement. This would mean that postgraduate training in the humanities should be delayed for a number of years beyond a first degree. This point was raised but not sufficiently debated for all the implications to be determined. It was agreed, however, that it merited further consideration.

6

POSTGRADUATE TRAINING OF RESEARCHERS

by Wendy Hirsh

A country's research capability is mainly a matter of manpower. We can always invest more heavily in laboratories or equipment, but it is not so easy to increase rapidly the supply of people with the theoretical knowledge, ability, imagination and motivation needed for research work. At present we assume that the need for researchers is best met by selecting some of our academically most able graduates and giving them three years in which to carry out one major research project and write a thesis.

Indeed, we expect the PhD to do more than contribute to the supply of research manpower, and it can be seen to have at least four possible functions:

1. Training for employment in teaching and research in the higher education system
2. Training for other, mainly research, employment outside academia
3. Providing students with the opportunity for study at a high level
4. Contributing directly to research

This chapter examines how effectively the PhD and alternative forms of postgraduate training in Britain satisfy these sometimes conflicting requirements. It also reviews current policy responses to the pressures on postgraduate training and identifies areas where issues remain unresolved.

THE DEVELOPMENT OF POSTGRADUATE TRAINING IN BRITAIN

Although the Masters degree has a long though somewhat uneven history in British universities, the PhD as we know it today is a comparatively recent innovation. By the turn of the century most universities, except Oxford and Cambridge, were offering 'genuine' Masters degrees, based on a period of further study. Doctorates were also awarded for original research, but these were gained after considerable periods of study (usually five years). Rudd (1975) traces the modern three-year PhD as an import from Germany. It was taken on somewhat reluctantly by the British universities in 1918 as a result of pressure from the United States and Canada, countries wishing to send students to Britain for such studies.

The Scale of Postgraduate Training

Rapid growth in postgraduate education was a dramatic feature of the 1960s, brought about by the creation of the first research councils and the exceptional growth in higher education as a whole. Postgraduate students represented one in sixteen of all students in 1959, and one in six students by 1972 (Rudd 1975).

Overall growth continued through the early 1970s before levelling off, although full-time home science student numbers actually fell between 1974-5 and 1979-80. This period was also characterized by an increasing proportion of overseas students who accounted for 37 per cent of the 19,300 higher degrees awarded by the universities in 1979-80, and over half of those in engineering and technology (USR 1981). Many courses would not be viable if overseas numbers dropped substantially. Thirty-two per cent of the higher degrees awarded by the universities in 1979-80 were PhDs, the corresponding figure for home students being 34 per cent. The polytechnics also expanded postgraduate courses during the 1970s, concentrating on business and technological studies.

By 1979-80 there were 83,000 postgraduate students, of whom 39 per cent were studying part time, 26 per cent were from overseas and 11 per cent were studying in polytechnics. Ninety-four per cent of home full-time science postgraduates were studying in universities and of these 63 per cent were taking research, rather than taught, courses. Of the part-time postgraduates, a much lower proportion (64 per cent) were in universities although they were just as likely to be taking research degrees as the full-time university postgraduates.

TABLE 6.1
Postgraduate students in universities and polytechnics 1979-80

		Home students	Overseas students	Total
SCIENCES	Full-time	17427	11883	29310
	Part-time	15419	2011	17430
	Total	32846	13894	46740
OTHER SUBJECTS	Full-time	14958	6188	21146
	Part-time	13310	1779	15089
	Total	28268	7967	36235
ALL SUBJECTS	Full-time	32385	18071	50456
	Part-time	28729	3790	32519
	Total	61114	21861	82975

Source
ABRC 1982

Purpose and Content
No less important than the substantial growth in postgraduate training over the last twenty years have been fundamental changes in its perceived purpose and therefore its balance and content. These have resulted from the considerable national discussion which has taken place concerning the relationship between training in science and engineering, and industrial employment. The issue at postgraduate level has centred on whether the PhD should be viewed as an apprenticship in academic research or be modified to provide both research and manpower more closely geared to industry. With an increasing variety of other postgraduate courses available (particularly Masters degrees), the issue also arises whether these alternative to the PhD may provide more suitable training for some kinds of research work.

The rapid growth in postgraduate students following the Robbins Report (1963) was at least in part justified by the demand both for university teachers and for highly trained scientists in industry. As early as 1965 the Arthur Report found that industrial employers willingly recruited higher degree graduates in engineering and technology, but were unwilling to send their own employees for such training. The growing concern in the late 1960s was that industry was suffering from shortages of qualified scientists and engineers (CMRST 1966). This was pursued in recommendations for increasing training in science and technology (Dainton 1968), reducing the 'brain drain' (Jones 1967) and making industrial careers more attractive (Swann 1968). Swann also questioned the value of the traditional PhD as preparation for industrial employment, and recommended shorter periods of postgraduate study based on advanced courses rather than research. Bosworth (1966) was thinking along similar lines for bridging the gap between university and employment in industry by much more flexible postgraduate training.

Meanwhile there were also wider pressures to improve collaboration in research between universities and industry (CBI 1970) which have inevitably influenced the type of research projects undertaken by PhD students. By the early 1970s it was clearly assumed that the employment by industry of PhD scientists and engineers was desirable, and that to this end their research projects shoud be more closely geared to industrial problems.

This shift in emphasis towards industry was reinforced during the 1970s by the development of new fields of industrial employment (such as computing for scientists and management services for social scientists) and the simultaneous decline in the academic labour market for PhDs. The Science Research Council (SRC) began to respond by limiting awards in subjects with little scope for industrial application and encouraging growth in such fields as statistics, operational research and computer science (SRC 1972). Taught Masters courses in such subjects were also expanded.

The 1980s were also characterized by a series of reports from government, the research councils and the academics (usually as represented by the Committee of Vice-Chancellors and Principals) arguing out the extent to which university research, including the PhD, should or could be geared to industry's needs. The recommended shift towards 'total technology' training as proposed in the Horlock Report (SRC 1971) was adopted in modified form and on a small scale by the SRC (1973), which also introduced Co-operative Awards in Science and Engineering (CASE), supported more taught courses and joint initiatives with the Social Science Research Council (SSRC) and considered differential grants for students in subjects of 'economic importance' (SRC 1975).

Much more radical proposals for industrially oriented postgraduate training were put forward by the House of Commons Expenditure Committee (Expenditure Committee 1974), and strongly opposed by the Committee of Vice-Chancellors and Principals (CVCP 1975) who reasserted the value of the PhD as a 'training for independent scholars and research workers at the highest level'. Government responded (DES 1976) by advocating planning for postgraduate education in response to 'the needs of the economy and society as a whole', but sat on the fence with regard to how these needs should be identified and met. Decisions on content and balance were left to 'the autonomous interaction of the institutions themselves, the research councils and employers'.

The SRC has continued to finance schemes for bringing postgraduate training closer to industry, although it has suffered from lack of student demand (SRC 1976). Meanwhile the pendulum still swings between those with a strongly industrial view of education (Finniston 1980) and the academics' determination to maintain some balance between applied and basic research (CVCP 1980 and 1981). The social sciences, although less publicly debated, have been subject to the same pressures to favour research aimed at meeting 'identifiable national needs' (Public Accounts Committee 1979). The arts and humanities, having no obvious relevance to industry, have not been the subject of any real public debate. The wisdom of encouraging postgraduate training in engineering and applied subjects, and PhD topics of direct interest to industry, can only be evaluated on the basis of whether there is evidence that industry has a real need for people with this kind of training.

THE EMPLOYMENT OF HIGHER DEGREE GRADUATES

Information on the first employment of higher degree graduates is published by the Universities Statistical Record (USR 1981) although it cannot be regarded, for various practical reasons, as a very complete or reliable picture. In particular it only shows the destination of those who were awarded higher degrees and therefore excludes failures and drop-outs. The first feature of note is that higher degree graduates still apparently have a relatively low level of unemployment (2.7 per cent for home students in 1979-80), although it is higher for advanced course students and in arts subjects.

Of home higher degree graduates entering permanent home employment in 1979-80, 33 per cent entered the education sector (18 per cent the universities), 39 per cent entered industry and commerce, and 23 per cent entered public service. High proportions of these graduates went into scientific research, design or development work (23 per cent overall and 59 per cent in engineering) and teaching and lecturing (23 per cent overall and 54 per cent in arts subjects).

PhDs are more likely than Masters graduates to enter academic employment or find jobs in research or scientific functions in industry (ABRC 1982).

Academic Employment
One function of the PhD is to provide training for those wishing to pursue academic careers. The possession of this qualification has become increasingly necessary for those seeking academic appointments (Robbins 1963; Blackstone and Williams 1972; Gibb 1977) and its effectiveness as a training for teaching in higher education goes apparently unquestioned. A large proportion of higher degree graduates, particularly PhDs, have traditionally found employment in the higher education system.

The boom period for academic jobs was the 1960s. According to Williams (1973) 42 per cent of all higher degree graduates entering home employment in 1965 found jobs in universities. The corresponding figure for PhDs alone was higher at 53 per cent (Williams et al. 1974). By 1971 the figure for all higher degree graduates had fallen to 22 per cent and by 1975-6 USR figures show a further fall to 18 per cent, the same as the 1979-80 figure. These figures all refer to those higher degree graduates entering home employment. The 1979-80 figure in fact represents only 7 per cent of all home higher degree graduates, and this only rises to 8 per cent by including polytechnic employment. Not surprisingly, the competition for university posts has become intense (Gibb 1977).

In addition to permanent teaching posts, the universities and polytechnics also employ researchers who often have higher degrees and are usually on short-term contracts. Such posts are mainly in science but also important in social science where they could account for about half the entry of postgraduates to university employment (IMS 1981a). The dangers of such short-term posts have been recognized both in Britain (Expenditure Committee 1974; Platt 1976) and in the United States (Cartter 1971). They can easily lead to an increasing backlog of good researchers who have little chance of gaining permanent academic employment. The research councils are beginning to intervene to a very limited extent, for example with the Special Replacement Scheme of the Science and Engineering Research Council (SERC, previously the SRC).

Sufficient data is available on university staff (through the Universities Statistical Record) to enable projections of new recruits to be made, based on various assumptions concerning future growth (or decline) in numbers of posts. Williams (1974) used fairly simple calculations to show that, even with continued growth, less than 10 per cent of higher degree graduates would enter university employment in the 1980s. Further modelling work (Hirsh and Morgan 1978) came out with similar findings. Growth of the order of 5 per cent per annum would be needed to restore the prospects of academic employment for postgraduates to the level which existed in the early 1970s. Even ignoring the acute short-term problems faced by universities and polytechnics, the academic labour market will only employ relatively small numbers of higher degree graduates for the foreseeable future. This will present particular problems for those subjects, such as the pure sciences and humanities, where higher degree graduates have been particularly dependent on university employment.

In addition to the fundamental reduction in the need for recruits to university teaching, the academic labour market is particularly sensitive to short-term policy fluctuations. The University Grants Committee (UGC 1976) drew attention to the drastic effect on postgraduates of freezing 500 academic posts in 1974-5. The postgraduate inevitably bears most of the burden of adjustment in any short period of reduction in university recruitment. This problem is particularly noticeable in small subjects where the universities have been major employers. For example, only about 50 PhD students in French were finishing their studies each year in the mid-1970s. This number was actually too low to maintain stocks of university teachers at a constant level, but clearly too high for university requirements in a period of cutback (Hirsh and Morgan 1978). This volatility of the academic labour market makes it difficult for universities, funding bodies or, indeed, students to plan on the basis of the future labour market for university teachers. In the short-term, cuts in university and polytechnic budgets seem likely to remove the academic labour market altogether for several cohorts of young researchers.

Non-Academic Employment

If we are to pursue a labour market-based approach to postgraduate training, then it is necessary to determine whether there is a real market demand for higher degree graduates outside the academic sector. The apparent willingness of employers to absorb such graduates does not, of itself, show that they are seen as having anything special to offer. In the arts, for example, higher degree graduates failing to gain academic employment tend to opt for school teaching, the Civil Service and a wide variety of other jobs where there is little evidence of a strong demand for their specific skills. In the sciences, PhDs may well apply for jobs which they could have entered with first degrees (UMS 1974).

The labour market for research social scientists is clouded by the large numbers of higher degree courses which amount to professional qualifications, such as those in town planning and educational psychology. The labour market for such qualifications is certainly well defined but extremely erratic in its demands. As the Director of the CSU put it to the Education, Science and Arts Committee (1980): 'there is in fact no course so irrelevant to the job market as one designed for a monoply employer who has just put up the shutters.'

Excluding such narrowly vocational courses, a recent survey carried out for the SSRC (IMS 1981a) found little specific demand outside the academic sector for postgraduate social scientists. The Civil Service, for example, tended to favour postgraduate economists, but would be recruiting only about ten per annum in future. Of all the social science postgraduates employed in industry, half had taken business studies and one fifth economics. Masters degrees tended to be favoured more than PhDs in subjects such as economics (UMS 1974) and psychology (Howarth and Harris 1974) but not many of their jobs could really be called 'research'. Employers saw a likely short-term drop in demand in most sectors and there was little evidence that stronger policies on the recruitment of social science postgraduates would develop.

The real nature of industrial demand for scientists and engineers with higher degrees is very difficult to determine. This is partly because diverse industries have widely different kinds of research and development activities. They therefore require not only varying subject backgrounds in their recruits but also have varying attitudes to the balance between specialist and general skills. The market is easiest to identify in those cases where industrial research is very similar indeed to that carried out in universities. The pharmaceutical industry, for example, uses research techniques mainly developed in the academic world and employs PhDs trained in these techniques in its research function (IMS 1981b). Within the wider context of industrial employment, it appears that the Masters degree is viewed as a suitable training for design and development work, but not so much for fundamental research (UMS 1974).

Very often, however, industry expresses its demands for trained manpower in terms far too specific to be met by any course as long as a PhD or perhaps even an MSc. For example, the Royal Institute of Chemistry (ABRC 1982) has drawn attention to 'a surplus of geologists, but a shortage of Petroleum Geologists, Geophysicists and Petroleum and Reservoir Engineers'. Such needs can only be met rapidly by short industry-sponsored courses.

In the case of engineering, there is considerable evidence that industry, although willing to employ PhDs, does not value them highly. The Finniston Report (1980) only dwells long enough on the engineering PhD to dismiss it and Swinnerton-Dyer (ABRC 1982) has also concluded that PhDs in engineering 'seem to get the same jobs at the same salaries that they could have got three years earlier when they graduated.'

In spite of industry's tendency to express opinions about qualifications in specific subject areas, the qualities of higher degree graduates which are actually valued by industrial employers appear to be more general. They include intellectual ability, maturity, breadth of experience and initiative and independence (ABRC 1982). This would tend to argue against attempting to produce highly specialized postgraduates in subject areas closely geared to current needs as expressed by industrial employers.

There are three further factors which reinforce this view. First, the research and development function in industry is notoriously subject to stop-go policies, making forward planning for particular kinds of recruits very hazardous. Secondly, substitution between subjects and levels of qualification, even in the research function, appears to be possible and even beneficial (Bosworth 1981). Thirdly, recruits into industry are actually entering careers in research which may span many years and many changes of technology, and quite often lead to research management or movement out of research altogether. Companies, in their desire to control manpower growth, are having to use all employees, including scientists and engineers, much more flexibly during the course of their careers.

Consideration of the labour market for higher degree graduates outside the universities offers little evidence of any research employment in the humanities (UMS 1974) and there appears to be a limited demand for those with extended professional training (eg in economics and business studies) in the social sciences. There is almost no evidence of any demand for PhDs in engineering but the same cannot really be said of other science subjects. The complex pattern of industry's needs for various kinds of research and development manpower appears to span both PhD and MSc graduates at present, but our understanding of these labour markets is still limited and based on the often contradictory views of employers. The practical problems of dealing with this kind of labour market and the views of employers on the skills they really value appear to argue against gearing the PhD to industry's short-term requirements for specialists.

STUDENT DEMAND
So far, higher degrees have been discussed in relation to the demand for highly trained manpower in the academic sector and elsewhere. The student view has largely been left out of the discussion, but is essential to the policy makers in two respects. Firstly, those bodies which support postgraduate training claim to take student demand into account in the way they allocate funds. Secondly, new types of courses aimed at new labour markets depend for their success on student response. It was our earlier disregard of student attitudes which led to the creation of undergraduate places in engineering in the 1960s which could not be filled.

The Level of Student Demand
In general there are more students who wish to take postgraduate study than there are places. Even allowing for multiple applications, Swinnerton-Dyer (ABRC 1982) estimated that 1.7 students applied for each postgraduate science place in universities in 1978-9. Application rates in the sciences were highest in biological science, followed by social and physical science, and lowest in engineering.

The research councils are by no means the only supporters of postgraduate students (other government agencies, local authorities and universities and colleges also contribute) but they do fund a high and increasing proportion of full-time students in science and engineering. The Department of Education and Science (DES) has a significant role in the funding of students in the humanities. All the research councils and the DES report a buoyant demand for postgraduate awards. The SERC has reported increasing surpluses of applicants over awards available (850 in 1980-81) and has only suffered from rather low student demand in engineering and the CASE scheme. The SSRC has recently had to impose severe cuts in postgraduate support, now down to about 880 awards each year (about half the 1974-5 number). It not surprisingly reports considerable excess student demand. The DES offered 884 studentships in 1981-2 and had three times that number of applicants. Budgetary cuts have left them unable to maintain the 'rule' of giving studentships to 20 per cent of those who obtained first or upper second class degrees.

In spite of apparently uncertain employment prospects, British students still seem eager for postgraduate study. The increase in part-time students might also reflect a shortage of funding for full-time study.

Reasons for Study

The reasons why postgraduate students embark on their studies were extensively examined for earlier cohorts of students in two large surveys (Rudd and Hatch 1968; Rudd 1975). Rudd found that research students had three main types of reasons for study. The largest group were the 'dedicated scholars' who were motivated by interest in the subject, although this was often coupled with the desire for an academic career. The second group were seeking to improve their general career prospects. The third group were 'drifters' who stayed on in university because they liked university life and did not want to do anything else. Students taking taught higher degrees were more likely than research students to be interested in general improvement of their careers, but a fair number were still seeking academic employment.

A later study of PhDs in mechanical engineering, mathematics and French was conducted when the academic labour market had started to decline (Hirsh 1978). As one might expect, the students in mathematics and French had shifted their rationalization for study towards that of purely intellectual interest. The home engineers, on the other hand, contained an alarming proportion of 'drifters' (42 per cent), possibly as a result of the relatively high availability of postgraduate awards in this subject. The small sample of post-experience and part-time engineers were mainly dissatisfied with careers in industry and were hoping to use postgraduate study as a route into academic employment.

The study also confirmed Rudd's view (1975) that students see themselves as encouraged by academics to undertake postgraduate study. Those coming from industry, however, were unlikely to have been encouraged by their employers.

Employment Aspirations and Expectations
It was not surprising that when Rudd (1975) conducted his study in the mid-1960s, 54 per cent of research students in pure and applied science and 83 per cent of those in arts and social sciences were hoping for academic employment. However, even in the mid-1970s, research students were just as likely to be seeking university careers (Hirsh 1978). Although the students in mathematics and French could rationalize their reason for study as purely intellectual, it did not help them to feel any less frustrated when the university job they hoped for seemed unlikely to materialize. Research fellowships were seen as a short-term alternative by the mathematics students, while those in French reconciled themselves to school teaching or the Civil Service. The engineering students saw industrial research and development as an acceptable alternative to academic research, but they did not regard industrial careers with any great enthusiasm.

The Dilemma of Student Demand
Any desire to escape from postgraduate policies based on labour market needs to those based on student demand raises very profound problems. The students attracted to PhD study seem to be very slow to respond to changes in the academic labour market. Rudd (1973) seems to have been right in his assumption that those who really want academic careers are very difficult to deter. Even the knowledge that university jobs will be scarce does not apparently prevent many PhD graduates from seeking them and feeling intense frustration when they cannot obtain permanent posts. In engineering, where student demand has virtually been met, many of the students expect to enter industry but without particularly positive motivation towards this career, or indeed towards their reasons for study in the first place. To put it bluntly, a policy of meeting student demand for full-time PhD study may be a way of allowing some students merely to delay entry to industry and others to cultivate lifelong feelings of frustration.

THE CONTRIBUTION OF RESEARCH STUDENTS TO RESEARCH
The immediate contribution which research students make to research output is not used as a justification for such study, but is a useful by-product to which the universities have become accustomed and one the research councils certainly acknowledge (ABRC 1982). Rudd (1975) found senior academics relying on research students for much of their research manpower and also, by taking on teaching duties, giving lecturers additional time to carry out research. Swinnerton-Dyer (ABRC 1982) found 60 per cent of university departments in the sciences claiming that PhD students made a significant contribution to research effort.

The nature of this contribution may well be different in the various subject areas. In biological sciences, for example, the necessity to conduct long experiments requires the use of research students or research assistants. In the arts, where academics tend to discriminate between research and that higher achievement they usually call scholarship, the PhD may on rare occasions result in a work of great importance, but more often had led to a lifetime's interest in a particular subject.

At least two of the trends in postgraduate training may well have an impact on research output, namely the shift towards applied research and the pressure (to be examined in the next section) to improve completion rates for study. The increased emphasis on applied research in the sciences seems mainly a reflection of the general emphasis in science policy on research with short-term applications. It is, however, likely to reduce the amount of basic research being undertaken in universities, which may have a longer-term effect on our capacity to innovate. The problem here is the old one of measuring the 'value' to society of basic research which may have unpredictable but potentially important consequences in terms of 'new knowledge, new lines of development work and indeed new industries' (CVCP 1981). Industrial funding of PhD work will probably also influence the choice of research topic (ABRC 1982) and academics are always worried (Select Committee on Science and Technology 1976) that their research output could become 'fragmented and subject to the whims of individual industries'.

This pressure towards PhD topics with applicable and predictable outcomes may be reinforced by the desire to improve completion rates for PhD study. While undoubtedly an attempt to improve the quality of research training, steps to improve completion rates may make it hard for students to take on 'high risk' projects which have the potential to yield very important results but with low chances of success.

Seen in the context of likely trends in university staffing, the role of the reseach student in producing research may well become more critical. Any reduction in staff/student ratios is likely to lessen the time spent by lecturers on research. Coupled with this, few young researchers will be obtaining permanent university posts (SRC 1980) and research assistant posts will also probably be reduced. Any reduction in the amount of research carried out by postgraduate students or attempts to make it strictly geared to industry's short-term interests will therefore contribute to the weakening of the basic research function in the higher education system.

PRACTICAL PROBLEMS WITH PhD TRAINING

The preceding review of the main functions of PhD training has highlighted many potential problems arising from the conflicting demands of its several functions. There are, however, serious weaknesses in the organization of PhD study which undermine its ability to function effectively on any level. The main sympton of these weaknesses is the relatively low proportion of PhD students who complete their thesis in the time allowed or indeed at all, especially in arts and social science subjects.

The SSRC found (ABRC 1982) that only 10 per cent of those beginning

PhD study between 1973 and 1975 had completed in 3 years, 19 per cent in 4 years and still only 40 per cent in 6 years. Parallel figures for scientists taking up SRC awards in 1975 shows 54 per cent completing in 5 years, but with higher completion in natural sciences than in engineering and mathematics.

Various commentators on low completion rates (ABRC 1982; SSRC 1980; Rudd 1975) have identified a common set of causal factors. These appear to be poor selection of students, choice of over-ambitious projects, lack of training in research methods, poor supervision, and social and intellectual isolation.

Suggestions for Change
Some method of selecting research students, paying more attention to their research motivation and less to their class of first degree, may well help exclude the 'drifters' who, Rudd (1980) claims, make up a significant proportion of 'drop-outs'. A fairly firm 'weeding out' after the first year has also been recommended (ABRC 1982) and where this is in force a high percentage of research students do seem to leave at that time. The Swinnerton-Dyer (ABRC 1982) figures of 50 per cent for the drop-out after a probationary year in engineering appear to concur with the finding of a very high percentage of 'drifters' in that subject group.

After the students have embarked on PhD study, problems are apparent in finding a topic of research which can be reasonably tackled in three years. There are connected problems in timetabling the research so that it actually gets finished in the time available, and particularly in allowing enough time for the writing of a thesis. Swinnerton-Dyer (ABRC 1982) found that students who selected their own topics of study were more likely to complete. The social sciences seem to have particular problems in finding topics of a suitable size. It is not immediately obvious why this should be a problem particular to the social sciences, and it might just be that social scientists have been unwilling to take this practical aspect into account in helping research students select and timetable their research. However, Swinnerton-Dyer did make the rather strange recommendation that social scientists (whose natural medium is the book) should be let off writing up a thesis and publish papers instead, whereas natural scientists (whose natural medium is the paper) should still continue to write a thesis! It would seem more immediately relevant to encourage academics in the social sciences to question the feasibility of the projects they allow their research students to undertake.

Many of these problems come back to the suitability and conscientiousness of the research supervisor. About a quarter of research students are dissatisfied with their supervisors (Rudd 1975; Hirsh 1978) and many more see their supervisors very infrequently, especially in the arts. Some method of supervising the supervisor (such as supervising committees and/or a dean of research students) is long overdue and has been again recommended by Swinnerton-Dyer (ABRC 1982).

Most groups agree in principle that some formal teaching in research methods and techniques would make the PhD easier to complete, and it might also counteract the narrowness of the PhD as a training in research. As Swinnerton-Dyer has pointed out, however, there are problems in the quality of such training where it is given and many research students (Hirsh 1978) seem to regard lectures and classes merely as an irritating distraction from research. For such training to be helpful, it clearly has to be very carefully geared to research students' needs.

Group projects might also improve research training and help to reduce the problem of social and intellectual isolation suffered by many research students. Rudd (1975) has identified possible problems in producing a thesis out of group projects, but Swinnerton-Dyer (ABRC 1982) is in favour of changing regulations if necessary to make group research a feasible method of PhD study.

Current policy is also moving towards concentrating research students (indeed research more generally) in large departments, functioning as 'centres of excellence' (Education, Science and Arts Committee 1980; ABRC 1982). Having other research students around should reduce isolation, although concentrating research could present part-time students with travel problems (Rudd 1975). One warning note is that among a survey of engineering students (Hirsh 1978), those working in the very largest departments were often extremely frustrated by the intense competition for laboratory equipment and technical help and felt inadequate to deal with the bureaucratic procedures to obtain the resources they needed.

One final practical problem occurs in the area of funding. The maximum time for which a student can expect to be funded is normally three years. In those departments where a Masters degree or diploma is treated as an essential prerequisite to PhD study, the student is expected to complete a major research project in two years. Swinnerton-Dyer (ABRC 1982) has highlighed the need for more flexible funding in such cases.

Time for Action
The universities have shown a persistant lack of will to tackle the obvious problems with the arrangements for PhD study, particularly the variable quality of supervision. It now appears that the research councils have become sufficiently concerned about low completion rates to take them into account when allocating awards to particular departments. This may at last get the universities to take their responsibilities for research students more seriously.

CURRENT POLICY TRENDS
Returning again to the more fundamental issues of the scale, content and purpose of postgraduate education, we now need to examine current policy developments against the backcloth of trends in employment and student attitudes. In practice, decisions on the scale of postgraduate education are at present largely a reflection of financial pressures within the research councils

and the higher education system. This financial constraint appears to relieve the research councils from providing a real rationalization for the actual number of postgraduate awards they offer. We do not know the extent to which they would, for example, seek to increase provision again if more money became available. It is, however, interesting to note that research councils tended to increase the proportion of their overall budgets spent on postgraduate training during the late 1970s.

Subject Balance
The fragmentation of financial support effectively prevents open national debate about the balance between funding in the arts, sciences and social sciences. The Advisory Board for the Research Councils (ABRC) considers issues of balance within the sciences. In practice science and engineering have been protected more than the arts and social sciences. Within the scope of each research council, however, decisions are taken in various ways on the allocation of student awards to different subjects. In spite of the rather flimsy employment evidence and manifestly low student demand, the SERC has mainly geared its policy towards encouraging postgraduate study in engineering by providing awards for nearly all applicants. Differential grants have been discussed from time to time as a way of encouraging more engineering students, but have not yet been accepted (ABRC 1982). There are signs that the SERC is now consolidating its views on subject balance, feeling perhaps that engineering has been pushed far enough. Swinnerton-Dyer (ABRC 1982) has taken the plunge and recommended that the SERC 'should not strain to fill places in engineering research'.

The Natural Environment Research Council (NERC) has adopted a very specific method of selecting projects for PhD study which gives close control over subject balance within their domain. The SSRC (ABRC 1982) tries to take labour market demands into account in allocating student awards to subject groups, although it is not yet clear how the new structure of the SSRC will affect subject balance (SSRC 1981). The humanities, being handled separately by the DES, seem to be the subject of very little open discussion on the issue of subject balance or indeed any other matter.

Within allocations to particular academic disciplines, the research councils have also responded to the wider pressures of science policy to encourage more applied projects as the topics of PhD study and to develop collaborative schemes (such as CASE). There appears to have been little attempt to evaluate the merits of pure or applied projects as training in research. The assumption appears to be that industrially-related projects must, by definition, provide more suitable training for those who will follow careers in industrial research.

The CASE scheme has had a persistent problem with student demand even when quota awards were in short supply (SRC 1977). This is not altogether surprising bearing in mind the apparent motivation of PhD students in engineering, who often seem to be using study as a way of deferring entry to industry. The SERC is still hoping to maintain its allocation of CASE awards, and the SSRC is about to introduce a parallel scheme.

Alternatives to the PhD
The main current alternative to the PhD as a research training is a Masters degree, either taught or involving research. For some reason there has been no real debate on the role of a Masters degree taken by research. The taught Masters degree spans specific vocational training (eg educational psychology), training in subjects not normally available at undergraduate level (eg operational research), and extensions of undergraduate courses for professional work in various subjects (eg economics). These courses vary enormously in the extent to which they might prepare students for research careers. On the whole, employers appear not to regard Masters graduates primarily as researchers (UMS 1974), and this is particularly so for university employment.

Taught courses have suffered in many cases from poor student quality and, according to students (ABRC 1982), poor teaching quality. It is, however, their apparently poor record in employment which is now causing the research councils to rethink their support. This is odd in view of the tendency which employers have to say that they prefer Masters graduates to PhDs. More evidence should be examined by the research councils on exactly where employment problems are occurring and particularly whether these problems are more or less prevalent with the narrowly vocational courses. Both the SERC and the SSRC (but not the NERC) are cutting the number of awards for advanced courses while trying to maintain research studentships. Support for advanced courses is also becoming much more selective.

The SERC is moving towards more radical alternatives both to the conventional PhD and the MSc. These range from a flexible series of short courses for young graduates in the Integrated Graduate Development Scheme, through various ways of encouraging post-experience training and industry collaboration (the Teaching Company, Collaborative Training Awards and the Industrial Fellowship Scheme). These schemes, apart from their slightly confusing proliferation of titles, seem to be a much more effective way of meeting industry's genuine short-term demands for postgraduate training. They are not, however, really aimed at the training of researchers.

This gives rise to the inevitable question whether the research councils should fund such diverse types of postgraduate training (Allen 1980). Both the SERC and the NERC expect industry to put in some of the money needed, but Swinnerton-Dyer (ABRC 1982) recommends that the DES should at least consider funding post-experience and conversion courses which are postgraduate by timing but not really by level. Loans have been considered as an alternative for postgraduate funding (Rudd 1975), but at present do not seem to find favour (ABRC 1982). Current arrangements also leave problems for part-time students who have been largely self-supporing.

UNRESOLVED POLICY ISSUES

Although the primary purpose of postgraduate training is now acknowledged to be meeting 'the country's need for trained manpower' (DES 1976), repeated reports have drawn attention to the problems of manpower planning approaches, pleaded for a 'looseness of fit' (DES 1976) and then directed attention to the need for concentration on the 'quality of those selected for awards, and of their subsequent training' (ABRC 1982). The question 'training for what?' is therefore repeatedly dodged, both in the case of the PhD and the Masters degrees.

In subjects with no real research labour market outside the universities (the humanities and certain areas of science and social science) the PhD has been largely regarded as vocational preparation for an academic career. This labour market is not only now fairly small but exceedingly erratic in its requirements', and the PhD graduate bears the brunt of the 'looseness of fit'. Either we abandon the idea of the PhD in these subjects altogether (as some 'scholars' would have us do in any case), or we continue to hope that PhD students will abandon their hopes of acadcemic careers, or that the government will start to adopt stable policies in the higher education sector.

In subjects where research jobs and indeed other kinds of employment exist outside the universities (engineering and some other sciences and social sciences) different issues emerge. These concern the extent to which the PhD can or should be adapted to serve the dual functions of training for academic and industrial employment. Even if the PhD can be geared to industry's needs, it is not clear that it will ever attract students with a strong industrial orientation. Are Masters degrees or the shorter post-experience courses that are now being developed better suited to meeting industry's short-term needs for specific skills and knowledge? If so, does the PhD in the sciences and engineering still have an effective role as a training in fundamental research?

Current policy on higher education in general, and postgraduate education in particular, seems firmly committed to evaluating such education primarily in terms of its contribution to the nation's manpower needs. Where this approach has been adopted in the past, the resulting policies have largely been based on ill-researched and often fictitious notions of the labour markets for particular qualifications in specific subjects. One can only agree with Lindley (1981) that the lack of better insights into industry's real needs 'is not a technical problem but an implicit choice in favour of ignorance'. Improved labour market information may eventually cause graduates in some subjects with very weak labour markets to reconsider the decision to study for three extra years when they are unlikely to find any job which uses the skills and knowledge which they will acquire.

More significantly, a deeper consideration of the nature of research employment in industry may question several assumptions currently embodied in policy decisions on postgraduate education. These include the assumption that a 'manpower need' in industry should be matched by a course in the higher education system designed around the specific skills and knowledge of the job identified. The second assumption is that employers can make reliable and consistent statements about current and future needs for specific categories of highly qualified manpower. The third assumption is that postgraduate education should be geared to the skills needed by researchers in their first jobs rather than the more general knowledge and attributes which will enable them to adapt over their whole careers. None of these assumptions stand up to serious scrutiny and yet they form the basis for our current attempts to relate postgraduate education in the form of the PhD and Masters degrees to the short-term needs for manpower as expressed by industry.

REFERENCES

ABRC (1982) *Report of the Working Party on Postgraduate Education* Advisory Board for the Research Councils

Allen, G. (1980) Postgraduate education in science and engineering and manpower needs. In SRC for CRAC *Higher Education and National Needs in the 1980s* SRC

Arthur (1965) *Enquiry into Longer-term Postgraduate Courses for Engineers and Technologists, 1964-65* London: HMSO

Blackstone, T. and Williams, G. (1972) Structural aspects of the academic profession in a period of expansion. In H.J. Butcher and E. Rudd *Contemporary Problems in Higher Education* London: McGraw Hill

Bosworth (1966) Committee on Manpower Resources for Science and Technology *Education and Training Requirements for the Electrical and Mechanical Manufacturing Industries* London: HMSO

Bosworth, D.L. (1981) Technological manpower. In R.M. Lindley (Editor) *Higher Education and the Labour Market* Guildford: SRHE

Cartter, A.M. (1971) Scientific manpower for 1970-1985 *Science* 172 (3979)

CBI (1970) *Industry, Science and Universities* London: Confederation of British Industry

CMRST (1966) Committee on Manpower Resources for Science and Technology *Report on the 1965 Triennial Manpower Survey of Engineers, Technologists, Scientists and Technical Supporting Staff* (Cmnd 3103) London: HMSO

CVCP (1975) Committee of Vice-Chancellors and Principals of the Universities of the UK *Study Group on Postgraduate Education* London: CVCP

CVCP (1980) Committee of Vice-Chancellors and Principals of the Universities of the UK *Research in Universities* London: CVCP

CVCP (1981) Committee of Vice-Chancellors and Principals of the Universities of the UK *Universities and Industry* London: CVCP

Dainton (1968) Council for Scientific Policy *Enquiry into the Flow of Candidates in Science and Technology into Higher Education* (Cmnd 3541) London: HMSO

DES (1976) Expenditure Committeee *Government Observations on the Third Report 1973-74 — Postgraduate Education* (Cmnd 6611) London: HMSO

Education, Science and Arts Committee (1980) *The Funding and Organisation of Courses in Higher Education* Fifth report from the House of Commons Education, Science and Arts Committee, Session 1979-80. London: HMSO

Expenditure Committee (1974) *Postgraduate Education* Third report from the House of Commons Expenditure Committee, Session 1973-74. London: HMSO

Finniston (1980) *Engineering Our Future* Report of the Committee of Inquiry into the Engineering Profession. (Cmnd 7794) London: HMSO

Gibb, F. (1977) Where have all the jobs gone? *The Times Higher Education Supplement* 6 May 1977

Hirsh, W. (1978) *Career Prospects in British Universities* University of Cambridge PhD

Hirsh, W. and Morgan, R. (1978) Career prospects in British universities *Higher Education* 7

Howarth, C.I. and Harris, M. (1974) The need for postgraduate education in psychology *Bulletin of the British Psychological Society* 27

IMS (1981a) *The Employment of Postgraduate Social Scientists* University of Sussex: Institute of Manpower Studies

IMS (1981b) *Qualified Manpower and its Role in Economic Expansion: Scotland's Health and Care Industry* University of Sussex: Institute of Manpower Studies

Jones (1967) Committee on Manpower Resources for Science and Technology *The Brain Drain — Report of the Working Party on Migration* (Cmnd 3417) London: HMSO

Lindley, R.M. (1981) The challenge of market imperatives. In R.M. Lindley (Editor) *Higher Education and the Labour Market* Guildford: SRHE

Platt, J. (1976) *The Realities of Social Research* Sussex: Sussex University Press

Public Accounts Committee (1979) *Research and Training in the Social Sciences* Thirty-fourth report from the House of Commons Committee of Public Accounts, Session 1979-80. London: HMSO

Robbins (1963) *Report of the Great Britain Committee on Higher Education* (Cmnd 2154) London: HMSO

Rudd, E. and Hatch, S. (1968) *Graduate Study and After* London: Weidenfeld and Nicolson

Rudd, E. (1973) Graduate study and the market for labour. In H. Greenaway and G. Williams (Editors) *Patterns of Change in Graduate Employment* London: SRHE

Rudd, E. (1975) *The Highest Education* London: Routledge and Kegan Paul
Rudd, E. (1980) *Dropping-out from Research Degrees* (Mimeo) University of Essex
Select Committee on Science and Technology (1976) Third Report *University-Industry Relations* London: HMSO
SRC (1971) Engineering Board *Report of Working Party on Postgraduate Training* (Horlock Report) London: SRC
SRC (1972) Engineering Board, Computing Science Committee *Policy and Programme Review of Research and Training in Computing Science* London: SRC
SRC (1973) Engineering Board *Total Technology* London: SRC
SRC (1975) *Postgraduate Training* (Edwards Report) London: SRC
SRC (1976) *SRC Bulletin* January 1976. London: SRC
SRC (1977) *SRC Bulletin* February 1977. London: SRC
SRC (1980) *Report of the Science Research Council for the Year 1979-80* London: SRC
SSRC (1980) *Report of the Social Science Research Council, April 1979-March 1980* London: SSRC
SSRC (1981) *A Change in Structure for Changing Circumstances* London: SSRC
Swann (1968) Committee on Manpower Resources for Science and Technology *The Flow into Employment of Scientists, Engineers and Technologists* (Cmnd 3760) London: HMSO
UGC (1976) *Annual Survey, Academic Year 1974-75* (Cmnd 6435) London: HMSO
UMS (1974) *The Employment of those with Post-graduate Qualifications* Unit for Manpower Studies
USR (1981) *Details of First Destinations of University Graduates 1979-80* Cheltenham: Universities Statistical Record (for the UGC)
Williams, G. (1973) The economics of the graduate labour market. In H. Greenaway and G. Williams (Editors) *Patterns of Change in Graduate Employment* London: SRHE
Williams, G. (1974) *Academic Tenure and the Numbers Game* (Mimeo) SRHE Annual Conference
Williams, G., Blackstone, T. and Metcalfe, D. (1974) *The Academic Labour Market* Amsterdam: Elsevier

SEMINAR DISCUSSION

Most of the discussion on this paper was about the problems associated with the PhD degree as a device for training researchers. There was a good deal of dissatisfaction with the degree, although it was claimed that the anti PhD campaign had been much more virulent ten years ago. Those who were negative about the degree claimed that although it provided cheap research labour, and enabled some students to pursue their own interests for a few years, it was singularly unsuited to training someone to do a job. Many industrialists preferred to give new recruits on-the-job training rather than take people with a PhD.

A few people thought that it was not until a person had obtained a PhD that they really knew their subject. They agreed there were problems with poor completion rates, but on balance thought the PhD still provided a good basis for someone entering a research career whether it be an academic one or otherwise.

Those who would retain the degree, but with modifications, suggested that the degree should be awarded for excellent work on synthesis as well as for the creation of new knowledge. Others spoke of the isolation of the PhD and urged greater development of collaborative research as a basis for it. Most were in favour of more formal training in research methodology.

There was also a good deal of discussion on part-time students, with the participants divided on whether this was a good thing or not. There was not much evidence presented either way, and it was difficult to reach any recommendation.

The number of part-time graduate students is growing and it is clearly important that the correlation between part-time and quality needs to be investigated. It is more likely that part-time postgraduates will be able to fulfil the requirements of Masters level courses than be able to provide the commitment and time that is required for a PhD.

7

CONCLUSIONS AND RECOMMENDATIONS

by Kenneth Durham and Geoffrey Oldham

The point of departure for the fourth SRHE Leverhulme seminar was a collection of six specially commissioned background papers. These form Chapters 1-6 of the present book, together with the discussions they provoked. They identified the four principal functions of research in higher education.

1 To contribute to the vitality of the nation's research capacity.
2 To train the next generation of researchers and to provide improved teaching for undergraduates.
3 To contribute to the solution of social and economic problems.
4 To contribute to fundamental knowledge, and through this to the attainment of cultural objectives.

Both papers and discussions considered the constraints which higher education institutions face in fulfilling these functions, and in meeting the often conflicting demands which are placed upon their research systems. Suggestions were made as to how the constraints could be removed, and consideration was given to what future research functions would be desirable. It was the responsibility of the two of us (chairman and convenor) to formulate a set of conclusions and recommendations.

There are a few other points to be made before we present our recommendations. First of all our concern is with higher education in the 1990s. Hence, although the recent government cuts clearly affect the current status of research in British universities and polytechnics, our recommendations are more concerned with the longer-term health of the research system than with finding palliatives to the present crisis.

Secondly, the recommendations are principally directed to the problems of natural sciences and engineering. This is because it is these areas which absorb most research funds. However, the social sciences and humanities were also considered at the seminar and special recommendations have been formulated for them.

Thirdly, most of the recommendations specifically refer to universities and are less relevant to the polytechnics. This was not because we considered the polytechnics to be unimportant in research, but because the total research budget for polytechnics is only of the order of 5 per cent of that for the universities. Also, unlike the universities, the polytechnics do not receive a research allocation from their central funding bodies. All of their research money is derived from grants and contracts. This gives rise to a different set of issues.

Fourthly, the terms 'research' and 'scholarship' seem to mean many different things; we have tried to clarify what types of research we are referring to in our recommendations, but the boundaries between these different meanings are often blurred.

We emphasize that the conclusions and recommendations are our own responsibility. We have been guided by the background papers and the seminar discussions, but the recommendations are not those of the entire group.

OUR RECOMMENDATIONS

Many demands are made on the research system in British universities and polytechnics, yet the higher education research system accounts for only 10 per cent of the total British research budget. This is considerably less than in most other OECD countries, and the seminar papers showed how the system is currently stretched to the limit.

There are three possible approaches for the future. First of all the range of demands on the system could be limited, so that with the same resources the system is asked to do less. Secondly, more resources could be made available so that the same demands are satisfied but the stress is lessened. Thirdly, the system can be made more efficient so that the same resources can achieve more results.

It is widely acknowledged that if Britain is to maintain even its present position within the world economy it will have to depend on its own inventiveness and innovation. This will require a thriving higher educational research system responding effectively to the various demands to which it will be subjected. We believe it unlikely that there will be a substantial increase in funds available for research; hence most of our recommendations are aimed at increasing the efficiency of the system. If these recommendations were implemented we believe that the university and polytechnic research system would not only retain a high degree of autonomy, but would be able to respond far more effectively to national and international needs.

The seminar demonstrated the pluralism which exists in research within British higher education. This is a strength and should be maintained. However, it does mean that recommendations cannot apply equally to all aspects of research in all institutions. We have ordered our conclusions and recommendations under a number of headings which represented the main themes to emerge from the seminar discussions.

STATISTICS

Our knowledge of the existing research situation in British universities and polytechnics comes from opinions and statistics. The statistical evidence assembled in the commissioned papers identified the main funding patterns for research in the basic sciences, but demonstrated the inadequacy of the present published statistics. This was even more apparent in the social sciences and the humanities than in the natural sciences and technology.

Unless good statistical data is available, policy making will be largely spurious. Our first recommendation therefore concerns statistics. It is addressed to each higher education institution as well as to the UGC and the research councils.

Recommendation 1
It is recommended that better systems for collecting statistics on research inputs to universities and polytechnics be devised and implemented by the institutions concerned.

This recommendation relates to research inputs. What really counts in research, however, is the output. We are aware of the notorious difficulties in devising suitable indicators of research output, but inroads have been made into this problem in recent years. Some of our subsequent recommendations will require judgements to be made on the quality of research outputs, and given the importance of this, our second recommendation is about indicators of research output.

Recommendation 2
It is recommended that more policy research is carried out to develop indicators of research performance.

UNIVERSITY RESEARCH POLICY

Universities are very jealous of their autonomy. Defenders of this autonomy claim that universities are, and should be, the bastions of truth and objectivity. They suggest that members of these institutions must be free to pursue inquiry wherever that leads and to be able to provide an independent critique of society. To a large extent we support these concepts. But they are in jeopardy when the resources available to finance them are inadequate. When this happens the funding sources frequently dictate priorities and shape the activities of the recipient institutions.

In Britain we have tried in the past to ensure academic freedom by having a buffer organization (the UGC) distribute funds to universities. The criterion it has used is essentially a per capita allowance for each student. The evidence presented at the SRHE Leverhulme seminar suggested that this is now proving inadequate as a way of supporting research. The research councils have helped supplement research activities in both universities and polytechnics, but they have their own objectives, and higher education institutions are only one of several mechanisms for enabling the councils to reach their objectives. Furthermore, the councils are themselves under increasing pressure to show relevance in the research they support.

Over the next ten to twenty years it seems inevitable that not all university science departments can be given sufficient financial support for them all to be at international frontiers of science. There are simply too many universities and too little money. We do not believe in a policy of 'equal misery' and under these circumstances there has to be more selectivity and more concentration of funding on fewer centres. The question is who will decide on where these centres of 'excellence' should be. We believe that the universities themselves should have a major say in the decision. The next recommendation is addressed to the universities.

Recommendation 3
It is recommended that each university should have a research policy.
This policy should help to:
1 Identify the balance of research effort within the institution that is to be devoted to each of the competing demands on that institution's research system: ie it would determine the balance between fundamental basic research, strategic research, the training of postgraduates, scholarship, and research directed to the solution of local, national and international problems.
2 Identify those departments and units whose past research performance warrants their being singled out as centres of excellence deserving special financial support.
3 Identify mechanisms to ensure that new research, and people with exceptional research talents, have an opportunity to succeed. This because universities should also aim to select on 'promise'.

It is recognized that it will be difficult for universities to make the required choices. The development of indicators of research performance might make the task more objective and hence more acceptable. So, too, would a move to establish a greater parity of esteem and promotion prospects between the different types of research. Although it will be difficult to determine priorities, if the universities do not make these decisions and formulate their own priorities, others will do it for them. Part of the price of autonomy is the responsibility for making tough internal decisions.

NATIONAL RESEARCH PRIORITIES

There is a need for a clearer identification of research priorities at the national level. This applies particularly to fundamental research and what is now called strategic research: ie research in areas identified as likely in the medium term to have relevance to the economy and society. A national research policy is required to guide the allocation of public money to fundamental and strategic research.

Discussion at the SRHE Leverhulme seminar showed that this is a controversial topic. Examples were cited of two apparently successful attempts to formulate national research priorities for the basic sciences. They were the 20-year plan for fundamental science in Japan, and the recent symposium to identify research priorities in France. Each of these heavily involved the scientific communities of the two countries and appear to have influenced their respective governments in the allocation of research resources. Britain differs culturally and politically from both Japan and France, but there are lessons to be learned from experience in other countries. Priorities cannot be left entirely to the government with its often narrow and utilitarian point of view. Rather we feel that there is a need in this country to find a mechanism which will allow the greater involvement in the articulation of research priorities of higher education institutions, the UGC, the research councils, the scientific community and the likely users of research — industry and government.

Recommendation 4
It is recommended that a forum be established to enable doers, funders and users of research to participate in the process of identifying fundamental and strategic research priorities in science and technology. These priorities should influence the allocation of resources by the research councils and ultimately by the UGC.
This forum should enable the views of the scientific community, government and industry to be brought together by a high level committee with representation from the different interest groups.

This recommendation is intended to help arrival at a consensus on the main priority areas where research funds should be concentrated. It should not be interpreted as being a device to plan or direct research itself. The purpose is to help pick the growth areas, not to stultify the individual researcher. Such a process is not without its hazards. A consensus may be difficult to achieve, and there is a danger that the potential users of research results will be too utilitarian in their approach. But the potential benefits from such a process should outweigh the disadvantages. The whole scientific community would be engaged in the process of setting broad priorities and the involvement of potential users from the beginning is likely to lead to the more rapid exploitation of the results. The contribution to improved morale among academic scientists should not be ignored.

The social sciences present a more difficult problem since it is likely to be less easy to agree on the crucial areas for support there than in the natural sciences. Indeed, there were strong arguments at the seminar, not merely against the concept of a national policy, but also against the development of an institutional policy. Nevertheless, we feel sure there is a need at least for some co-ordination of research in the social sciences so that a proper system of priorities can be established.

Recommendation 5
We recommend a similar forum to suggest priorities for research in the social sciences. It should comprise academics, civil servants and representatives of local authorities and the community at large.
We do not argue that all public monies for research be allocated according to these priorities. There must be ways of supporting exceptional talent even when the proposed research does not fit predetermined priorities. This point will be considered again in a later recommendation.

Recommendations 3, 4 and 5 suggest how priorities might be

CONCLUSIONS AND RECOMMENDATIONS 215

determined at institutional and national levels. Implemented on their own they are unlikely to match. The national priorities may well call for a limited effort in one area, whereas many universities may identify this area as one which they intend to designate as a centre of excellence. Alternatively, there may be other areas of national importance which no university, acting autonomously, designates as a priority area. Marine biology and oceanography appear to be examples of this at the moment. To resolve this potential dilemma will require a process of consultation, and a measure of co-ordination will be required between individual universities, and between the universities as a whole and the sources of public funds for basic and strategic research.

It is not clear what would be the most appropriate framework within which this iterative process could take place. Possibly the Committee of Vice-Chancellors and Principals would be appropriate. It is therefore to this body and to the UGC and research councils that the next recommendation is addressed.

Recommendation 6
It is recommended that a process of consultation between universities, and between the universities and funding bodies (including research councils and the UGC) take place, in order to ascertain which institutions will be the designated centres for research in particular disciplines.

This approach will require some loss of sovereignty for the universities. Not all will be able to do all that they would like to do. But if Britain is to maintain research excellence in a wide range of scientific fields there will have to be more selectivity and concentration.

We believe that Recommendations 3 to 6 together would help rationalize the allocation of resources within the university research system with the minimum of outside interference.

FUNDING RESEARCH
So far we have considered the way in which priorities for research should be formulated. We now turn to methods of funding. The present method, based on the dual support system, appears from the evidence presented at the SRHE Leverhulme seminar, to be inadequate. The notion that allocation of resources for research should be based largely on the number of undergraduate students does not appear to be suitable, unless there is a direct correlation between undergradaute teaching and research.

There was a good deal of discussion at the seminar on the relationship between teaching and research. The generally accepted wisdom in the past has been that the two are intimately related. This view was challenged, and most participants agreed that there was no evidence to support it. Some studies which have examined the issue have concluded that the reverse may be the case.

If we are no longer bound by the convention which insists on the inextricable link between teaching and research, then a more rational approach to funding research can be proposed.

Recommendation 7
It is recommended that a new system of university funding be introduced which distinguishes between undergraduate teaching and the support of scholarship on the one hand, and postgraduate teaching and research on the other.

In our scheme the UGC would continue to fund both teaching and research. It would, however, use different criteria for each. The funding of research would be linked to the designated research centres at each institution and there would be a measure of 'resonance' between the general support for research provided by the UGC and the specific project funds provided by the research councils. The recommendation would mean that in consultation with the universities and research councils the UGC would become more selective in its allocation of research funds.

There is a danger that the system as recommended would reward only past excellence in research. Therefore in addition it is essential to add a mechanism which will enable each institution to encourage new ideas and young researchers.

Recommendation 8
It is recommended that the UGC should stipulate that up to 10 per cent of the total research grant to each institution should be available to promote new initiatives. The funds should be allocated at the discretion of a research policy group within each institution.

A separation of the criteria for supporting research from the criteria for supporting teaching would also allow the creation of more research appointments. Such appointments should be for terms of five years, and the possibility should exist for staff to move from teaching posts to research posts and back again. Many staff would continue to do teaching and research, but the above scheme would encourage flexibility and should improve productivity. The present system of appointments assumes that all staff spend a part of their time doing research. It is doubtful whether this is so and the research productivity of many staff, in terms of publication at least, seems to be low.

UNIVERSITY/INDUSTRY RELATIONS
As the full severity of the recent government cuts in education has become apparent, so has the interest in university/industry research relationships increased. The important question whether industry could be a third source of research funding was explored at some length. The general view of the seminar seemed to be that although there is room for some collaboration with industry which will result in financial benefits for universities and polytechnics, the scope for large-scale finance from industry is limited.

There was, perhaps surprisingly, agreement between academics and industrialists that the university researchers' prime task is to do fundamental or strategic research. It was felt that universities were not problem-solvers for industry and that only rarely, and in a few areas, is it likely that the academic will be able to move easily with his ideas into industry. Such occasions are to be welcomed but the opportunities should not be over-estimated. Industrial research requires a flow of knowledge and understanding from university research and the onus for exploiting this must lie with industry itself.

There are, however, potential areas of collaboration which would jeopardize neither the security aspect of industrial research nor the sovereignty of the university department. When industry is assessing whether to move in to a new area, it often needs a major scientific input into the analysis. This it can either get by setting up its own research or by commissioning quite fundamental research in an appropriate university department. This would give a resource flexibility to industry while the university department would receive funding for a limited period without any direct interference. Another potential benefit from this kind of collaboration might be exchange for short periods of time between university and industrial researchers.

At the same time, industrial problems usually require a multidisciplinary attack and this is particularly difficult to sponsor in highly specialized British universities. Although we make no specific recommendation we feel that university departments in the natural sciences in particular might give thought to the possibility of collaboration on fundamental problems sponsored by industry. The polytechnics appear to suffer less from this particular weakness.

THE SOCIAL SCIENCES

Although many of the recommendations that we have made apply equally to the natural sciences and the social sciences, there are some significant differences between the two. The natural sciences often proceed by intense specialization whereas in the social sciences the issues are often broad and complex and require different methods of analysis. Although both the natural sciences and the social sciences help us to attain a better understanding of nature and the world, and both in different ways provide tools to help solve society's problems, it is the social sciences which provide a critique of society. Much of social science is ultimately about power relationships and is not so easily amenable to consensual national policies. This critical role is important and it is one of the reasons why academic groups are needed to do long-term policy research.

The seminar identified several problems facing social science research in Britain. The most obvious is the drastic cut in funding during the past two years. Other difficulties identified were those of ensuring that research capability exists in important policy domains, and of promoting interdisciplinary policy research. It is to these latter difficulties that we address the following recommendation.

Recommendation 9
It is recommended that a number of social science research groups be identified as worthy of special support. They should be groups capable of contributing to the solution of critically important policy problems. Those selected groups should then qualify for long-term (8 years) support from both the UGC and the research councils. The process of identifying the groups would involve consultation between universities, the UGC and the research councils.

This would enable a limited number of social science policy research groups to flourish, and help resolve the problems of lack of continuity in inter-disciplinary research. What is proposed is analogous to the SSRC Designated Research Centres, but involves more UGC core funding as well. The existence of such centres would also facilitate greater university/government interaction since it would make it easier for government departments to place contracts for shorter-term policy-related problems.

THE HUMANITIES

The discussions on research in the humanities were some of the most stimulating of the seminar.

Academic research in the humanities not only contributes to the cultural enrichment of society, but it can also provide a better understanding of foreign cultures and societies. In this it may have even a narrowly defined utilitarian function. There is also the function, most probably not of overwhelming quantitative importance in the 1980s, of training the next generation of secondary and higher education teachers of humanities.

There are, however, very significant differences between research in the humanities and research in the sciences. Scholarship, implying reflection and synthesis of a wide range of knowledge, is a much more important activity in the humanities than it is in the sciences; research in the humanities is still largely an activity of lone individuals, as compared with a greater emphasis on teamwork in the sciences; the cost of humanities research (with very few exceptions) is much less than that in the sciences; and the integral link between teaching and research seems to be closer than in the sciences.

As a result of these differences, the recommendations made earlier should not apply to the humanities. Instead:

Recommendation 10
It is recommended that the UGC continues to allocate funds to universities for work in the humanities primarily on the basis of student numbers.

There was some discussion on the need for the humanities to have their own research council. We do not feel able to make a positive recommendation on this matter. We are convinced, however, of the importance of maintaining high quality scholarship and research in the humanities in British universities.

Recommendation 11
It is recommended that the case for a research council in the humanities be fully explored by a representative group from the universities, the UGC, the DES and the British Academy. The appropriate group to convene such a committee would be the British Academy.

POSTGRADUATE TRAINING

Universities and polytechnics play an important role in training new researchers. For the past fifty years the PhD degree has been the device whereby most researchers in the natural sciences, and more recently in the social sciences and humanities, have obtained their research apprenticeship. In recent years there has been a good deal of dissatisfaction expressed about the PhD. It has continued to serve as a useful stepping stone to academic appointments, but many employers have claimed that the graduate with a PhD is often over-specialized for their needs, and they have preferred to recruit people with other qualifications. In the social sciences in particular there is also the problem of poor completion rate, with many students failing to complete their doctorates and others taking five or more years to do so.

This leads us to make the following recommendations on postgraduate training.

Recommendation 12
It is recommended that the PhD degree be judged with more modest expectations of contribution to original knowledge than is now demanded by many universities. There should be more explicit training in research methodology, and more opportunities for research to be done as a part of a team. The experience of working for a PhD should encourage flexibility, and enable the researcher to move between areas of work within the same discipline. In other words, the PhD should be seen more as a training experience than as a major contribution to knowledge.

Britain is the only Western European country where fees for higher education are not allowable against income tax.

Recommendation 13
It is recommended that fees for both undergraduate and postgraduate education should be a tax deductible item.

THE POLYTECHNICS

There seems to be no national consensus about the role of research in the polytechnics. Certainly, a very large part of the activity of most polytechnics is concerned with teaching mainly because of the requirements of their students. One view at the SRHE Leverhulme seminar was that local authorities see no reason why they should fund research. The argument could be paraphrased as 'Don't get above yourselves by doing research'. But from the viewpoint of individual polytechnics the ability to do research provides increased status and autonomy. The polytechnics do have an important role to play, certainly when judged by the standard of utility. Their links with industry are generally stronger than universities and they are more flexible in that they more often are prepared to use experience as a qualification for entry to a degree or higher degree course. Many polytechnics already have a policy for selection of research and for allocation of priorities.

Recommendation 14
It is recommended that the research function of polytechnics be recognized as important, particularly with regard to their contributions to industry. Each polytechnic should encourage the pursuit of research, and to this end should have an explicit research policy.

If it is recognized that the research function of polytechnics is important, then from a research standpoint it would make sense for the polytechnics to be funded centrally rather than locally. The notion that polytechnics should serve only the needs of local industry does not seem to be appropriate for research since much of local industry is now in the hands of national or even international companies and looking nationally for its research assistance.

IN CONCLUSION

We believe that the need for Britain to rely on its scientific and technological wits will increase over the next two decades. This means that demands on the higher education research system will increase, and the intention of our recommendations is to improve the capacity of the system to meet these demands. The recommendations, if implemented, would also slightly strengthen the research function in comparison with the other functions of higher education, such as teaching, and this we think is desirable.

We recognize that the precise ways in which the recommendations are implemented remains to be worked out. What is important is for a full and public debate to take place about the issues. These conclusions and recommendations are our contribution to the debate.